A Time to ....

'If the poll tax is dead it was killed by non-payment, a tactic which each of the three main parties insisted was pointless and wrong . . . This weekend each and every one of those non-payers should feel proud of themselves . . .'

The Observer 23/3/91

'Introduced two years ago in Scotland and last April in England and Wales, the poll tax has been the most expensive mistake in modern political history . . . (resulting in) one of the most spectacular U-turns for any government this century.'

The Financial Times 21/2/91

'They're the backbone of a campaign which has undoubtedly put the uncollectable into the poll tax . . . The Federation has succeeded where most political parties have failed. By biting the bullet and advocating non-payment it has been able to channel genuine grievance at the poll tax into effective, if illegal, action.'

The Evening Times 21/3/91

A Time to Rage

Tommy Sheridan
with Joan McAlpine

Introduced by John Pilger

Polygon
EDINBURGH

© Tommy Sheridan and Joan McAlpine 1994

Introduction © John Pilger 1994

Published by Polygon
22 George Square
Edinburgh

Set in 10½ on 13 Bembo by ROM-Data Corporation Limited,
Falmouth, Cornwall
Printed and bound in Great Britain by Short Run Press, Exeter

British Library Cataloguing in Publication Data is available

ISBN 0 7486 6174 3

Contents

Foreword

In this fine book Tommy Sheridan writes of the poll tax: 'The Victorian working class were supposed to touch their cloth caps and stay at home making rag mats on polling day. The twentieth-century Tories hoped people would take their names off the electoral register in order to avoid the tax. Most never did. It was clear from the start that the tax was odious. The real challenge was how to defeat it.' And defeat it he did, as one of the leaders of a mass movement, the All-Britain Anti-Poll Tax Federation, that undoubtedly set in train the dumping of Margaret Thatcher.

I am honoured to write these words at the beginning of Tommy's book. He exemplifies the kind of political opposition that the Labour Party has abandoned; and he is a source of inspiration for young people, and the rest of us, who are sometimes consumed by a sense of political impotence. This is not meant to elevate a single personality; Tommy Sheridan speaks for many like him, who have fought the ruthlessness of the British establishment in a variety of ways, such as the legions of working-class people, including the old and the alone, the disabled and the unemployed, who gathered their courage and refused to pay the poll tax. This book is as much a tribute to them as it is a record of Tommy's own development as a socialist. Certainly, his description of the way people have endured the poverty imposed upon them is moving; and his understanding of the nature of modern internalised poverty is unusual. 'Sandra's stress levels', he wrote of a not untypical resident of his native Pollok, 'are often determined by how her giro is stretching'. He describes a world in which almost half the jobs available to working-class people have disappeared in a dozen years 'like a blanket being drawn over the place'; and the refusal of those like himself to accept the remedies and false democracy offered by the official political opposition.

I first spoke to Tommy shortly after his release from Saughton jail in Edinburgh, where he had been imprisoned for six months for breaching a court order and forcing the cancellation of a poll tax warrant sale. From his cell he had successfully campaigned for a seat on Glasgow district council standing in the 1992 general election as a Scottish Labour Militant candidate, in Glasgow Pollok; and for one who was denied the hustings, he did pretty well. He told me that in prison he had kept a copy of *Revolt on the Clyde*, William Gallagher's account of Red Clydeside. 'It reminded me', he said, 'that John MacLean also fought a parliamentary campaign from prison – for the Gorbals in 1918. I left my copy with my cellmate, Ron, who'd looked after me.'

Tommy uses the term, 'It makes me so angry', a great deal. It is odd to hear this from one as erudite; and it is not difficult to understand the source of his popularity in Glasgow, where the people among whom he lives talk about conditions there at first with despair, then with an anger that is denied by Westminster politicians. Tommy's greatest achievement, a friend told me, 'is that he has politicised people whose apathy Labour depends on. He has done a very traditional thing: he has made the connection and shown people that we all lead *political* lives'.

I asked Tommy about this, and also to answer the standard Labour leadership argument that, for a left-wing party to win government, it had to appeal to a Toryism among large sections of working-class people. 'Oh that's a static, defeatist view of people', he replied. 'If you study the social attitudes surveys, you're left in no doubt that the population at large is to the left of the Labour Party. For instance, people believe there is one law for the rich and one for them; but an issue like that needs to be articulated. Also, most people do not support the so-called 'free market'; they want a publicly planned economy. Even *The Economist* has said as much'.

Tommy's belief in people's right-to-know, perhaps more than anything else, has underpinned his and Scottish Militant's success.

'A radical', he told me, 'only becomes dangerous when people start listening, and wanting to know more, and what *they* can do. At that point, apathy has gone, maybe forever. *Inform* people and you have a new agenda'. Labour's witch-hunts have given Militant a distorted reputation; and it is interesting that in Scotland, where the close-knit nature of the society makes divisions among working-class people more difficult to forge than in England, Militant has little of its media reputation south of the border. Perhaps people living on the edge in Scotland understand that the legacies of Labour's witch-hunts are the very authoritarianism of which Labour leaders have accused Militant, and that the espousal of socialism itself is now tantamount to 'entryism' in the Labour Party. Tommy is credited with recruiting some 100 new members to Labour's branch in Pollok. They were all ordinary people not necessarily inspired by Militant's programme, rather than by the commitment of Tommy and his comrades to the community. And Labour witch-hunted about forty people from this branch, including Tommy.

This touches on the very notion of 'extremism' in British politics. I asked Tommy, an accredited 'extremist', about this. 'The middle ground that Labour wants to occupy', he said, 'simply doesn't exist. Wanting to give people jobs is now extremism. Wanting schools that will educate children against a background of the world, not as fodder, is now extremism. Wanting a health service that doesn't let people suffer and die on impossible waiting lists is now extremism. Of course, the real extremists are those who have created such conditions, not those who oppose them'. I would add that the opponents of change are not the only identifiable class enemy; but almost equally those less menacing, even decent collaborative voices who remain silent on the great issues and who guard the enemy's faith by failing to protect the very people for whom they claim to speak. We should celebrate those who break this silence. The author of this book is one of them.

John Pilger

Acknowledgements

It would be impossible to name everyone who played a role in the course of the campaign which unfolds in the book. Save to say that it is dedicated to all those who refused to pay and especially those who were penalised. We have tried to include as many characters as possible in the pages which follow. To those not personally mentioned, I apologise.

The following acknowledgements are by no means exhaustive: Janice Glennon, Evelyn Beattie, Elaine Boden and John McFadden all of whom sadly died in the course of the campaign. Jean and Steve from Maryhill, Raymond, Ian, Mary, Agnes, Mary McQuaid, Margaret Mary, Ann Campbell, Denise Cassidy, Ann Curran and her family, Brian Lewis, John Bryson and Andy from Cumbernauld. Betty and Dave Curry who adopted me as one of their own.

May I also record my love for my mum, dad and sisters Carol and Lynn. My girlfriend Gail and my two grannies, Rose and Babs.

May I lastly, record a huge debt and unflinching admiration and respect for Joan McAlpine whose determination, stamina and talent made this book possible.

Tommy Sheridan

During the course of writing this book, Tommy Sheridan and I paid a visit to the People's Palace, Glasgow's social history museum. We saw John MacLean's desk, some fading trade union banners, photographs of Govan housewives demanding municipal housing and striking apprentice boys with placards saying, 'It's not so Squair to ask for Mair'. But the exhibits we were looking for had been removed. These were the banners of the local anti-poll tax unions, which the former curator, Elspeth King, had displayed before she was forced out in 1991. In vain we moved up to the third floor. But the space had been given to a temporary exhibition on Glasgow trades jointly supported by the Scottish TUC and the CBI. The exhibition boards made it difficult to view Ken Currie's magnificent panels depicting the city's radical history. The paintings had been moved higher onto the ceiling and hung at an angle which made you squint. 'They've got to be out of reach,' explained an attendant. 'Do you realise how much they're worth these days?'

If financial factors put Currie's images of striking weavers and shipyard poets out of sight, then political considerations attempted to put the anti-poll tax movement out of mind. Here was the biggest campaign of civil disobedience this century. A campaign which started in Glasgow. Yet it had no place in the official citadel recording the people's past.

It is the role of journalists to give a voice to the unheard. The written word should celebrate what museums deliberately ignore in order to sell people a sanitised version of their history. That's why I agreed to this book. It is based on many long hours of conversation with Tommy Sheridan and dozens of ordinary people who never made the headlines but nevertheless won the campaign. Very few newspaper reports between 1988 and 1993 explained who the anti-poll tax federation actually were. They were sometimes dismissed as 'the mob' or 'the rabble' or 'professional agitators'. But the turning points in our history have always been determined by men and women whose names we do not know.

The *sans culottes* who ran through the streets of Paris during the French revolution were also known as the mob. The thousands of individuals who gathered in Eastern European cities two centuries later will remain forever anonymous.

This book is intended to rescue from invisibility some of the participants in a mass movement closer to home. These people are heroes and Tommy gives them a voice. They will not be erased from history.

I would like to thank all the people who lent their support to this project. Foremost, I would like to thank Marion Sinclair and

xii A Time to Rage

her colleagues at Polygon for their belief in the book. John Pilger, in our view the greatest investigative journalist of the last thirty years, paid us an enormous compliment by agreeing to write the foreword. My colleagues at the *Scotsman,* Catherine Lockerbie and Bob Campbell, were encouraging from the outset, as was Bob Wylie of *Scotland on Sunday.* Roy Templeton at the *Greenock Telegraph* for articles and photographs. My friends, Margaret Gribben and Jane MacKenzie, helpfully read over some of the initial chapters and provided continual encouragement. None of these people should, of course, be held responsible for any of the views expressed in these pages.

I would like to thank all those people whose personal testimony forms the backbone of this book. Alan McCombes helped organise the transcription of their taped interviews and Angie Black, Eileen Clocherty, Lorraine Earl and Sheena McDonald helped enormously by typing some of these for me.

Finally I would like to thank my husband, Patrick Kane, my parents Jim and Esther McAlpine, sisters Maureen and Laura McAlpine and parents-in-law May and John Kane for the time they spent looking after my daughter while I was bent over the word processor. Most of all I'd like to thank Grace for doing without her mother for long stretches of her third summer.

Joan McAlpine

Author's Preface

This book is intended as a celebration of the mass campaign of poll tax non-payment. The campaign that not only forced the Tory government into a humiliating reversal of policy but which was responsible, more than any other factor, for the downfall of Mrs Thatcher. A celebration of the courage and determination displayed by the millions who participated in the campaign and refused to pay the 'unjust, unfair and immoral' poll tax. Still bloodthirsty Tory authorities and 'Uncle Tom' Labour ones throughout Britain continue to persecute and prosecute the poor. Many casualties have been sustained in the battle. From those with bank accounts frozen, wages arrested, benefits arrested and council allowances witheld, like myself, through to those imprisoned in England and Wales. All proud warriors in a proud and just campaign. A campaign that has prevented every attempted warrant sale and must continue to do so as well as promoting the case for a poll tax amnesty for non-payers.

The Anti-Poll Tax campaign involved civil disobedience on a mass scale and was genuinely mass-based. The woman and her government who had done so much to make effective trade union and political action illegal were cast into turmoil by millions of ordinary people who refused to obey the poll tax law. Political leadership of this campaign was vital. Militant provided it. Our programme and tactics on how to beat the poll tax became the property of millions. It was a leadership secured through debate, democracy and discussion, not cunning or subterfuge. And it was an experience which revealed the power the working class has when united in political action. Despite their cheerleading media and their obedient judiciary and police forces the all-powerful Thatcher government was defeated and she was forced to go. Cause indeed for celebration.

However, this book is also about condemnation. Condemnation of capitalism itself, a social and economic system which thrives on inequality, exploitation and injustice.

Although there are many other single issues just as offensive as the poll tax, from the fuel tax to water privatisation through to the attacks on single parents and the welfare state, it is the system itself which deserves exposure and condemnation. Capitalism is put on trial in the pages of this book. It is found guilty of failing to provide jobs, homes, services and equality of opportunity. But these are possible given the rich era of resources, wealth and technology which now exist. The system is rotten and corrupt to the core. Yet it is a system which finds cosy refuge in the arms of the political parties from Labour and Liberal to the SNP. Scottish Militant Labour offers it no refuge and condemns it as outmoded and bust. We promote instead the inherent logic, sanity and justice of genuine socialism. This book above all else is arguing the case for genuine socialism.

1 'It's the poor wot gets the blame.'

'You're no longer poor? There's more in the pot?
You're being cared for? Content with your lot?
So things are looking up, then? They're not:
It's a drop in the ocean, that's what.'

From 'Ballad of a drop in the ocean' by Bertolt Brecht

When I was eight or nine I sometimes went to meet my father coming home. He'd cross the footbridge over the White Cart River not far from our street. The bridge is sixty foot long and was built for men like my dad. It was a shortcut from Pollok, the big post-war housing scheme where we lived, to Paisley Road West, and buses for the Govan shipyards or Rolls Royce in Hillington. It connected us to the world of work. Sometimes it was hard to see my old man. There were so many bodies streaming over the bridge at exactly quarter past five every night. So many men.

That was twenty years ago. In those days we played in the river on rafts built from wooden pallets we'd acquired from building sites. We even went swimming. But if you stand at the foot of the bridge today you hardly see a soul. The water is full of tyres and old shopping trolleys, despite the clean-up efforts of the local angling club. You meet the odd single parent pulling her buggy over the bridge to get to the special offers in Safeway. Or somebody on their way to sign on the broo which is now in Hillington. The manufacturing industry which dictated where we lived and how we lived has gone. The same people live here. Everything else has changed.

I suppose the bridge is a bit of a symbol of our isolation, our fragile concrete link to the outside world. You'll see something similar in Easterhouse on the other side of Glasgow. As you turn off the M8, there's a sign which says 'Welcome to the township of Easterhouse'. It struck me the first time I saw it. I thought: that's true, these places *are* like townships in South Africa. You might not need a passbook to get in and out. But you need enough money for the bus fares. Your Transcard is your passbook. Otherwise you're stuck in your scheme.

Glasgow has four big peripheral areas – Easterhouse, Drumchapel, Pollok, and Castlemilk. All suffer entrenched poverty and poor housing which also affects many smaller schemes around the city. It's just more concentrated here. Having said that, I like living in Pollok. I love the insularity. I love feeling part of something. I admire the people: their resilience, their humour, their sense of values. If I ever have a family, I couldn't imagine bringing them up anywhere else. But there's an increasing ghettoization taking place in these areas. And it's not just the physical barrier of the White Cart, following the curve of my street before turning towards Paisley and spilling into the Clyde at Renfrew. Life on my side of the water is totally different from normality – or what the media tells us is normality.

The barriers were not so visible at first, when everyone was employed. My earliest memories of Pollok are happy. Lots of kids and trees to climb. A bit of space. My parents Alice and Tommy moved here with me and my older sisters, Lynn and Carol, in 1966. I was two. Linthaugh Road was paradise compared with the two rooms and a scullery we left behind in Govan's McKechnie Street.

Now we were on the top floor of a modern tenement. Pollok has the highest concentration of flat-roofed tenements in Glasgow. Sketched on the architect's board, it must have looked like something from one of those early Spanish holiday brochures. The round windows, the verandas, the wide boulevard: all very Mediterranean. But without the sun.

My mum is quite a spiritual person. In the early years she'd go out to the veranda just to admire the changing seasons. The rent was £10 a month – a lot in those days. Sometimes she'd have to make a choice midweek. Would she buy that packet of soap powder she needed – or take the bus to visit her mother in Govan? She missed her mum, my gran Rose. Then she looked down the street, at the gardens and the trees and felt it was worth the sacrifice.

My mother has an interesting background. Her grandfather, Alexander Cameron, was a shipwright, carpenter and union agitator. He was a naval petty officer in the Battle of Jutland during the First World War. When he came back to Govan he was shocked at the conditions men worked under at Alexander Stephen's shipyard. There were no toilets and the yard stank and bred disease. Alexander kicked up a fuss. He started campaigning for toilet facilities. When he got his books Mr Stephen personally told him he'd never work on the Clyde again.

By all accounts he was a proud man, self-educated and articulate. He was forced to take the hunger trail to Australia. The farm work waiting for him was practically indentured labour – men were treated like slaves. Alexander, being the type of guy he was, rebelled against this. He must have banjoed someone, because he left Australia with the police chasing him and ended up hoboing round the world for twenty-eight years. This meant my great-grandmother, Alice Dailley, was left alone in Govan with her two children. She scrubbed subway stations for a living, getting up at five every morning before the trains began. She'd be doing that when there was snow on the ground. Kneeling on the cold steps meant her legs ulcerated. The varicose veins burst. Even then she had to go out and work.

All hell broke loose when her long-lost husband made contact again. He was in South Africa, working in the gold mines. Alice thought he was dead. There was a big dilemma over whether she'd have him back in her bed: 'I've done without a man all these years', she told the family. But she was a right good Catholic and, in the end, she took him back as a lodger. My mother remembers a man embittered by his experiences. His back had twice been broken while mining. He believed children should be seen and not heard. Her gran's house, which had been full of love and children, was never the same again.

My mother is named after Alice Dailley and she inherited her sense of values. Everyone in Govan knew the old lady and came to her for help. I was told of the day she sent my mother to buy butter, milk and cheese for a lassie who'd appeared at the door with wee bits of weans. 'I'm not going messages for her!' said my mother, who was then a child herself. 'Her man drinks.' Alice put her against the wall and said: 'You will not be the judge of whether a child eats'. If you needed, you got. That was the unwritten motto.

Things were not much easier for my parents' generation in the 1950s. There was the NHS if you took ill. But you still had to work hard. My mother's first job on leaving school at sixteen was in a dairy. She had to get up before six just like her gran. My father was a moulder to trade. He worked in Harland and Wolff's yard but moved to Rolls Royce as a storeman when there was no longer a demand for his skills. You had to take what you could get. Still, everybody thought it was the bees knees at the time, a job for life, big factory, security, that kind of thing. My mum had several jobs: cleaning, serving in pubs and shops. I remember her working in a butcher's.

We were not poverty-stricken. We were a normal working-class family. Financially it was always tight, though you don't realise these things till you get older. Every penny they earned went into the house and my mother liked everything to be just right. They never went out socialising. Mum worked nights so she could be there for the children during the day. Dad took over when she left for her stint in *The Bay Horse*. That was the price of 1960s prosperity. We seemed comfortable, but it was a grind for my parents.

Mum was always struggling against the penetrative dampness in the houses which were not designed for the Scottish weather. She bought storage heaters to see if they would make a difference. But she had to give them up because of the bills. So our bedrooms stayed icy. She seemed to spend her life looking over her shoulder at the electricity board. What am I doing wrong? she'd ask. We don't drink, we don't go on fancy continental holidays. Am I a bad manager?

Much later she staged her own rent strike over the issue. She demanded the council take her to court – so she could argue that they'd broken the tenancy agreement. She won her case but the settlement was a pittance because she was working by then and didn't get Legal Aid until she stopped work due to ill health.

Even before she won the case, they'd admitted culpability. They put false walls in the house to try to hide the damp. It's still hopeless, though the rooms have shrunk.

As kids, we looked forward to a better future. Pollok was built on a country estate and part of the deal when the council bought the land was the retention of parkland and trees. So although the buildings are ugly, it's quite green.

When we weren't playing kerbie – throwing a football from one side of the road to another, we'd hang around closes. We called ourselves the Brocky Boys, the closes being in Brockburn Road. Ironically, now I'm a councillor, I often get complaints from constituents worried about groups of young boys hanging about closes. It's a bit of a dilemma because, of course, I was that soldier. But I can understand their worry. Nowadays, there is lot more aggression. Sure, we were rogues, back in the 1970s: camping out overnight after lying to our parents. Doing commando runs through the back greens in the pitch dark. Getting up at six to steal rolls and milk from outside the local newsagents. It all seems pretty innocent with hindsight. Today, kids that age are carrying blades. Thirteen year-olds, all tooled up. There's a culture of fear. Kids are frightened of being attacked, so they carry weapons. Adults are frightened of the kids, so they stay indoors.

When I was growing up in Linthaugh Road there were different kinds of childhoods. Adolesence for some was glue-sniffing and petty crime. But for me, and lots of others, life revolved around sport. Especially football. Pollok United, the boys' club we played for, is worth mentioning. It was a good example of how communities can come together to organise themselves. Collective action can be a social thing, like a football team or a pensioners' lunch club. Or it can be more explicitly political. Either way, working-class people tend towards collective action even when the odds are stacked against them. That's what this book is all about.

In Pollok the people were up against their environment. The scheme was considered a paradise when our family arrived in 1966. But like other social-planning nightmares around Glasgow, it was only paradise on paper.

It's a familiar tale. The adults missed stopping for a chat at Govan Cross. They missed going to the pictures, the dancing, the shops. In Pollok there was no centre of organisation. Nowhere to stop and chat. Nowhere to have a drink or a dance. Only churches, schools and a bit of windswept turf.

But people got together and tried to build new communities. We first heard about the boys' club when I was nine. Our neighbour, Mr Little, suggested I join. Every Saturday my dad came to watch me play. When I was ten, he began to take the team. He did that for fifteen years, along with his brother, my Uncle Jim. Eventually he was elected club president. Probably because he's a very passive, easy-going guy – not like me. He's not a particularly political animal. More a get-on-with-life person. He was a shop-steward for a short time, but only because there was no one else to do it. But commitment to the community is political in itself.

It takes a lot of enthusiasm to run a boys' club. With adult amateur teams, the guys have to go down and line the park, fork the park, put the nets up. But there's even more work when kids are involved. You have to keep the strips clean and make sure they all have a decent pair of boots. They have to have parental permission to be there in the first place. At the end of the evening they must get up the road safely. It's a big responsibility.

Whenever I was looking for some pocket money on a Friday night, I knew I'd find my dad in the laundrette in Paisley Road West. He'd be washing three or four sets of strips. He was exiled there because they'd have blazing rows in the house if he used the pulley and my mum couldn't get her washing done.

The club was marvellous for the area. There were lots of teams for different age groups, right up to eighteen year-olds. Hundreds of young boys were taken off the streets. It gave them a chance to vent their anger and frustration. Certainly it shaped me as a person. My two closest friends from the age of nine, Monty and Billy, were great footballers. By the time Billy was twelve, Manchester United had shown an interest in him. They flew him all over the world: to Switzerland, France and Canada. He had a tremendous future ahead of him and eventually signed for Rangers at sixteen. He's currently with Dunfermline.

Billy was very disciplined at an early age. That rubbed off on myself and Monty. When I was about twelve I started doing karate twice a week. It was a brilliant thing for disciplining your mind and body. It gave me a lot of confidence. Monty felt a bit out of things, with me doing the karate and Billy wrapped up in the football. So he went off and formed the Pollok Young Loyalists flute band. He originally played with an Orange Band in Bridgeton. But they argued over uniforms or something. Anyway, it didn't come between us. We fell out after Old Firm games, but only for a wee while.

Lots of social activities spun off the football club. Most Friday nights we held discos at Howford school to raise money. Young teenagers from all over Pollok came to these Howford discos in their glad rags. Teddy boys, punks and poseurs. We were poseurs, which meant wearing your sweater casually round your neck – along with straight-legged cords and Kickers. Of course we could never afford the real French Kickers, with the wee leather label on them. We wore lace-up boots that looked pretty much the same.

One of the great characters I remember from this time was a boy called Tam McGurk. Monty got really friendly with him. He was one of the roguish types of guys, always in some kind of trouble. But he was a great laugh. He had that real Glasgow wit. When he was fifteen they put him away for something. He went sniffin' glue soon after he came back. They pulled his body out of the Cart. He thought he could walk on water.

Tam's funeral was in St James' Chapel and Monty didn't go. I went to see him afterwards and he was crying. He didn't go because it was in the chapel. It was so stupid, he really wanted to be there.

Young people's lives are still so riven with division, both territorial and sectarian. It's 'I'm with the Young Team or the Krew or the Kross or the Bushwackers'. 'I'm a Tim and you're a Teddy Bear.' It's all about wanting to be part of something. That's why others might want to be in a band. Nobody wants to be on their own. I just wish they all wanted to be in Scottish Militant Labour. Maybe they won't all join. But we can at least campaign for better youth facilities. That's one way of bringing them together.

Pollok was full of gangs when I was young. I used to run behind what was called the Spe. It meant Swing Park End. I wasn't in it, we just ran behind the big guys like Alky, Tub, Brad and Fin. They wore Crombie jackets and Doc Martens and carried big blades. You'd see them showing off their chibs in the woods. But I never saw any of these weapons being used.

I was never a fighter. All I was really interested in at that time was earning a wage, playing football and chasing women. When I say women I mean girls my own age, although it was always more impressive if you got off with someone older than you. Every weekend we would hold record sessions in Monty's house. Record session was the euphemism for a party, except you played lots of slow ballads by Rod Stewart and The Commodores. These gave you the opportunity to increase your status in terms of the number of girls you'd been with.

At around fifteen the girl I was going steady with thought she was pregnant. To think of it now, I was a selfish wee creep. I remember thinking I was going to join the army to get away. I even went up to the recruiting station in town. I'd always been attracted to that life. I loved army films and the thought of being able to do all those five-mile assault courses with the pack on your back. It's the same appeal as running a marathon, being able to push your body to a certain level. The camaraderie appealed as well. I like being part of a crowd.

This crisis with my girlfriend was really serious. I remember I even prayed – which is almost as bad as wanting to enlist. In the end it was a false alarm. Just as well cause her parents were really strict and religious. We would have been marched to the altar. I remember a song by Squeeze that was in the charts at the time – Up The Junction. It really evoked life for so many of my contemporaries: getting someone pregnant at sixteen or seventeen, settling down, discovering after a year you hated each other's guts. Then the guy would get up and leave and the girl is left with her life ruined. Women always come off worse. My mum would have skelped me if she knew how I was behaving towards girls. She never brought me up to be like that – but peer group influences are very strong.

My mother was left to be the disciplinarian in the house because my dad was very easy-going. But she was the biggest influence on me politically. During the 1974 miners' strike she explained why I couldn't play with my toys in the blackouts. These men had to go down dark holes in the ground. They were trying to get a decent wage. I thought 'That's rotten' and supported the strike.

My mother was a strong trade unionist. After working a while in pubs like *The Bay Horse* and *Argosy* she began to organise workers in the bar trade. Eventually she was an official in the Transport and General Workers Union. She was very prominent in a strike they had against Tennent Caledonian over union recognition in the early 70s. The company thought the workers would lose because they couldn't picket every pub. Instead they picketed the brewery and won the strike.

I was still a kid and resented the amount of time she spent away from home. She takes great delight now in reminding me how I used to moan 'I hate thae unions.' I also used to worry about her involvement in what was then called the battered wives' movement – it would be domestic violence today. We never saw anything like that in my house. My father never lifted his hand. But people in school talked about how their fathers took belts to them. Anyway, I'd have visions of these aggressive husbands turning up at the battered wives' meetings and having a go at my mum.

All this activity eventually led her into full-time education. She went to Newbattle Abbey, which was a residential college especially for mature students. Then she went to Jordanhill to do social work. It must have been very hard for her. There was an attitude in family circles of: 'That's terrible, she's leaving the weans.'

When working-class women become involved in political activity or education, it often causes a lot of resentment. Men feel threatened as women become a bit more dominant. In my own mum and dad's case it was more a question of incompatibility. Like so many in their generation they were encouraged to get married without really asking whether they were suited to a long-term relationship. My lasting impression was of a wonderful mum and a wonderful dad, but not much of a couple. They split up when I was eighteen but it was all very amicable and they're still good friends.

It was my mum who encouraged me to get an education. My dad was more chuffed that I got trials with football teams. I had an idea that I wanted to be a mechanic like my uncle, although I've always been hopeless at anything technical. But my mum came back from a parents' night once and said the teachers felt I was setting my sights too low. So she pushed me.

The one subject I really enjoyed was modern studies. It was a real eye opener. John McMenamin and Danny Corbett were both younger than the other teachers. They made jokes. The style of the class was different. John McMenamin wrote to me when I was in prison. I wrote back and said "You do realise you're partly responsible for all the trouble I've caused. . . ."

They gave lessons in truth. Things on television began to make sense. Learning what apartheid was, how the blacks were murdered, imprisoned and denied the vote, was a real eyeopener. America was no longer the land of the free after modern studies. John Wayne was always a bit of a hero of mine. But the teacher said he only got all those good parts because he had grassed on his mates during the McCarthy witchhunts.

Apart from Modern Studies, I wasn't that interested. I got a job when my 'O' grades were finished. I wasn't really expecting to stay on at school. I worked in Burton's menswear and found I had a talent for selling ties.

I went back to school and sat Highers but again left with thoughts of employment and not university. I got a job as a labourer with Pickfords removals. I enjoyed the routine of getting up in the morning and going to work in your overalls. It was a good crack. I would have stayed there if my exam results hadn't worked out. But I got the grades and went to university in 1981 at the age of seventeen.

My mum saved me from the deference factor that comes with social inequality. The idea that 'education isnae for the likes of us.' That's ingrained into working-class children at a very early age. Few of their role models are educated. The value of education isn't understood or even accepted among a lot of families in the schemes. Reading books isn't something that comes naturally. They are encouraged to think this way. Just consider the waste. All the brilliant minds, all the talents. Neglected and left to wither.

Monty was really clever. He got seven 'O' grades. But he left school at sixteen to bring some money into the house. He was slaving as an apprentice turner and fitter in this engineering shop. It wasn't a good job and wasn't expanding his mind. In the final year of his apprenticeship, he got paid off. That's when he decided to get some Highers and go to university. Eventually he graduated in social administration. But it caused problems in the house. Monty's father was very community-oriented. He helped run the boys' club with my own dad. Like many of his generation, he saw Monty's decision as a kind of betrayal. He actually said: 'Is a boiler suit not good enough for you?'

Stirling University was a real culture shock. My mother encouraged me to go there because it had a radical reputation. You might remember a big demo in the early 1970s when a student threw eggs at the Queen.

A lot of the students came from very wealthy backgrounds. I always remember someone in a tutorial who asked: 'What is the dole?' It was my first experience of anyone like that. I just couldn't imagine the kind of life they led down in the Home Counties.

Education for me was a politically-transforming experience. I was very nervous throughout the first year. I was the first one in my family to get to university. My mother had expended a lot of time and effort to get me there. So I was worried about failure and studied all the time.

And it was like getting keys to open doors. In school, Modern Studies had whetted my appetite but it only gave a fleeting impression of the world. We learned about Martin Luther King, but not Malcolm X. Waterloo, not Peterloo. Labour history was not on the curriculum until I got to Stirling.

I was encouraged through my courses to learn about Marx. Here was a theory, a view of the world, which related to my own experiences. Everything came together. I began to enjoy the idea of education in and of itself and became totally convinced of Marxism as an outlook on life. It armed me politically, and told me inequality was not rooted in human nature. Before history was written, society did not have divisions – although everyone was very poor. It was only when these primitive communist societies turned to agriculture that they divided into opposing groups. This happened when extra food was created. (This is what Marxists call a surplus.) A powerful group emerged to control it – like the king and his family. The food was traded for other goods: pottery, leather or cloth. Money then made its appearance. As trade grew, so did demand for more and more goods or commodities as Marx called them. These were manufactured by people who sold their labour for a wage – the working class.

This was – and is a quick summary of – capitalism. It was an improvement in some ways. It meant technology advanced quickly, more new commodities appeared, and society made some progress. The problem was inequality. Working-class people were forced to sell their labour for less than the full value of the commodity they made. The difference – the surplus value – was pocketed by the capitalist.

Capitalism means a small group own and control the wealth created by a larger group. The ruling class of capitalists maintain their grip through a power structure called the state. This might include the army to frighten people, or religion which tells them to accept their fate. The law is an arm of the state which justifies the ownership of property – allowing the ruling class to hold on to the wealth. The media performs a similar role.

In developed capitalist societies there is a lot of surplus. So the state which guards it has to be very big and sophisticated. The British state, for example, offers the illusion of democracy. It tells people they are in control – but all the while keeps the surplus in the hands of that same small group.

Through reading I also learned that struggle between different classes has been a symptom of every society since primitive communism disappeared. There was the slave revolt in Rome led by Spartacus in 73 BC. Or the Peasants revolt led by Wat Tyler against the original Poll Tax in England in 1381. The French Revolution of 1789 saw the middle classes overthrow the aristocracy. But revolution will not change society if it simply replaces one ruling élite with another.

We have to change the system so wealth can be shared among the people who created it in the first place. At university I learned that this was not fairy-tale idealism. It wouldn't mean going back in time to impoverished, primitive societies. Britain is a very rich country with a large surplus. According to the Organisation for Economic Co-operation and Development, which brings together the world's biggest economies, the UK has the sixth largest industrial output in the world. We are the fourth largest producer of chemicals in the world and the fifth largest producer of machinery and processed food. We are the seventh largest producer of textiles. Put simply, if all that was divided equally we wouldn't have to live in damp houses.

While I was learning all this as part of my politics and economics course, I was also getting a political education through the Militant Tendency. I had joined the Labour Party at the age of seventeen because it was the organisation for the working class. My parents were both members.

I was attracted to Militant because its student members seemed to come from the same kind of background as mine. That was reflected in the views expressed in their paper, which I agreed with. Also, they dressed more normally than the other far left groups. That probably sounds narrow-minded. It *is* narrow-minded, but that's how I thought.

Hazel Sutherland was the Militant person responsible for keeping in contact with me at university. 'Here's a pamphlet, did you read the last one I gave you?' she'd say. I was always letting her down. Football came before political meetings. But she came back every time. I grew to admire her tenacity.

Militant was also active in Pollok. I remember being really impressed with Terry Fields when I heard him speak in Partick Burgh Halls in 1982. The theme was 'Defend the socialists, expel the Tories'. As I remember, Jim Devine of the health workers' union COHSE, now Unison, was on the platform.

It was during this period I discovered Glasgow's labour history. Even when you read Marx, or learn about revolutions elsewhere, it seems very far away. But there was very nearly a revolution in Glasgow in 1919 just after the First World War. The workers had gone on strike, demanding shorter hours. In January they assembled in George Square and raised the Red Flag. The government sent tanks into Glasgow to put down the revolt and imprison the leaders. This forty-hours strike was led by men who had been members of the Clyde Workers' Committee formed in 1915. The CWC was a group of shop stewards who brought together workers across different shipyards and engineering shops on the Clyde. They took on the Government in 1916 and were such a threat that ten members were deported to Edinburgh.

The leading figure, I discovered, was John Maclean, who was imprisoned for speaking out against the war. He was born in Pollokshaws, just a mile away from where I lived. Why did we not know about him? He was a great Marxist teacher who held economics classes all over the West of Scotland. Lenin appointed him the Bolshevik government's first consul in Britain after the Russian Revolution in 1917. The more I read, the more angry I got. We hear about other cities which have suffered military occupation. Why not Glasgow in the 20th century? Our heritage has been wiped off the curriculum.

It's vital to have this sense of history and pride – something to relate to. It tells you that people have always been struggling. The struggle we are now involved in to change society has been going on for several hundred years.

Coming back to Pollok from Stirling was heartbreaking. The place was getting progressively poorer. I'd notice the despair on women's faces and it turned my stomach.

My time at university coincided with the big recession of the early 1980s. It hit our traditional industry really hard although it had been declining for some time. Between 1971 and 1983, Glasgow lost forty-five per cent of its manufacturing jobs, according to figures compiled by the district council. Iron and steel making were wiped out in those years. Clyde Iron, Tollcross, Hallside and Clydebridge works, along with Parkhead Forge, all shut between 1977 and 1983.

Singer's once huge sewing machine plant in Clydebank was closed. Goodyear Tyres disappeared from Drumchapel. Wills, the tobacco firm which dominated the East End, cut back severely. As did Rolls Royce in Hillington.

Lots of people in my parents' generation lost their jobs. Uncle John was the car mechanic I had hoped to be – a really skilled man. Now he drives the lorries which fix motorway lights.

It was like a blanket being drawn over the place. The Howford discos stopped. There aren't so many boys' teams now. That's partly due to the cost of hiring a school. Charges have gone up from £1 to £6 a night. If you take several teams, you're talking around £30 a week, a lot of money.

And unemployment also demoralises people. Some think: What's the point? What are we building for? Pollok is better than many places because Militant is strong here. People are defiant, more willing to have a go. But often enthusiasm is not enough. The changing nature of employment can put barriers in the way of community organisation. Lots of people take work when they can find it, cash in hand, on a day to day basis. Labour is being casualised. We're going back to the treatment the dockers' union fought to end – men queuing each morning hoping they'd be hired.

One guy I know recently started taking local boys' teams. He can't guarantee being around each week. Sometimes he'll be out on a Saturday, driving a Mercedes for weddings for an extra tenner. What can he do? Like anyone else, he wants a bit on top of his benefit. His life is at the whim of the market. We often hear the working class today compared unfavourably to their predecessors in the 1930s. Why is it that the poor of that period still managed to run their cycling clubs and their temperance halls? Did they have a stronger sense of solidarity?

These questions fail to take into account the closeness of the links between lives and work. Take the pit villages of Lanarkshire. They had a welfare state going before Beveridge even thought it up. Ambulance services were run on penny wage deductions which also funded silver bands, libraries, debating societies and football teams. When the mines closed in the 1960s, all that went. Lanarkshire's just a shell now. People still have a pint or a game of bingo at the Miners' Welfare, but very often that's it. These places are ghost towns. When you don't have the employment and industry to organise around, you don't have the same community spirit. You see it in the city, with the closure of factory and railway clubs.

Unemployment levels were similar in the 1930s. But the poor were not as marginalised as they are in the 1990s. Now, unemployment is highly concentrated in the schemes over several generations. My friends and neighbours are cut off from the very prospect of work. That's the difference.

These people have been marooned by capitalism. That gives right-wing thinkers an excuse to blame them for their own poverty, calling them an underclass. American writers like Charles Murray say this underclass have become welfare-dependent, they lack the work ethic, are criminally-inclined, immoral, cut off from normal values. Now you hear those insults traded in Britain – by the social security minister, Peter Lilley, among others. Unfortunately, the chorus of moral indignation includes voices from the Labour Party. Some things never change. As cockney soldiers sang in the trenches during WW1: 'It's the same the whole world over/It's the poor wot gets the blame/It's the rich wot gets the gravy/Ain't it all a bleedin shame.'

How many researchers in the Adam Smith Institute have experienced the strain of budgeting on a low income? How many know the indignity of having to beg for money because the mattress on your child's bed is rotting with mould? Have they felt the constant edginess of worrying if your powercard will last till Monday when you get your benefit? This is real life for every family in my close.

The little boy downstairs from me loves pigeons. Sean is two years old and could spend hours peering over the windowsill, watching the birds settle on the balcony. His mother, Sandra Harvey, says he's daft about animals. But he's never been to the zoo. He's never been on a holiday or a family day trip. He just watches the pigeons.

Sandra is thirty and trying to bring up four children on benefit. She thinks it's important for them to go outside Pollok for a bit of stimulation. Her daughter, Suzanne, went to the safari park with the school recently. But only after she had carefully put aside fifty pence a week for several weeks. The kids are always asking to go swimming

and rollerskating. Swimming is rare as it costs around £2 for a trip
to the pool. They have never been rollerskating.

All Sandra's children have suffered from asthma, but Sean is the
worst. She's on first-name terms with the accident and emergency
staff at Yorkhill Children's Hospital. Asthma can be triggered by
moving from a hot to a cold room. The bedrooms in our tenements
are freezing cold. Sometimes, in winter, all the Harveys sleep in the
livingroom. The kids wear woolly jumpers in bed at night. Sandra
wonders why the older ones still wet the bed in the winter months.
That creates extra expense, like new mattresses. More debt. She has
to find £7 a week for the baby's disposable nappies. She used
towelling nappies on all the rest. But Sean has eczema, the condition
which often comes with asthma. Urine burns into his skin.

Sandra lost a daughter at one week old a few years ago. The baby
had a heart defect. The pressure of it all resulted in Sandra taking
epileptic fits for the first time in her life. She never knows when they
are going to happen. Once she collapsed in a fit while pouring tea
and scalded herself from the wrist to the elbow. Another time she
fell and split her head on the corner of the fireplace. She is terrified
it will happen when she is alone with Sean. Sandra's stress levels are
often determined by how her giro is stretching. Epileptic fits could
be triggered simply by not having enough milk for the weekend.
During her last pregnancy she received a milk token for an extra
pint a day. That's to ensure she has enough calcium. But she gives
it to her children.

Think of all the advice women today are given while they are
pregnant. In one of the bestselling books on this subject *Vitamins
and Minerals for a Healthy Pregnancy*, the author, Dr Richard Gerson,
writes; 'Good health comes from nutritional awareness, physical
fitness, stress management, self-responsibility and sensitivity to one's
environment. Everything you do affects your unborn child, from
your state of mind to the food you eat.' The one thing he doesn't
mention is money, and the security it brings. That's the thing a
woman must have before she can develop nutritional awareness or
stress management. That's what she needs to buy the Vitamin C rich

food which Dr Gerson says will develop the baby's tissue and immune system.

All the foods he recommends – spinach, wheatgerm on your cereal in the morning – that's all out of the question for Sandra. She has more immediate considerations: like whether she should borrow from relatives to feed the kids over the weekend. Is it any wonder that low birthweight babies are seventy per cent higher in deprived areas like Pollok than in Eastwood not far away? The Greater Glasgow Health Board's figures show that infant deaths in Glasgow's poor areas are double those in the rich suburbs.

Recent research by Professor David Barker at Southampton University has shown that what happens to a baby in the womb affects its chances of getting heart disease and strokes in adulthood. Maybe that's why death rates for people under sixty-four in Glasgow's schemes are twice the level of the wealthiest areas.

Sandra's family mainly get corned beef, sausages and mashed potatoes and mince on very rare occasions. There's hardly a pick on her kids. She buys all her food from Capital Freezeway, because it's cheaper than the supermarket.

Most working-class families in Glasgow fry their food or open a tin of spaghetti. Fat fills you up and keeps you warm. It's easier to manage. I remember when my mum was studying away from home my father fried everything. He'd even put the eggs in the chip pan till they were almost black.

Basic economics is more important than culture when it comes to diet. Supermarkets have a wider variety of healthy food. When your giro comes in, you have to deduct money for your powercard, your gas bill and your catalogue. You are not going to spend what's left on a bumper shopping at the supermarket. If you did that you'd be penniless until the next giro arrived in a fortnight. Nobody can trek to the supermarket each day, buying dribs and drabs. Certainly not a woman with kids in prams and no car. So you go to the wee row of shops round the corner. One day it's a pint of milk or a loaf of bread, next day it's a packet of sausages and a tin of beans. These shops are more expensive because they have a captive market. The food is poor quality: the few fresh vegetables will be old and unappetising. Yet this is the only way to budget. And in a lot of schemes, there is no choice because there is no supermarket anyway.

The end result of this still stares you in the face. It might help explain a recent survey by Glasgow University which found that residents of Drumchapel were four centimetres shorter than their contemporaries in neighbouring Bearsden.

In the 1930s, when nostalgics now insist we had a better class of working class, there was also a debate over how much the poor required to live. George Orwell's *The Road to Wigan Pier* talks about the public row over the Means Test in the 1930s. This cut benefits to a minimum and split families by forcing anyone who was working to leave home. One middle-class person wrote to the *News of the World* claiming it was possible to survive on four shillings a week – as long as you didn't spend money on fuel and ate all your food raw.

Such letter writers accused unemployed miners at the time of squandering their means-tested dole money on luxuries. Sounds familiar? And what were these excessive items? Tea, jam and sugar. The killjoy correspondent thought the money would be better spent on extra carrots. Orwell wrote at the time: 'When you are unemployed, which is to say when you are underfed, harassed, bored and miserable, you don't want to eat dull, wholesome food. You want something a little bit "tasty".

There are many Tory politicians and journalists who still think the definition of poverty should be the absolute minimum a family needs to feed itself. Even though the rich have become much richer in the last hundred years, these people believe the working class – who are, after all, responsible for the economic growth this century – should survive on the subsistence level of the 1890s.

'Most people in this country, including the unemployed, live in what the labourer of a hundred years ago would have considered unimaginable luxury', wrote Geoffrey Wheatcroft in the *Sunday Telegraph* in 1991.

Often I'll hear journalists sneer about the satellite dishes attached to the balconies of council flats – the feckless poor wasting their income on luxuries. Paying for Sky TV is actually cheaper than taking a family of four to the movies every fortnight. Going to the pictures means bus fares into town and a taxi back – most families can't afford a car. After you pay for the tickets, juice and ice cream for the kids, you're lucky to get change out of £30. That's the cost of a month's subscription to satellite TV. It's cheaper than traditional forms of working-class entertainment.

Accusations about the unemployed going to the movies or wearing cheap, fashionable clothes were also made in the 1930s. Orwell wrote: 'The youth who leaves school at fourteen and gets a blind alley job is out of work at 20, probably for life; but for two pounds ten on the hire purchase he can buy himself a suit which for a little while, and at a distance, looks as though it has been tailored at Savile Row. The girl can look like a fashion plate for an even lower price. You may have three half pence in your pocket and not a prospect in the world, and only the corner of a leaky bedroom to go home to; but in your new clothes you can stand on the street corner, indulging in a private daydream of yourself as Clark Gable or Greta Garbo, which compensates you for a great deal.'

Perhaps our detractors believe we should do without luxuries altogether? Like the man in the 1930s *News of the World* who would have us give up cups of tea for extra carrots. No television. No visits to the pub to meet friends. No jam or sugar. That's the logical conclusion. Would the people casting stones be willing to deny themselves in this way? I don't think so. So why should we?

Poor people want the best for their families, so they are literally swimming in debt. The catalogue, the Provy (Provident) cheque and the illegal moneylender have succeeded the pawnshop and clothing club of Orwell's day. The government encouraged this by expanding consumer credit in the 1980s.

A quarter of all households with debts in 1990 had incomes of less than £150 a week, according to a survey by the Policy Studies

Institute. This compares to just 3 per cent of households on £400 a week. Strathclyde Region's Money Advice Centres asked why clients had fallen into debt. A fifth blamed redundancy, the same number who said low income. Another 17 per cent blamed the breakdown in relationships and one in ten said poor health was the cause. Well over half of those seeking help for debt in Strathclyde have kids.

Sandra usually asks me to keep the kids' toys at Christmas time. Especially if it's something bulky like a new bike or a board game. She admits she gets most of her stuff from catalogues. And she admits she can't afford it. But working-class parents, quite rightly, want to give their kids a good Christmas. I loved that time of year as a kid. All my uncles and aunties came round for a big party and everyone was dead warm. But I hated the run up to it, because of the tension in the house.

I remember one year my mum hadn't been keeping well. She smokes like a chimney at the best of times and this year she'd had a big operation. I honestly believe she thought she didn't have long to go. So she wanted to give us a Christmas to remember and got herself into all this debt. We all got leather jackets, which were a big status symbol at that time, *real leather!*

I still get quite cut up seeing what Christmas does to young mothers. They just want to give their kids so much. They take on loans they know will never really be cleared. Not unless Prince Charming whisks them off, like Richard Gere in *An Officer and a Gentleman*. I've yet to see that happen in Pollok. But I'd never condemn parents for spending the money. In fact, I'm proud of that spirit. Why shouldn't our kids have a good Christmas?

It's ironic that people who blame us for getting into debt also support an economic system which encourages us to consume. Capitalism has to keep creating new markets. Right now, Sandra's wee boy is on at her to buy him the trainers with the light that flashes on and off as your foot hits the ground. They cost about £80. She took him to buy shoes in Paisley Road West and he refused to wear the ones on the sale rack. He thought he'd be laughed at in school.

Advertising bombards kids with the latest Nike Jordan trainers and Adidas sweatshirts. It tells them they're less of a person if they don't have the new rave gear. Then the State doesn't give them any dole money. If they do get work, it's a youth training scheme at 50 pence an hour. A real job will not pay much more. Employers know they can pay sixteen and seventeen year-olds what they like as the alternative is often destitution.

Why wonder if teenagers get involved in theft, in pushing or using drugs? What other future do they have? It's an earner. I don't condone these things, but you have to try to understand it. If poverty doesn't kill you slowly through heart disease and stress, it finishes you off quickly with hard drugs. Scotland has 20,000 injecting drug addicts according to the Home and Health Department in 1993. That's twice the rate for the rest of Britain, France, Italy and four times as many as in the Netherlands. Drug abuse is now the biggest single cause of death among young people in Glasgow, according to the health board. You can't be like Neil Kinnock after the riots on Tyneside in 1991 and say: 'There's absolutely no excuse.' The statement is spot on but it was directed at the wrong villains. There is 'absolutely no excuse' for a system which robs young people of their own self-worth.

The other night I came home from a meeting and saw glass on the road outside my house. A crowd of weans of about thirteen or fourteen had set about the ice-cream van. About thirty of them charged out of a close, smashed all the van's windows and stole the popcorn. Don't ask me why it was just the popcorn. Obviously it wasn't very funny for the people in the van at the time.

The other day a wee boy was taken to hospital with concussion after he'd been attacked by some other kids. When I was coming up the stairs a group of ten years-olds said to me: Hey, Tommy, have you got a stick? We want to give X a doin' for what happened to Y. One window across the backgreen from me has been replaced – I don't exaggerate – about fifteen times in the last month. It's the close nearest the corner so the kids know they can run away and hide. There's nothing else for them to do.

They still play football. In fact, that's about their only aspiration, to be the next Ally McCoist. You look at their wee skinny legs and think: Well, the dice are loaded against them. I still like to take the boys around my block over to the fields for a game when the light nights come in. We do lots of exercising and training and hopefully they go home exhausted. Sometimes I ask them what they want to do when they grow up. It's a question that just doesn't inspire an answer. They say: There's nae jobs. If you had asked me that question at fourteen I'd have said I wanted to be a mechanic. But these kids have no expectations at all. And that hopelessness, that demoralisation, has not happened by accident.

Since 1979 there has been a deliberate attempt to diminish young people's ambitions in order to make them a more pliable workforce. This country has given up pretending to compete with Germany or Japan in terms of high-tech industry. The government has decided our competitors are low-wage economies like Taiwan.

Education is being tailored accordingly. In 1984 a leaked report from an official at the Department of Education warned against educating working-class children to high levels: 'If we have a highly educated and idle population we may possibly anticipate more serious conflict (than the Toxteth riots).' This appeared in a book called *Selection, Certification and Control* by Patricia Broadfoot.

Young working-class people have always been educated to have low expectations. But this is reinforced today as they are expected to go into low-paid jobs. According to the low pay unit seventy per cent of young people earn low pay and their average earnings have been slipping since 1979.

Whenever I speak to young people I encourage them to stay on at school. Not to get a job, because Highers won't necessarily get you a job. But so they understand, if nothing else, why they can't get a job.

The other thing I learned from university was the importance of organisation. That did not come through books. It certainly didn't come through student politics, which can be a bit of a game, removed from the lives of working people. It was through the miners' strike, which began in 1984. Although I was becoming more politically aware, I was not really politically committed even after joining Militant. I was still playing football every weekend and working two nights and weekends as a fitness instructor in a health studio.

Before I returned to university in 1984, I was regularly going down to the picket line at Killoch Colliery in Ayrshire with a team from Glasgow. I went back to university determined to carry on that activity. The local pit at Fallin was solid – no need for a picket. The miners were picketing the Castlehill pit near Castlebridge in Fife. To go with them, we'd have to get up at five to catch the bus to the Stirling Miners Welfare. At first I think the miners were suspicious of our motives. You can understand that – only five per cent of the university population are from manual backgrounds. And there is some truth in the saying that everybody's radical at university until they get their first accountancy job. But the men soon realised we were also working-class people who were on their side. They began to send the bus into the university to collect us.

Throughout all this, we began to attract students to Militant. People who had steered clear of campus politics saw us doing something practical, showing physical solidarity with the miners. I befriended lots of young miners and was really impressed with the way they organised themselves, without the need for bosses and managers. It showed me a future way of life. Not just on the basis of street collections and trying to stretch resources, but on the basis of the spirit demonstrated. It must have been like that during the Paris Commune in 1871 – trying to provide for everyone without any hierarchy, without anyone creaming off the surplus. The Parisians took control of their city after a long siege by the Prussians. They held elections and for two months the revolutionary city belonged to its citizens, or Communards as they named themselves. Marx called it the harbinger of a new society.

For me, the miners strike of 1984–85 was the harbinger of a new society. Just as the General Strike might have been for an earlier generation. The 1926 General Strike was in support of the miners whose pay was being cut by 20 per cent. But it was called off after nine days by the leaders of the TUC.

The miners in 1926 stayed out for eight months. They formed their own committees to look after everyone's needs. In East Fife – just one example – the local motor club offered them couriers and transport. Silver bands from Methil and Buckhaven played in towns up and down the east coast of Scotland, raising hundreds of pounds for the soup kitchens. The Clydeside MP John Wheatley wrote in 1926: The miners are fighting alone. But they are fighting the battle of the whole nation. That's how we felt in 1984–85. It was my last year at university. I was writing a dissertation about Marx's labour theory of value and spending most days organising picket buses, support meetings and collections. Miners' support groups were set up all over the country. The fourteen groups on Merseyside raised £1 million. There were collections of food outside supermarkets and, people raising money to take miners' families on holiday.

No one went hungry. Miners' wives were able to serve hundreds of meals in the welfare halls each day. Even the *Financial Times* called it, 'The biggest and most continuous civilian mobilisation in Britain since the second world war.' So many people recognised that their interests were connected to the miners' fight. They recognised the political nature of the strike.

Like everyone else involved, I was gutted when it was all over. The miners had fought themselves to exhaustion. I will always remember one pit delegate, speaking, I think, as the silver band led the miners back to work: 'This is the end', he said. 'The end of the beginning.'

What he meant was that the strike had ripped away the curtains of British society. It exposed the class nature of Britain to hundreds of thousands of people. Up until then they probably thought the police were just there to catch criminals and handle lost property. They probably thought the state was a neutral body which administered pensions and child benefit. They thought the media gave a well-balanced account of the news. After the strike nobody with any political consciousness could have doubted that the state was 100 per cent tied up with the Tories. Capitalism used the police, the judiciary and the media against the miners.

Defeatists, who include most of the leaders of the labour movement, said the strike was a failure. They still argue against taking any action unless success is guaranteed. Of course the main reason the miners had to return to work was because these same leaders refused to back the NUM, just like their 1926 predecessors.

Ordinary people had much more faith. That's why the strike was still worthwhile. Each struggle is a preparation for the next. If you do not fight, you simply end up demoralised. The strike did not just mobilise miners. It was not merely an industrial dispute over pit closures. It was a class confrontation involving pensioners, the unemployed, black people, students, and ordinary workers. There is a story, repeated up and down the country, of a man who put a tenner from his newly-cashed giro into the miners' support bucket: 'Are you sure you can afford to give that?' asked the collector. 'I can't afford not to', he replied.

He was right. Within three years of the strike ending the 1988 social security reforms were put in place. Benefits were snatched from the ill and handicapped. The unemployed had to beg for discretionary social fund loans. The gulf between rich and poor continued to grow. The Child Poverty Action Group in 1992 revealed the number of children living in poverty in this country had doubled since 1979. The government's own records show the gulf between the earnings of the richest ten per cent and the poorest ten per cent are wider than when records began in 1886.

Statistics like those show why it was important to support the strike. They link the interests of those aristocrats of labour, the miners, with the unemployed, the old, the unskilled and the low paid. Miners were being hit by a state bent on impoverishing the Polloks, the Easterhouses, and the Castlemilks as well as all those pithead communities. A state determined to destroy the manufacturing industry on which these places had depended: just as it was determined to close pits.

It was all part of the one miserable plan. But when the next stage, the Poll Tax, came along, we were ready for them. I graduated in 1985, the year the strike ended. I headed straight back home to Pollok: one of the thousands of young activists who had been politicised by the experiences of the previous year. Communities like Pollok could learn from 1984. When the next attack came, we would be prepared. Now it was the turn of the dispossessed working class to fight back.

2 Pollok fights back

'A time to rage, with righteous anger,
A time to rise, to point the finger'

(Ann Narky)

I had been back in Pollok for a year when I met big George
McNeilage again. It was the most significant thing to happen since
my return. We last spoke across the table in our form class at Lourdes
Secondary School. His big eyes were usually half shut, either from
drinking, or from exhaustion after a night's housebreaking. He was
a rogue, but a friendly rogue. Then I walked into a Labour Party
Young Socialists meeting on 'The Lessons of Chile' six years later
and he was sitting there. Except now his eyes were wide open.

I was then trying to build up the membership of the Pollok
branch of the Labour Party from an all time low of six. We needed
some youth and energy. George certainly had the energy – it was
where he channelled it that posed a problem.

I got on alright with George when he came to school. Our paths
seldom crossed after four o'clock. While I was away working
towards my karate brown belt, he'd be crouched underneath the
water tower up in the woods. Water towers are distinctive landmarks
in most housing schemes. They are geometric structures stretching

up from long concrete legs. Around thirty young boys would gather
in the stinking space beneath the tower, sniffing glue out of old crisp
bags. The ground underneath would be littered with that kind of
debris, along with piles of empty gas canisters.

He is one of nine children and lived in Dormanside Road, which
was then a notorious street round the corner from me. His mum
tried to bring them all up on benefit since the mid-seventies. That's
when George's father fell off a boiler in Ravenscraig, the big Scottish
steel plant. He never worked again.

George got his first taste of alcohol at twelve and says he was a
seasoned drinker by the age of thirteen. The housebreaking started
around that time. The first house he did belonged to a customer
who never tipped him in the three years he delivered her *Evening
Times*. After that first time, he didn't discriminate. All that was
required was a house with an open window. He'd steal jewellery
and videos. Mostly from poor homes around here in Pollok. He
would also cross the White Cart to Cardonald where better-off
workers live in cottage-type council houses or small bungalows.
Really rich pickings required a trip to the red sandstone villas of
Pollokshields, home to Glasgow's accountants and solicitors. Then
he had to be careful not to make a sound. He'd avoid the crunch of
the long gravel driveways and creep over the lawn.

George was what you call a creeper, a cat burglar. He'd sneak
into houses at two, three and four in the morning while people were
in their beds. He'd crawl across the bedroom floor to take the
wedding rings sitting on the dressing-table. He began to do it for
the buzz. He'd go out when there was £300 sitting under the carpet
in his room. Sometimes he would be lying at the foot of someone's
bed and they'd turn in their sleep and call out: 'Who is it?' George
would reply, cocky as anything 'It's only me!' and listen as they
rolled over and began snoring quietly again.

He left school at sixteen and got a YTS place with Govan
Shipbuilders. That only lasted a few months. He was paid off after
an accident when a drill bit lodged in his knee. George lived to get
a buzz. By 1981, when he was seventeen, he was taking all sorts of

tablets: uppers, downers, acid, speed, even travel sickness pills. Anything to get stoned. He was caught red-handed one night in 1984 and got four months' detention for housebreaking.

While he was inside, George began to look at his life and ask where he'd gone wrong. He felt terrible about what he'd done to his mother. She must have spent most of her time praying for him. While he was in jail George began to read the Bible. He was determined to change. But he came out into the same environment and was straight back on drugs.

Then he got involved in a Save the Children youth project in Pollok in 1986. Jim King, the project leader, took the young people away canoeing and hill walking – things George had never done in his life. He'd tell George he had a good heart and head and should go to college. That's what led to us meeting up again.

George felt a bit out of place at college. One day he was doing his usual rebel bit, staying in the class for a fag when everyone else was having dinner. He saw a copy of the *Militant* newspaper sticking out of a bag belonging to one of the guys from the scheme. He began to read and was impressed enough to ask the guy – Davie McDickens – about it when he came back. He told George about the meeting on Chile that Tuesday night in the Linthaugh Advice Centre.

George didn't want to come by himself and dragged a mate along. But in one of those stranger than fiction ironies, his mate spotted an open window on the way, and decided to go and screw a house instead of debating Allende's economic policy.

George argued against housebreaking by this time, saying it was stealing from our own people. But the boy headed for the window and George went to the meeting alone.

He said it changed his life. He'd always felt something was wrong, that his family and friends were hard done by. But he'd never heard any arguments for socialism. He never thought of Labour as a party which would transform the way he lived.

Then he heard a guy, Colin Fox, talk about Allende's attempt to do just that. At first he felt uncomfortable because it was all quiet ones from the scheme. But at the end he was really uplifted: I thought this must be the young ones in the Labour Party. They're totally different from the ones you see on television.

When I'd recovered from the shock of meeting George there, I started to make conversation. He ended up coming up to my house for a coffee and I asked him to go out flyposting with me the next night for a meeting we were having on South Africa. His finger got caught in the shutter of a shop. He lost his grip and was hanging there by his finger – it would have been severed had I not managed to grab him.

George embraced Marxism with an almost evangelical zeal. He became the Militant branch paper organiser at the first meeting and doubled the sales in a week. Everybody knew him. They'd say: 'You must be getting a turn out of this!', and he'd reply, 'This is my paper, you know! It costs me £1 a week out my giro.'

George might have changed. But his peer group was the same. He started slipping. He raised £300 to take a group of young people down to London for a Tories Out demonstration. But he blew £100 of it on smack. In the next few weeks he started going down again. That was when he jagged the jellies. Jellies or eggs are properly called Temazepam, a legally prescribed tranquillizer. Abuse of Temazepam is a Glasgow epidemic. It is so easy to obtain that younger kids who have never touched smack start to buy it. The rate of abuse is linked to poverty. Many of the people who sell it are also desperate. There have even been reports of pensioners flogging their prescriptions.

Injecting Temazepam is very dangerous. When George used it the powdered capsules would be split open and mixed with water. It now comes in jelly form and has to be melted down. It can congeal in the veins and lead to amputation. It also makes users very aggressive. George did some things that night he still won't talk about. He must have been really low when he did it because he's always been scared of needles. He came to see me afterwards. Tears were welling up, he kept saying how horrible he felt inside. He thought he'd let me down and let Militant down. But the very fact that he came and said that, and was so upset, showed that he wasn't lost. There's been a bond between us ever since.

After that night, the two of us were together constantly for about six months. George got stuck into reading. He had always been a great reader when he was a young kid. His mum encouraged him with C.S. Lewis stories. But he lost his way in secondary school and was dismissed as remedial.

Now he devoured the written word: biographies, old school-books, war stories, history. He got a loan of Nan Milton's book on John Maclean and his reaction was the same as mine the first time I read it. How did they keep this from us? How dare they! After a while he was racing through all our pamphlets: Lenin on imperialism, Trotsky on fascism. He'd write down questions to raise at meetings. He was becoming more politically developed than people who'd been in the organisation for years. But he was also exhausting.

George was clean – drug free – after a few months. Militant gave him some self-respect for the first time. A new football team was started in Pollok. George became captain. He was voted player of the year, then player of the league, then player's player. When we were on the field, he would overturn the manager's instructions. Everyone listened to him. He was brimming with confidence for the first time in his life.

I go into all this detail about George because his story is not unusual. His enthusiasm brought teenagers into Militant who might otherwise have been jagging the jellies or stealing from their neighbours. They helped transform Pollok into the most class-conscious housing scheme in Britain. And they were the frontline troops in the biggest civil disobedience movement seen in decades.

George was there when we first discussed how to stop the Poll Tax in a council flat in Lyoncross Road, Pollok. Our local unemployed group used the converted house for meetings. Tommy Martin, who had worked in the yards, was there. He always puffed a cigar, so I suppose it was a 'smoke-filled room.' There was Bill Bill who had also been in the shipyards. Gordon McCrae was a labourer of about twenty-six. Then there was George and I. It was November

1987 – the year Margaret Thatcher vowed to eradicate socialism from Britain.

The group often talked about the causes of unemployment. Too often people blame themselves. The government had launched Job Clubs, where people had to go to phone as many employers as possible – the underlying message being they could work if they tried hard enough. They are not told that capitalism deliberately creates a pool of spare labour to keep wages low. They are not told that world trade moves in cycles. The desire to make the most money in the shortest possible time results in factories over-producing. Suddenly they have too much of everything, so prices plunge. In order to protect their profit margin, they lay off workers like Gordon and Tommy.

So it was perfectly natural that our unemployed group, between sessions of pool and Marxist economics, would get around to talking about the Abolition of Domestic Rates (Scotland) Act, which had been passed in parliament earlier that year. The group went on to organise the first anti-poll tax meeting in Pollok.

By late '87 a few scattered groups were talking about refusing to pay the tax. One started in Maryhill, and there were a few in Edinburgh, the most important and biggest being the Militant inspired Labour Movement Campaign Against The Poll Tax. Govan Against the Poll Tax was just up the road. The Govan group was formed from all the local community councils. John Foster, a communist, was secretary. Many of the people involved in it – the late John McFadden, Tommy Stewart, Eddie Gray and Dick McGlave – had been shop stewards. Tommy and Eddie had been directly involved in the Upper Clyde Shipbuilders work-in of 1971 which had links with the tenants' movement.

Our discussions in the unemployed group and within Militant concluded that this new tax was something everyone could unite around. Up until then, the government had zapped its enemies one at a time: General Galtieri, the miners, the health workers. Now they were coming for all of us at once. So I began to gather as much material about this head tax as I could lay my hands on. I read stuff

from Labour Research and pamphlets by the Rowantree Founda-
tion. It was effectively a transfusion of wealth from the poor to the
rich. In Scotland, two million people would be brought onto the
local tax register for the first time.

Women who were not working, young people earning £55 a
week, disabled people dependent on relatives – all had to stump up.
A Scot called Douglas Mason had dreamt it up. (Mason now has a
new scheme. He was quoted in the *Scotsman* in September 1993
saying the poor should not have children.) The Duke of Roxburgh,
who sits down to dinner in Scotland's biggest occupied castle, was
to save £2,200. The Hughes family down the road from me, with
five working adults in low-paid jobs, would lose £800 a year.

The Community Charge first slithered out of the Adam Smith
Institute in the early 1980s. This right-wing thinktank devised it to
replace domestic rates, a local tax based on the rented value of
property – the bigger your house the more you paid. Scotland was
to get the poll tax in 1989 – a year before England. We were a
testing-ground. The Tories had nothing left to lose up here. But
they forgot that the Scottish people had nothing left to lose either.
An army like that is fearless. The new tax was the culmination of
everything Thatcher stood for: greed, inequality, heartlessness. It
was more than a vindictive attack on the working class. Thatcher
hoped it would realise her dream and purge Britain of anything
smelling remotely of socialism.

She wanted to destroy Labour local authorities. Even before Keir
Hardie took his seat in parliament as the first Labour MP, a kind of
municipal socialism was being built in cities like Birmingham and
Glasgow. The city fathers recognised that the pursuit of profit was
causing chaos. Children played in open sewers. Cholera was rife.
But private companies did not want to see good money piping clean
water to poor areas. So local authorities did the job instead. When
gas and electricity arrived, competing private companies dug up the
same roads to lay wires and pipes. Some streets became impassable.
It made sense to have everything provided by one company, owned
by the public. So, again, local corporations took over the job.

Eventually the same logic was applied to tramcars, buses, public baths, and football pitches. There were even municipal meat and fish markets where hygiene could be enforced – all things which made life better for everyone. Housing was the biggest achievement of municipal socialism. Private landlords threw up tenements so close together that no sunlight penetrated the single rooms shared by whole families. Glasgow was the most overcrowded city in Britain. In 1911, eighty per cent of families in the West of Scotland lived in one or two rooms. It became clear that decent affordable homes must be subsidised by the council.

All those decades of local authority achievement angered Thatcher and the forces of big business which she represented. She hated the caring, collectivist values of municipal socialism. Her business friends wanted a big slice of the cake – even if that left the rest of us with a few stale crumbs.

Between 1979 and 1988, the government hammered local authorities, forcing them to cut back the public services they provided. In those years central government funding to councils – the Rate Support Grant – fell by £28.5 billion in the UK and £6.5 billion in Scotland alone. They sold the best council houses. Government funding of public housing, the Housing Support Grant, was slashed from £371.4 million to £46.5 million. One in three Scottish local authorities got nothing at all to repair homes.

The Poll Tax was the culmination of this process. It only covered a fifth of a council's income. If the government continued to cut funding, councils would have to raise the tax to astronomical levels. The government could stop this through the imposition of Poll Tax capping to keep the level of the tax down and force instead the wholesale reduction of council services to meet the shortfall. So the poll tax was designed to close nurseries, end the home-help service to frail old people, and cram school pupils into even bigger classes for second-rate education.

The Tories thought the tax would stop people voting against them in local elections. Most voters prefer not to have Tory councils that sell off their cemeteries to property companies. The government would love to return to the pre-1918 days when only property owners could vote.

The Victorian working class were supposed to touch their cloth caps and stay at home making rag mats on polling day. The twentieth-century Tories hoped people would take their names off the electoral register in order to avoid the tax. Most never did. The Department of Social Security and housing departments were instructed to supply the names of claimants and tenants. Hundreds of thousands ended up in the worst of both worlds – registered for the tax on the one hand, off the electoral register on the other. It was clear from the start that the tax was odious. Everyone saw it as the rich nakedly gorging themselves on the poor. The real challenge was how to defeat it.

The more I read, the more convinced I was that a mass non-payment campaign would bring down the Tory flagship and its captain. Sober voices everywhere said the Community Charge would be uncollectable. Professor Gordon Hughes of Edinburgh University carried out a survey for the local government trade union, NALGO, in 1986–87. The survey showed that a clear majority of households would become poorer. Another survey, by Dundee University for the Scottish Consumer Council and the Convention of Scottish Local Authorities, concluded that trying to collect small sums from every adult in the land would lead to costs out of all proportion to the sums collected. The researchers doubted that 18 to 24 year olds would pay – few had been eligible for rates. Most young people owned nothing of value, said the report, and so it would be impossible to recover their debt. (You cannot be jailed for poll-tax debt in Scotland.) So that bogeyman was slain before we had begun. There was much talk about wages and benefits being arrested or furniture being sold off. To do this the regional council must obtain a court warrant. The warrant could only be enforced by a sheriff's officer. There were only 193 of them in Scotland – such a small group of anglers couldn't catch every fish in the sea. It would take them well into the next century to hook a million non-payers.

The new Debtor's Scotland Act 1987 also became essential bedtime reading. If you were unlucky enough to be snagged by a sheriff officer, the new law only allowed him to arrest a proportion of your wages, depending on earnings. Before the Act your entire pay packet or salary cheque could be frozen.

Warrant sales were the ultimate sanction. Sheriff officers had the power to enter your home and sell your possessions to pay the debt. Would Strathclyde Region – the biggest bastion of socialism in Western Europe, with a Labour majority of eighty-seven – take such barbaric action against the poor? Surely not . . .

In fact, in 1987, many people still hoped regional councils would refuse to implement a tax designed to cripple them. It would be like cutting off their own fingers. We also believed trade unions representing council workers should instruct their members not to co-operate with the Poll Tax. Militant sketched out its strategy: 'Don't Pay. Don't Collect. Don't Comply' over the winter of 1987–88. We had good precedents. For as well as ploughing through Consumer Council reports and Government white papers, we revisited our history books.

The years between 1915 and 1922 saw the women of Glasgow take on a government and win – thrashing a few landlords and sheriff officers in the process. These were the famous Clydeside Rent Strikes, organised by the Glasgow Women's Housing Committee. Thousands of people flocked to the city shipyards and engineering foundries for munitions work during World War One. With an eye on the main chance, landlords duly raised the rents for the over-crowded tenements. So, in 1915 the women of Govan, led by Mary Barbour, went on an illegal rent strike. Public sympathy was immediate. While their sons and husbands were fighting in Europe, wives and children were being evicted. Despite its illegality, the unofficial protest spread across the river to Partick, to the closes around the giant forge at Parkhead in the East End, and among the families who sweated in the locomotive works of Springburn. It was backed by the shop stewards of the Clyde Workers' Committee.

The CWC threatened to strike unless fair rents were imposed on the racketeers.

The rent strikes were devised by the women themselves. They stayed in control. Tenants' Defence Leagues were formed for each close. Sheriff officers, who served eviction notices, were chased by crowds of angry women, pelting them with flour and pease meal. One patronising cartoon of the time in *The Bailie* magazine still gets across some of the atmosphere. The Battle of Partick depicts the leader of a tenants committee, a woman with forearms like mangles, surrounded by frying pans, irons and pokers. She is reassuring a cowering neighbour who has been threatened with eviction: 'It's a' richt, Mrs McStinger, we've pit the Sheriff's Officer in the Washin' Hoose b'iler an' lichtit the fire.' There's a case that John Wheatley, then a socialist councillor, championed which made headlines in 1915. The McHughes family in Shettleston were in debt. The husband had been injured in the war and his wife fell into £1 rent arrears. A huge crowd gathered to stop the attempted eviction. Estimates at the time ranged from 400 to 4000. They chased the factor back to his offices and burnt his effigy. Eventually the police stepped in and told the sheriff officers not to carry out the eviction order.

Twenty thousand Glasgow families joined the protest. It spread to Aberdeen and Dundee. In Birkenhead, Birmingham, London and in Belfast too, tenants began standing up to their landlords. The socialist newspaper *Forward* told its readers: The rent issue is now a national issue and must be settled nationally. Just before Christmas that year a Partick landlord – despite opposition from a very nervous government – tried to evict 18 families who were working in Beardmore's shipyard at Dalmuir. He also tried to have their wages deducted through the small debts court. The Glasgow Women's Housing Committee planned to storm the court *en masse* with weans in tow. Five major shipyards and one big munitions plant struck work on the day of the hearing. Loads of others factories sent delegations of workers.

The court was beside the City Chambers and George Square was mobbed. They set up makeshift wooden platforms for speakers including John Maclean and Mary Barbour. When the landlords lost the case Maclean immediately put a resolution to the ecstatic crowd demanding the government forbid any rent increases for the duration of the war. The government later introduced rent controls. The rent strikers won that concession by challenging the idea – enshrined in law – that property rights come before a family's right to feed and clothe itself. They broke the law. So did the shipyard workers who threatened to strike if evictions were carried out. So did Maclean and the ILP councillors who marched to the court house.

If those rent strikers could protect their neighbours in those dangerous times, then so could we. We could refuse to pay our Poll Tax like they refused to pay their rent. We would form similar defence committees covering every working class area. And we hoped to get the same support from Labour politicians as those women received in 1915.

Coincidently, the year the poll tax became law in Scotland was the 200th anniversary of the Calton Weavers' strike. The Clyde Valley Weavers Association had withdrawn their labour after employers tried to reduce the rate for the muslin they produced – they had already suffered a pay cut of seven shillings a week and could take no more. On 2 Sept 1787, troops from the 39th Regiment of Foot fired on a crowd of several hundred strikers in Calton, then a village to the East of Glasgow. Three died in the field, which is now covered by Tennent Caledonian's Brewery. Another three were murdered in the wood nearby. The strike leaders were later tried for sedition and one was whipped through the streets of Edinburgh.

Of course the weavers were breaking the law by encouraging workers to withdraw their labour. In doing so, they helped free future generations. Appeals to law and order remain weapons of social control two centuries later. But these days the state does not need to turn troops on people or whip them publicly. It has more subtle means of oppression.

Parliamentary legislation had overtaken bayonets and rifles as the preferred method of control by 1987. Thatcher won her third general election victory in that year. Although the party was reduced to ten out of seventy-two MPs in Scotland, she was more determined than ever to impose her divisive philosophy.

A fresh round of legislation threatened to deliver Scottish council houses into the hands of private landlords through a giant government agency called Scottish Homes. Hospitals were to become trusts, despite overwhelming opposition from doctors, nurses and patients, who all saw it as a step towards private health care. A planned review of the benefits system would snatch £640 million from the weakest members of society. Housing benefit would be cut and emergency grants replaced with discretionary loans. Ravenscraig, Scotland's only integrated steel plant, faced closure by a privatised British Steel. This in a country, which, according to the government's own figures, lost 32% of its manufacturing industry between 1979 and 1985. The Poll Tax was just the last straw.

Thatcher planned to do all this with ten Scottish seats. Labour, on the other hand, returned fifty gallant members, upon whose slippery shoulders the hopes of Scotland's working class were perched.

Sensing the mood in the housing schemes – not least the impoverished Drumchapel on the Western fringe of his Glasgow constituency – the Shadow Scottish Secretary, Donald Dewar, mustered as many fighting metaphors as a political training in the debating chamber of Glasgow University Union would allow. 'We will stretch the Tories to breaking point and turn the screw as time goes on', he said immediately after the election. Bill Speirs, then chairman of the Labour Party in Scotland also flexed his adjectives: 'The Scottish Tories are in for a hard time', he threatened. Doomsday had arrived. This was the buzz word in Scotland for the scenario where Labour hold a huge majority in Scotland but are defeated in England. Donald took a list of demands to the then Secretary of State for Scotland, Malcolm Rifkind.

We supported his demands: Save Ravenscraig; Scrap the Poll Tax; Cancel the planned social security changes; Invest in health and education.

Malcolm and Donald, both successful lawyers, jousted for about forty-five minutes behind closed doors. Dewar emerged having laid down his verbal weapons. 'I did not expect the government to capitulate on a short term encounter,' he clucked. 'It may well be it will have to be decided at the ballot box at some future time.'

I suppose it must be easy to wrap yourself in the white flag of surrender when you do not have to live with the consequences of defeat, like Donald's constituents in Drumchapel. Could they afford to sit in their prison-grey homes watching the damp blur the wallpaper pattern, waiting for the ballot box to speak at some future time? They would bear the brunt of benefit changes – begging for social fund loans to replace torn sheets or broken cookers or buy new underwear for a sick, incontinent child. They would be the ones faced with crippling poll tax bills. Three miles down the road, in his pleasant flat in Glasgow's West End, Donald would also contemplate his loss. Perhaps a little loss of face? But no reduction in his salary. And possibly even a considerable saving in the switch from rates to Poll Tax.

Still, Labour's self-styled Fighting Fifty MPs had to be seen to be applying some muscle to the poll tax problem. On October 21, 1987, they launched 'Stop It, The Scottish Campaign Against the Poll Tax'. Brian Wilson, a new MP with radical credentials, was to be chairman. Wilson had been a freelance journalist. He had travelled to Nicaragua and wrote sympathetically about the revolutionary Sandinista government's attempts to improve literacy, health care and sanitation.

The 'Stop It' launch was very high-profile. Popular Scottish figures like Elaine C. Smith, the actress, were there. So was Billy McNeill, the saintly manager of Glasgow Celtic. Elaine always made it clear she would refuse to pay. It was difficult for her, and many others, to see that 'Stop It' was just another spoiling tactic.

The Scottish National Party began raising the tactic of non-payment a month before 'Stop It' was launched. Many ordinary Labour members also supported the tactics and not just in Pollok. Yet 'Stop It' refused to discuss non-payment on the grounds that it was an admission of defeat. 'We aim to stop the bills coming through the doors in the first place', said Wilson. Just how their forest of fact packs would persuade the most resolute government this century to see sense remains a mystery.

Victor Hugo said: 'Greater than the tread of mighty armies is an idea whose time has come.' The time had come to rage. Although the behaviour of our political leaders in 1987 gave us good cause to despair, the mood of the people was very different. They were not defeatist. There was plenty of evidence that they were prepared to break the law to challenge the system. This was apparent even before the general election in the tremendous support for the Caterpillar workers during the winter of 1986–7.

The multi-national Caterpillar Corporation announced it was pulling out of Scotland after previously telling the workforce it would be investing and expanding. So the workers occupied the factory illegally. George and I took a minibus full of young people from Pollok to visit them in Uddingston, Lanarkshire.

'Members who do not support the occupation do not enter' said a big sign on the gate. Inside, the workshops were all clean and tidy. There were signs around the plant dating back to an earlier production drive by management: 'Make it Happen and Get Involved.' They had assumed a whole new meaning under the occupation.

The workers, led by their shop stewards, Frank Kelly, John Gillan and John Brannan, attracted widespread sympathy across Scotland. Workplaces held collections and Glaswegian pop musicians produced a record called 'Making Tracks' to raise funds. No one ever defended Caterpillar's property rights. As far as everyone was concerned, the factory and the machinery belonged to the workers who spent their lives and labour making profits for this multi-national.

The workers built a tractor themselves, sprayed it pink and called it the Pink Panther. They wanted to give it to War on Want. They were told this was illegal because it did not belong to them. To me, that showed the absurdity of capitalism – that the property rights of a huge company come before the needs of the starving.

Jimmy Airlie, the Scottish organiser of the AEEU union, put

heavy pressure on the workers to end the occupation. He wanted to negotiate a settlement with the American management – then holed up in the Hospitality Inn. The union can support no action which is in breach of the law, he told the press. If the people of Scotland could support illegal action, why not the union leaders? Six years later Airlie was trying to pull the same trick on his members at Timex.

Jimmy Airlie was the leader, along with Jimmy Reid, of an earlier occupation: the UCS work-in of 1971. It inspired a whole generation. Tony Benn says it was a turning point in his political life.

If you visit the second floor of Glasgow's social history museum, the People's Palace, you can see black and white pictures of the two Jimmies, arms linked before the gates of the shipyard. You'll know them because their faces have been worn away by thousands of pointing fingers. Is it just curiosity? Or is the Glasgow public expressing its feelings about the men who sold the jerseys?

Our experience told us folk were more than willing to have a go, not just at the Jimmy & Jimmy photograph, but at the whole system. This is true even of very localised issues. In Pollok around this time a busy bus route was redirected past a school despite protests from teachers and parents. We got together with tenants, activists, and parents, and literally sat down before the double-deckers. Our Labour regional councillor, Bill Timoney, came to show a bit of support – from a safe distance. He had a good view of us being arrested. Now he's watching his seat, because people remember who stood up for them in the past.

Pollok's Labour Party Young Socialists branch – the one responsible for George's conversion – used similar methods to support struggles further away from home. We had been campaigning hard in support of the uprisings in the South African townships at that time. The COSATU trade union had formed and there was a boycott of white stores. Young Socialists were supporting a boycott of Benetton's stores. The Italian clothing company was exploiting cheap black labour in South Africa. It was particularly galling because their advertising campaign, The United Colours of Benetton, featured both black and white children. They suggested world harmony could be achieved if only everyone wore the right sweater.

We decided to occupy the Benetton branch in Argyle Street. George and the newly recruited youth from Pollok along with the other Young Socialists from the West of Scotland couldn't afford these clothes and shamed the trendy customers. In the end, the police took a hammer to the plate glass door to get us out. George wouldn't move. I was practically dragging him away for his own safety. He still had an almost violent anger in him. Now it was captured for a cause.

This kind of activity, locally and nationally, convinced us the time was right to revive the old tactics of direct action. We had absolute confidence that anti-poll tax unions would be as successful as the rent strikers tenant's Defence Leagues. We heard they organised this way in the townships of South Africa during the rent boycotts. Just imagine: street committees *pieceing* Scotland's dismembered communities back together. If any sheriff officer dared approach, the word would pass from door to door. Gardens would fill with crowds of local people defending their neighbours.

The idea of mass non-payment was first raised by one of our older firebrands, Chic Stevenson, at that time Labour Councillor for Queenslie, who proposed a motion at the annual conference of Militant in Scotland in the Autumn of 1987. He urged the delegates to make the poll tax and the campaign against it a major theme of our work in Scotland. Chic's passionate appeal was met with unanimous approval. Months of detailed discussion in the branches of Militant then ensued. This discussion culminated in a special Scottish Conference in April of 1988. It took place in the Govanhill Neighbourhood Centre and was attended by Peter Taaffe, Militant's National Leader and introduced by Bob Wylie, then Militant's leader in Scotland. The conference was indeed fateful. It discussed the details of our future strategy including the necessity for mass non-payment and the building of a Scottish-wide network of local anti-poll tax unions and regional federations. The only contentious issue was non-registration.

There was a debate about whether we should encourage people to refuse to register for the tax in the first place. I initially supported non-registration. But I changed my position halfway through the debate. Others argued, successfully, that non-registration fines were so high, and so many were already on the electoral register, that it was a bit of a non-starter. We decided to support those who refused to register, but not to encourage it. To be honest, I never did register for the tax. I just couldn't bring myself to do so.

Regular discussions took place throughout Militant in Britain. Certainly there were some differences of emphasis and perhaps even doubts but these were ironed out during the course of debate. The role of the trade unions in the campaign was one of the main issues.

We pointed to the rent strikes. The stand made by the women involved trade unions and the Independent Labour Party. The rebel spirit expressed by the pan clashers and flour throwers of 1915 sparked the movement which resulted in the forty hours strike of 1919, and the dispatching of tanks to Glasgow. The women of Govan struck a match and all sorts of radicals and revolutionaries gathered around the flame.

Our community-based resistance was also a product of its time and place. The rundown of British manufacturing, accelerated since 1979, meant you could not rely on factory meetings to organise the working class. The Billy Connolly scenario of walking from the school gate to the shipyard gate – then joining the union and working in the same place till you die or retire. It just doesn't happen any more. Many of my neighbours had not had a steady job since leaving school. Where was their trade union? Who defended them? Who listened to them?

Had we waited for an instruction from the labour movement leaders, we might never have passed the starting line. Sure, we would speak to shop stewards and try to organise in the workplace. But even if we lost on the industrial front, we could still win if everyone linked arms with the family in the next close. Thankfully these issues were clearly understood at the Scottish Conference and the motion calling for mass non-payment was supported unanimously. This was something of a relief to the Pollok crew. We'd already gone ahead and booked a hall four days later for what we hoped would be the founding meeting of the Pollok Anti-Poll Tax Union.

We had no money to build for the meeting. So we got a couple of megaphones and blasted the whole scheme. In Brockburn and Calfhill Roads the front rooms of the tenements face onto the back greens. So we'd campaign from the middens. Everyone would turn down the telly and hang out their windows to listen. There would usually be a bit of crack: 'Away in and make the tea!' was the stock reply to good-natured heckling.

George was working on the railways at the time – his first real job, on a wage of £85 a week. Every night when he got home he'd follow the campaign trail through the gardens and drying greens, over the fences and hedges. Sometimes he brought his guitar and serenaded them with anti-poll tax songs, something by Bob Dylan or Bob Marley's Redemption Song: 'Emancipate yourself from mental slavery. Only ourselves can free our minds . . .' There was even a bit of slapstick when the bins once gave way beneath him. We didn't need to harangue people into delivering leaflets. George would nab a crowd of boys down the football pitches. 'How aboot gien us a haun?' he'd ask, explaining the poll tax and the way it would affect them. Within half an hour the street would be covered.

Many young people joined up. Colin McGregor (Coco) and his brother James were fifteen and seventeen at the time. There was Eddie Gribben (Radar), Tam Diamond and Brian Kidd (Kiddo). They all ran about in a gang called The Bushwackers. They'd spend weekends fighting boys from the same neighbourhood but divided by a gang boundary like a street or a stretch of water. The poll tax brought them together.

The meeting was called by the unemployed group, with backing from the community councils and the tenants' associations. The shop stewards' committees at the local Leverndale Hopital and the Civil and Public Servants Association at the Cowglen Savings Bank, the biggest employer in the area, were represented. So was the local branch of the Fire Brigades Union and the Labour Party branch through myself as secretary.

I bumped into the Labour regional councillor, Bill Timoney, on the steps of the school as I was going into the meeting. 'So do you think you'll get many coming, son?' he smiled. 'Aye, I hear it's no' bad, Bill,' I replied. We walked through the glass door into the assembly hall and his face fell. For a minute I thought he was going to hide in an empty classroom. But it was too late. He'd been spotted and would have to speak to all these angry voters. There were about 400 people crammed into the hall. The janitor was rushing around looking for extra chairs. Anyone who didn't arrival early was squeezed up at the back. Poor Bill knew he'd have to say something.

Folk at the meeting confirmed all the anecdotal evidence about the strength of our support. I looked round the hall at the mothers of my friends, all respectable, all saying they wouldn't pay this tax.

Jack Jardine, a guy in his fifties who had long been active in the tenants' movement, rose from the floor. He asked if anybody had passed the factor's office recently. Had they seen pensioners coming out in tears because they had been refused housing benefit? The social security changes had removed housing benefit from a lot of people with small occupational pensions. That affected former Rolls Royce workers in Pollok. Now they were being asked to pay the poll tax as well. They'd had enough.

It wasn't just pensioners who were reeling from the benefit cuts that month. A *Glasgow Herald* article in April 1988 revealed half of Pollok's 11,000 inhabitants relied on benefit. Those people were set to lose £750,000 in that month's changes.

I remember making a point in my speech that night – which I have repeated often since. We shouldn't have a Grand Ol' Duke of York campaign yet again. Leading people up one side of the hill only to tell them to turn round and head back down. It mustn't be another verbal soufflé type of thing, like Dewar and Speirs after the election. We had to actually *do* something. Everybody opposed the Social Security Act. What did they do? Everybody opposed the treatment of young people. What did they do? Everybody opposed the closure of Gartcosh steelworks a few years previously. But what did they do? They marched and signed petitions and came together in a united front of vocal opposition. They did nothing concrete, nothing to damage the establishment. Unity in inaction is not worth having.

The response was absolutely overwhelming. They were applauding to the rooftops. People like George's mum. Such a timid woman. She's probably never uttered an aggressive word in her life. There she was with all her neighbours, supporting non-payment. I thought: This has got potential!

Then Bill Timoney got up and waxed lyrical about the iniquities of the tax. Immoral! Unjust! Unfair! He repeated the three adjectives familiar from standard 'Stop It' speeches. Dick Douglas, the Labour MP who eventually defected to the SNP because of the tax, used to talk about how this was an abuse of vocabulary. If it was immoral, unjust and unfair, why pay it?

Timoney said he was not objecting to illegality in itself. But non-payment would hurt local authority services. We made the point that if the poll tax was successfully introduced it would wipe out local authority services. That was the Tories' point. Timoney was asked why the regional council was so determined to collect the tax. 'It's all right for you,' he said. 'I could be surcharged! Who will pay my fine?'

Chic McPherson stood up. He's a marvellous guy who's written more letters to the poll tax registration officer, Jack Woods, than a lifer writes to his partner. 'I'll pay your fine, Bill,' he said. 'And I'd be proud tae share a cell wi you. But you'll no' get ma vote unless you stick wi us, the people of Pollok.'

I pointed out that forty-seven Liverpool city councillors were surcharged for refusing to set a rate. This was a policy of resisting Tory cuts which was earlier agreed by all the Labour local authorities. Only Liverpool and Lambeth saw it through to the end. Anyway, none of the Liverpool councillors lost their homes or their possessions. The Liverpool labour movement went out on the streets and raised the money to pay their surcharges, which totalled £500,000. Of course, it would have been unfair to impose this financial worry on Bill. But he had been elected by the people of Pollok and if he was not prepared to stand beside them, he should have made way for someone else. Someone with the courage to defy the law. Someone more in tune with the people. Bill never came to our public meetings after that. We founded the Pollok Anti–Poll Tax Union that night, electing a committee which would later issue membership cards. There was one card for each house – fifty pence covered the whole family. The meeting voted to build mass non-payment across the country as well as Pollok. That gave me the authority, as secretary of the new union, to speak elsewhere. So began my life as a Poll Tax nomad.

Pollok was to be an inspiration to other areas. We built the union through street meetings. Outside my close in Linthaugh Road at first. Eventually all over the constituency – bus stops, traffic islands, shops, patches of spare ground all provided impromptu venues. We'd publicise the meetings with wee strips of paper cut out of big photocopied sheets. It was very cheap. Women could bring the kids – it would be just down the road. When you have a million tasks to juggle at night – getting the weans' school clothes ironed, making sure their homework's done, cooking dinner, sorting through the bills – it can be hard to put aside three hours to attend a political meeting in the community centre. This way took only half an hour.

Jack Jardine raved about these meetings. He said it reminded him of his childhood in Govan. A communist called Peter McIntyre held big meetings from the fountain at the cross. He was elected a councillor in 1945 and was involved in the squatters' movement after the war – when families without decent homes would occupy big houses. Jack said big crowds would come to listen to McIntyre just for the patter.

Jack himself was a leader of the apprentices' strike which began on Clydeside in 1952 when he was seventeen. The strike involved exploited young workers in thirty-four firms. The Clydeside

Apprentices Committee in 1952, like the Clyde Workers' Committee during WW1, was very politicised. The Young Communist
League leafleted for the strike and one of its members, Jimmy Reid,
was a spokesman on the committee. Jack helped build it by agitating
his way down the Clyde, from Govan to Greenock and Port
Glasgow. He was in the yards without management permission.
Police hauled him out more than once.

The anti-poll tax movement was to emulate the apprentices
strikes which spread from Scotland to Birkenhead and Sheffield in
England. We were also organising outside the established structures.
We were telling different groups of workers their interests were the
same.

Jack was one of many older people whose experience was
invaluable to our campaign. They were the link with the old ways
we were trying to revive.

One of the first people elected to our committee was Meg
Callaghan. Meg is in her seventies and at that time ran the pensioners'
lunch club in the basement of Calfhill Court, the high flats where
she lived. She took away a pile of posters and information leaflets to
give out with the mince and tatties. Outraged eighty year-olds
displayed them in their windows.

Meg is a Rolls Royce widow. As it turned out, she had been
brought up in the ILP. She remembers marching beside Manny
Shinwell and Jimmy Maxton as a young child. Her parents sent her
to Socialist Sunday School. As a teenager she spent weekends in
socialist rambling groups – the ILP were very keen on social and
cultural activities to complement the politics.

Her late husband was a bonus checker with Rolls Royce. When
they were first married, he was a trainee chemist and, sad to say, a
man with Conservative sympathies. He would rib her about her ILP
affiliations and, like so many woman, her political activity stopped.
She was kept busy raising her children and working in a local
box-making factory. She assembled cartons for De Luxe whisky
which was then shipped to America. The box-makers moved away
and the site is now occupied by Texas Homecare DIY store. She

has never abandoned her socialist beliefs. In fact, she was delighted in 1987 to make up for the lost decades: "The wheel keeps turning and it always comes back in the one direction," she says. Meg's involvement was significant but shortlived. Her son had a sensitive job with the Home Office and worried that his rebel mother could get him the sack. 'I'm afraid my family have to come first,' said Meg. We still keep in touch.

There were lots of people like Meg across Pollok who saw this as a reminder of the radicalism of their youth. Grace Moran, then a forty year-old cleaner, was one of the names on our phone tree. She's soft-spoken and describes herself as not wanting to go to extremes. It turned out she had been a member of the Young Communist League YCL in her teens. Her mother, Margaret Gray, worked for British Rail for many years, making the beds on the sleepers. She remembers going to hear Willie Gallacher speak at the St Andrew's Halls in Glasgow: 'The way he gripped the audience you'd think communism was just around the corner.'

Other supporters described themselves as non-political. Margaret Williams was fifty-seven when she became involved. She stays in a terraced council house in Cowglen across the road from the Pollok Centre, a big shopping mall. Her sons and grandsons love fishing and there is usually a fibreglass boat sitting in the driveway.

Margaret had just been widowed when she first came to our meeting in the library down the road. That year she had also stopped working as a geriatric nurse in Crookston Home. Twenty years of lifting patients had given her arthritis in her neck and back.

Margaret often ran buses taking patients on day trips and she'd raise money with the other nurses by holding jumble sales. When the Cowglen Anti-Poll Tax Union held a raffle, she would go over to the Pollok Centre and beg prizes. The chemist donated talcum, the shoe shop gave a pack of tights. All her nursing work made her good on the doorsteps. But the arthritis meant she sometimes couldn't speak when she reached the top flight of a Priesthill tenement. Her grandsons, then aged twelve, nine and eight, would give up a night's fishing to help her out with leaflets.

Rose McCann, another grandmother who lives near Margaret Williams, was also not political. But previous brushes with authority meant she was a determined woman. Everything is political. Early one morning she heard one of her children shout Waaater! She panicked, thinking it was a fire. But when she gathered her family downstairs they discovered the kitchen and living room under four foot of filthy black water. The burn near the houses had finally burst its banks. It had been threatening to do so for years.

Rose was then in the tenants' association and called a public meeting to try to force compensation from the district council. It knew the risks when it built the houses. It was January, and after the mire subsided, the water on the walls turned to ice. But the tenants never got compensation. Rose lost the things she'd spent twenty years accumulating. But she had become political.

Rose worked as a domestic with Securicor and then with the local hospital. She had never owed a penny in her life, yet knocked on thousands of doors encouraging people not to pay the poll tax. There were four adults in her house at the time, as her elderly father was still alive. She usually paid £600 in rates but would have to find £1,400 in Poll Tax.

Women were at the forefront of the campaign. They were in control of the family budget and had to find the extra money for the new tax. The women of Pollok had good precedents. Rolls Royce was the first company in Britain to give equal pay. In 1955, when their wages dropped to 76% of the male workers, the women went on strike. There was a long tradition of female shop stewards, several were involved in the poll tax movement.

Our APTU, as it became known, grew so quickly we soon had to divide it up. We were on the way to the equivalent of the Tenants' Leagues or the South African street committees. Before long, we had an APTU for every part of the constituency. Pollok itself had a union, followed by Bonnyholm, Brockburn, Arden, Carnwadric, South Nitshill, Priesthill and Cowglen. Eventually we even formed a Pollok Federation. By May we had distributed 426 membership cards alone in Pollok. The following month it was up to 700.

We created an impressive phone tree. Every street had someone you could call if you were worried about the tax. We delivered thousands of bulletins with long lists of phone numbers on one side and information on the other. Worried in North Pollok? Call James McGregor, if he's not in, try his mate Eddie Gribben, or Madge Kenny, or May Logan or Caroline Halligan or George McNeilage.

As the campaign branched out, so did the phone tree. We developed it further when the sheriff officers became active later in the campaign. It joined people down the wire from the Shetland Islands to Dumfries – ringing out in a thousand housing schemes on the way. Robert Burns talked about the Tree of Liberty. Without it, "life was a vale of woe where men and woman laboured: 'To feed the titled knave, man/And a' the comfort we're to get/Is that ayont the grave, man.'" Maybe the toil hadn't ceased in the late 20th century. But neither had the quest for liberty – and our tree was technological!

Pollok was drawing attention to itself. Whenever a television company wanted to do something on the tax, they knew they could get good visuals in Linthaugh Road. Practically every window carried a poster. The Glasgow *Evening Times* printed a Gall cartoon featuring two kids on their way home from school. One is saying: I've got an Auntie Margaret in Maryhill, an Auntie Mary in Castlemilk. My Auntie Poll Tax stays in Pollok . . . We were all pretty pleased with ourselves.

Proud as we were – we didn't want to be the only ones. A later Gall cartoon told the real story. It featured a determined middle-aged woman dragging her reluctant husband into one of our meetings. Pollok wasn't mentioned. The caricature represented working–class women across Scotland. Everybody, everywhere, had an Auntie Poll Tax.

3 Building the federation

Jack Harvey is a colourful big bear of a man. A joiner to trade, he set aside his tools for two years to build the anti-poll tax campaign. Towards the end of 1988 he got a call from a reporter from Radio Merseyside. The young guy sounded very public-school. He was from the Home Counties, making his name on the provincial stations. Now he wanted to venture even further north, to see if there really was a Revolt on The Clyde. He arrived with a portable tape recorder and an armful of suspicions:

'There is a feeling in journalistic circles that Pollok's a set-up,' he said by way of introduction. 'I don't think this myself, Jack, you understand, but some people in the media cannot quite believe it is for real . . .'

He wanted to meet people from another area and asked Jack where he lived.

'Castlemilk'.

'What's it like?'

'One of the biggest housing schemes in Europe. Sprawling, massive. 30,000 souls. Rundown tenement housing and five multi-storeys.'

'Sounds good to me', says the young cub. 'Let's go.'

Three quarters of an hour later – it can be a long drive – they piled out of the car at the foot of the tower blocks in Mitchellhill. These mark the far southern edge of Castlemilk, between the city boundary and the Cathkin Braes. Mitchellhill is some height and the panoramic sweep of Glasgow unfurls like a big grey blanket at your feet. Looking down from one of those livingrooms in the sky, you might really think Glasgow belonged to you. But only for a second, until reality and poverty hit you again.

Radio Merseyside randomly chose the middle tower block and they took the lift to the top floor. Jack was nervous. No anti-poll tax union had been formed in Mitchellhill at that time. Would this media opportunity backfire? Should Jack have stalled the guy, giving himself time to set something up?

They began chapping doors. All the way down they went, all sixteen floors.

Every single person who answered said they were not paying their poll tax. One man in his mid thirties, who was very clearly ill, invited them inside. Each breath was laboured, his cheeks were sunken, he had difficulty standing up. Perched on the bed in his two-roomed flat, he held out two skinny arms and said: 'Look around. Look at the state of the place. Look at the state of me. Look how much I have to live on. How can I pay this tax?' Both Jack and the reporter got quite choked up as the tape whirred.

'Couldn't you get me someone who's paying, for the sake of balance?' said Radio Merseyside. But Mitchellhill was adamant. Definitely not! No way!

They reached the ground floor not having found one poll tax payer. They knocked on one of the last doors and a young woman said worry over penalties would make her pay, although she opposed the tax. Jack carefully explained her rights. We wouldn't let them take her furniture and so on. She listened, thanked them anyway, and closed the door. It was too good to be true thought Jack, settling for 99% defiance as he rapped on the few remaining flats. Then, just as the two of them were turning to leave, the girl flung open her door again. 'Hey Mister! Score me off. I've had a think about it and I'm no payin' either!'

Our campaign was well underway by the time Merseyside met Castlemilk on the airwaves. Drums were beating across urban jungles of Scotland in 1988–89. In old Glasgow – Bridgeton, The Gorbals, Anderson, all around the big schemes, in the forgotten towns of Lanarkshire, little bands of people were tramping from door to door setting up anti-poll tax unions. At first our Militant activists called meetings in areas where they lived. Eventually individuals with no political affiliations were asking me to speak at the launch of their own unions. If you have a background in the labour movement, meetings tend to run along a certain groove. You're introduced. You speak. People listen. There's a stilted discussion, a summing up, maybe a vote. Then you all go home. But these meetings called by tenants' associations and community councils were full of people for whom standing orders might as well relate to the army parade ground.

After the introduction by a local community activist, you'd extend fraternal greetings to your class: 'Brothers and Sisters' . . . Some joker would invariably shout: 'I'm no your brother, pal!' So you'd qualify that with a quip and move on a few sentences. Then someone stood up waving a registration form or whatever, saying: 'Haud on here, can you tell me' . . . You had to learn to use different language, to jump the worn groove of the average Constituency Labour Party meeting.

Nobody argued in favour of the tax. But every hall had a wee woman who said: 'I agree wi ye, son. But it'll never work. Yeez'll never dae it.' The wording was identical each time. Jack Harvey had a theory that they were planted. But the raucous nature of the meetings meant the entire audience usually turned on the spoiler.

In a typical political campaign involving trade unions, you'll get shop stewards reporting developments to their workmates. Views are exchanged in the canteen. Activists might agitate outside the workplace. Slowly, ideas take root. But the anti-poll tax movement saw ideas spread much more quickly. Women went to meetings with neighbours and friends. They spoke about it afterwards. They'd spread the word to more neighbours at the supermarket or the school gates: 'Did you go tae that meeting aboot this Poll Tax? It set ma mind at rest. They told us you cannae get the jail for no payin' . . .'

The level of public support was incredible. Queenslie Anti-Poll Tax Union followed Pollok's method of issuing membership cards. They were sold door-to-door each Sunday night. The area covered Cranhill, another rundown part of Greater Easterhouse. Often people said: Could you come back tomorrow night when I've got my family allowance cashed? There wasn't so much as fifty pence left in the house. Union canvassers gave them a card anyway. Queenslie kept its membership register. It read like a voters' roll for each dilapidated row of tenements. In Bellrock Street alone there were seventy names, each one covering a family.

The campaign run by Sheila MacDonald in Springburn, Glasgow, was a good example of how things worked. Sheila is a grandmother who stayed in high flats in Royston Road, in the old Garngad area, for many years. Everybody knows her locally because she was a school dinner lady. She was also secretary of the social club attached to St Roch's parish church. A collecting can for the Little Sisters of the Poor sits on her windowledge. Sheila says she tries to live up to her faith. She ran a food co-operative for a while when the bakeries and butchers of Royson Road started to close. She was involved in a Save Our Steamie campaign when the district council closed the local washhouse. The anti-poll tax union was simply an extension of that kind of grassroots activity.

Outraged about the tax, she got together with some neighbours and set up a stall outside the Post Office in Royston Road. They collected names and gave information. Big meetings were held in the tenants' hall. I addressed audiences of 200 in Royston, as did Jim Sillars, who won the Govan by-election that year for the SNP.

The women who came to the fore during the campaign were a gritty combination of energy and commonsense. Scratch the surface and you'd find fire. Often the past held some secret struggle, long buried beneath years of rearing children. The most vivid example surfaced during a press conference with three generations from the one family. The grandmother, Jessie Kane, the daughter, Flo Reilly, and the granddaughter Janet Thompson, were all marching against the tax. Flo set up one of the thirteen anti-poll tax unions in Easterhouse. She was a Hofman presser for years, creasing several million pairs of trousers. Now she works with handicapped children. Flo and Jessie live in a typical, damp Easterhouse tenement. Open the door and their house is immaculate, never lacking human warmth or chocolate biscuits. Jessie had a loathing of the Tories – intense even by Easterhouse standards. At the height of the campaign, the APTU sent her a joke invitation to Margaret Thatcher's garden party and reminded her to buy a hat. 'Hat!' she said. 'It's a hatchet I'll be taking!'

When it was time for questions at the press conference one reporter asked if the women were militant – if they'd been involved in previous battles. 'Never in my life', said Flo, truthfully. 'Have we, mum?' To everyone's amazement the old lady blurted out: 'I hit a councillor once.' Flo and I looked at one another, thrown by this departure from the script. Jessie had never even told her daughter the story.

Back in the 1950s, Jessie reared her family in a room and kitchen basement flat in Anderson. One daughter was in hospital for 10 years with tuberculosis of the spine. The girl was one of the first TB patients to benefit from the drug streptomycin. At last her parents could take her home, but Jessie needed a decent house for the convalescing child. So a delegation from Glasgow Corporation arrived to inspect the tiny flat. A female councillor surveyed the gaping window frame and the huddled children and said: 'It's not so bad as to give you a transfer. You'll just have to put your daughter in a home.' Jessie lost her temper. Her neighbours, who had all come to offer support, chased the woman down the street with milk bottles crashing at her heels. But Jessie got a new house. An early example of angry women and direct action getting results!

A sense of history was often carried to meetings. Not just personal

battles, like Jessie's, but memories of working-class solidarity. Mining villages, or former mining villages, were a case in point. Blantyre
Miners' Welfare gave the anti-poll tax union its hall for free. The
hospitality was incredibly generous. You'd end up having a second
meeting in the social club afterwards – with the guys who'd been
playing pool during the speeches.

Dunterlie, a housing scheme in Barrhead, Renfrewshire, was
another strong area for us. The town was badly hit by the demise of
the Paisley threadmills and the closure of the Linwood car plant in
1981. Shanks once had a huge sanitary ware factory in Barrhead
which was run down and eventually closed.

Dunterlie suffered historic neglect. Tenants were used to taking
on the local council and were equally combatative over the poll tax.
Phil Treish, a former painter and decorator, could claim a lot of
credit for that. Phil is a member of the Communist Party of Britain
and has worked hard to keep the tenants' organisation fighting and
active – even when the council set up its own, compliant tenants'
group.

When poll tax registration officers targeted Dunterlie in 1988,
locals tied their garden gates together. They then posted sentries at
either end of the street. The official made off and returned with the
police. 'Why are these gates tied up?' demanded the cops. 'It's all
the dangerous dogs, we have to keep them out of the gardens,' they
replied.

In Castlemilk, working-class anarchists joined local Militants like
Larry Flanagan and Flora Edmonds, in getting the the anti-poll tax
union off the ground. Big John Cooper became a stalwart of the
national campaign, along with his wife, Carol, and son, John junior.
John senior is a giant of a man, a former car worker. We have our
political differences but John and the Glasgow Anarchists are still
with the campaign and still offer physical and financial support.

John always felt his housing scheme had been abused by the
municipal Labour machine. Castlemilk once had the highest concentration of public housing in Western Europe. The scheme was
completely dry apart from the Labour Club so you joined the party

to get a drink. Anything more ideological was discouraged as became clear from the later witch-hunt of Militant members in the constituency.

John often talked about his involvement in the local Claimants' Union in the late 1970s. The Claimants' Union movement was about radicalising the unemployed as well as informing them of their rights. He resented the way the Labour councils neutered these groups by setting up Unemployed Workers' Centres. These were apolitical places, employing full timers who were invariably leaned upon by their right wing pay masters. In John's view, another local initiative had been killed. He was also very active in the Castlemilk Miners Support Group during the big strike. He felt, as I did, that these support groups showed the potential of ordinary people to organise.

Rural as well as urban areas set up unions. Community solidarity in some smaller places was so strong it occasionally overwhelmed the broader principle of a national campaign.

Keith Baldassarra, one of Militant's organisers in Pollok, remembers speaking to several hundred people in Auchinleck, an Ayrshire mining village. Emphasising the mass nature of the campaign, he praised the good work of groups in Edinburgh. 'Never mind Edinburgh! Whit aboot Auchinleck! cried a voice from the crowd. So Keith diplomatically dropped the next bit referring to 'Our brothers and sisters in England and Wales . . .'

Indignation was bubbling away in even more remote places. Jack Harvey visited Leadhills, the highest village in Scotland. He drove there one winter night, slowed by the mist and occasional flurries of snow. To get there you must first cut off the M74 just as Lanarkshire becomes Dumfriesshire. Then you negotiate red tarmac roads twisting up through the Lowther Hills. The village hasn't changed much since the eighteenth century. Even the lending library set up by the lead miners is still there, with its yellowing volumes on theology and politics. The last mine closed in the 1960s. Some of the heathery land round about is owned by the Douglas-Home family, who use it for shooting.

Tea and empire biscuits were being served when Jack arrived at the village hall. It was all very civilised. He concentrated on warming up and mulled over a low-key speech on how to set up a committee with limited numbers. Suddenly people appeared, shaking the sleet from their shoes. Folk from the surrounding villages had descended on Leadhills. Many looked quite genteel and Jack, who by his own admission is a coarse big bloke, cut out the rabble rousing which went down so well in the housing schemes. He needn't have bothered. Leadhills was as livid as Glasgow's Blackhill. 'I'm a headmistress,' said one lady, shaking her finger. 'And I'd just like to tell you how appalled we all are and how much you have our full support. We're all so impressed by the work of the federation and you Glasgow people!' Resounding cheers and stamping of feet followed. Jack thought: If this is how a headmistress feels in the Lowther Hills, the revolution must be round the corner!

Anger makes you wise – if you direct it properly. Blantyre, Leadhills, Drumchapel and Royston were all separately ablaze with strong feelings. But little fires, no matter how brightly they burn, eventually flicker and die. We had to kindle more anger, stoke up the flames and create a Scottish inferno. We had to build a federation.

We did not waste time. On 6 June 1988 a group of us got together in Glasgow's Virginia Chambers to organise a conference. There was myself, Stewart Petrie from Pollokshields Against the Poll Tax, Jim Keegan from Bridgeton, Teresa Donaghy from Anderson, Doreen from Govanhill and others. Mohammed Sarwar, now a Glasgow district Labour councillor, was co-opted onto the committee to provide a link with the Asian community, who would be badly hit by the tax. Unfortunately, however, he never attended any of our meetings.

We wanted the conference to establish the Strathclyde Anti-Poll Tax Federation. We set a date for 10 July – just one month away. I spent two laborious weeks handwriting letters of invitation to anti-poll tax unions, tenants' groups, shop stewards' committees and community councils. Money was so tight we did not always have a typewriter. We attempted to create headed notepaper on someone's office computer. But to use a Glasgow term, it was all a bit 'haunknitted.'

None of us knew what to expect when the time came for the conference in the City Halls. Would people take such a shoestring organisation seriously? Would they pay us the compliment of turning up? It was nerveracking.

We could not have hoped for a better response. There were 330 delegates from ninety-six different groups. Almost half the delegates represented forty-four APTU from all over Clydeside: Drumchapel, Renfrew, Gorbals, Mount Florida, Bridgeton, Cumbernauld, Kilsyth, Cambuslang, Shettleston, Clydebank and many others. Community Councils who sent delegates included Govan, East Govan, Cranhill, Sighthill, Brockburn, and Paisley North. Twelve tenants associations and ten community or-ganisations were represented. Just some of these were: Braeside Action Group, from Greenock, The Argyle Community Associa-tion from Anderson in Glasgow, Milton Information Group from the north of the city, Birkenshaw Tenants from Lanarkshire, The Cambuslang Tenants' Action Combine and the Garscadden Tenant Management Co-operative from the heart of Donald Dewar's constituency.

Participation from the Labour movement was healthy. We had twelve trade union branches and three trades councils. These in-cluded Glasgow 38 Branch GMB, printers from West of Scotland Sogat and clerical workers from Nalgo's branch in the Southern General Hospital. The Leverndale Hospital joint shop stewards committee sent delegates, as did teachers from the Langside branch of the Educational Institute of Scotland. Glasgow Trades' Council Youth Section also sent representatives.

We also had students' associations including the body represent-ing all the student associations in West Scotland (WOSNUS). Pollok was well represented, not only through its mushrooming APTU, but also its community and youth groups. One of the best indications of the success of the conference was attendance at the creche. It entertained fifty children that day.

I was elected secretary and Drew McEwan, then a member of Erskine Labour Party, was voted chairman. No one dissented when we voted to build a mass non-payment campaign across Scotland and to disrupt the registration process which was then underway. We also voted to put pressure on Strathclyde Regional Council not to impose fines or penalties on those refusing to register or pay.

More than anything else, we were determined to keep the federation democratic and accountable to its members. We could not lose touch with the roots that give every movement its momentum. So we took the unusual step of holding a monthly meeting to which all the groups could send a delegate. These aggregate meetings sometimes numbered one hundred and were extremely lively.

Our City Halls success contrasted sharply with the conference of Labour's 'Stop It' campaign in Glasgow the previous week. It only attracted 114 delegates. 'Stop It' was running out of steam before the tax was introduced. Their conference was top-heavy, with Labour speakers like John Mulvey, the leader of Lothian Regional Council and John Mullin, chair of finance at Strathclyde Regional Council. This top-heavy approach was apparent when they belatedly tried to set up a Glasgow south-west 'Stop It' group in the summer of 1988. The area already had almost a dozen street-by-street unions which were up, running and part of our Federation: Penilee, Govan, North Pollok, Nitshill, Bonnyholm, Brockburn, Cowglen, Cardonald College, Ibrox, Darnley, Dormanside. All directly involving the real experts, ordinary people, doing things for themselves.

Coincidentally, I debated with the 'Stop It' leader, Brian Wilson, in Shettleston in May of 1988. He was careful not to condemn law-breaking in itself. He argued against non-payment in terms of *tactics*, a well-worn device of political intellectual types: 'Do you really think 100,000 people refusing to pay will bring down this government? Don't be daft,' he scoffed in his affable way. He failed to grasp – probably deliberately – that a campaign of defiance would politicise its participants. Their confidence would grow as more people joined. That's how we would get bigger. That's how we would win.

Brian's debating sophistries could not stop the clamour for non-payment. It was something he had to acknowledge and led to 'Stop It' launching the Return to Sender campaign. Return to Sender encouraged individuals to send registration forms back to the regional assessor, the person in charge of compiling the register of poll tax payers. The returned form should include a barrage of questions like: Why do you need to know my date of birth? We supported Return to Sender as a useful way of clogging up the system. It involved people before the real test began.

The record of the Labour leadership told us 'Stop It' was probably as far as they were prepared to take disobedience. But we still hoped for official trade union support. The Transport and General Workers Union was making very sympathetic noises at this time. So in those weeks running up to our July conference we chased the Scottish Trades Union Congress in the way a besotted schoolboy might pursue a woman who's just not interested. At first they refused to attend. They blamed the structure of the federation. We wanted the anti-poll tax unions to dominate the Fed by sending five delegates while everyone else had two – another way of ensuring control remained in the schemes. When the STUC objected we gave everyone five delegates. It was a compromise. But we felt it was worth it to get the full weight of the Scottish Labour movement – representing 910,000 workers – behind non payment.

Clearly, no amount of crawling would have been enough. The STUC drew us a look and turned away with another excuse. We were not particularly bothered if union leaders like STUC general secretary, Campbell Christie, and his deputy, Bill Speirs, gave us the brush off. The trouble was, they had written to local trade union branches instructing them to shun us.

By mid 1988 the STUC took over the official campaign from 'Stop It', which was by then a laughing stock. Christie and Speirs said they would build a united front against the poll tax. The STUC extended a fraternal hand to organisations who were in favour of non-payment: the Greens, the Scottish Tenants' Organisation and the Scottish National Party. Remarkably, they froze out the federation, which was doing all the ground work. Christie called for a Week of Action in September 1988 and refused to rule out non-payment. Like Brian Wilson, he kept saying the tax could be stopped before its introduction in April 1989. The months ticked by and what started as a united front was eventually exposed as just another stalling device.

When they could no longer quibble about conference details, the Labour establishment tried to dismiss the federation as a Militant front. This accusation was a bit patronising to Sheila MacDonald, Phil Treish, the Castlemilk anarchists, and all the ordinary folk who made up the Fed. But this salvo backfired on Labour because being identified with non-payment built respect for Militant. On the eve of the July conference an expose in the Glasgow *Evening Times* did us more good than harm.

The crunch came on 18 September 1988 when the Labour Party in Scotland held a recall conference in Govan Town Hall to discuss their attitude to Poll Tax. We were all outside singing and heckling the commissars in the red silk ties who now controlled the party. Hugh Cochrane, a *Glasgow Herald* journalist who covered the event, noted that men out-numbered women at the conference by five to one. What a contrast to the meetings I'd addressed in recent months! No wonder the women demonstrating outside began to sing Donald whaur's yer trousers? when the Shadow Scottish Secretary ran the gauntlet. Inside, Dewar had told delegates: 'A party which believes it will soon be in power and responsible for legislation cannot repudiate obligation under the law. You cannot argue for the rule of law when the right people are in charge and have the luxury of picking and choosing when they are not. The party which takes this course forfeits respect.'

Responsible? Is that what you have to be in the face of poverty? How many weans will it feed? So Labour didn't have any anger or guts . . . but at least they were responsible. He also referred to respect. A party which turns its back on the people who built it deserves no respect. Choosing whether or not to pay the poll tax may well have been a luxury for Donald. We just couldn't afford it.

Dissent was given little space at that conference. Supporters of non-payment were branded extremists. Dick Douglas, the Labour MP whose passionate stand against the tax embarrassed his party, was not even allowed to speak. Dick had always been regarded as a bit of a right-winger on things like defence. 'After a lifetime of being called a moderate I now find myself being called a Trot Nat,' he said when it was all over.

The result was a *fait accompli*. A majority of delegates from Constituency Labour Parties voted in favour of the Transport and General Workers Union motion that Labour should lead a campaign of mass non payment. But the motion was defeated by a union block vote of 512,000 to 225,000. This result sealed Labour's humiliation at the Govan by-election which followed only a few weeks later.

The result was a setback for morale. Scots felt deserted. The Fed got little media coverage. So no one appeared to be leading the non-payment campaign. It was such a betrayal. The STUC's promised week of action was almost as farcical as the Labour Party conference. Instead of calling a one-day strike, they asked workers to down tools for eleven minutes. Guys in the shipyards at Govan and Yarrows said that was how long it took them to reach the gate. It was hardly long enough for a tea-break.

Instead of firing us all up, this non-event was a further attempt to extinguish the flames of rebellion. In March 1988 a MORI Poll in the *Scotsman* newspaper showed 42% of those questioned would support a non-payment campaign. But after the conference decision and the STUC Week of action another MORI opinion poll for Scottish Television showed only 8% in favour of non-payment.

Apart from the conference decision, Labour Party figures had been doing their personal best to scaremonger on behalf of the government. The late Norman Buchan, regarded as a left-winger, wrote a hand-wringing piece in the *Glasgow Herald* on the inequality of the tax and the unfairness of capitalism generally. He wrote elegantly and emotionally, even enlisting the support of Dundee mill-worker May Brooksbank who sang:

> 'Oh dear me, the world's ill-divided
> Them that work the hardest
> Are aye wi least provided.'

That song should encourage all good socialists to cry: Yes, the world's ill-divided and we must set it to rights. But for Buchan, it was just an excuse for more breast-beating. If we choose to engage in the wrong battle, the movement itself will be dangerously weakened, he wrote. What movement? It wasn't moving. It was crippled by its own inertia. Labour was dying on its feet – or should I say knees. If the poll tax was the wrong battle then when would the time ever be right to fight?

Brian Wilson also used his *Glasgow Herald* column. 'My persistent concern in all this nonsense about leading people into non-payment campaigns is for those who will genuinely believe that the poll tax will disappear if they ignore it, and who will then find themselves landed with fines and costs – on top of their cruel poll tax bills.' Labour local authorities looked no more likely to resist the attack. We wanted regional councils, the bodies charged with collecting the tax, to adopt the slogan: Better to Break the Law than Break the Poor. This was used by the Poplar councillors of the 1920s who were jailed for refusing to set a rate which would cripple East London's working class . . . Liverpool councillors of the 1980s were surcharged for following the same line.

But right from the start regional councils made it clear they would co-operate with the poll tax. Charlie Gray, the leader of Strathclyde Regional Council, said the tax would cost the council another £8.6 million to administer. Rather than refusing to comply even on these grounds, he demanded more money from the Scottish Office. He should have told them: 'Look, we're setting a rate. We're going to levy and collect it, so there's still money coming in.' Then Lothian, Central and Tayside regional councils would have followed Strathclyde's lead. The tax would have been dead in the water.

Charlie Grey has eventually arrived at this conclusion but too late now in 1994.

With Labour politicians prostrating themselves before the government, we turned instead to the trade unions. Given the STUC's behaviour, we did not have grounds for optimism. We called on the unions not to comply with the administration of the tax. Certain groups of workers were particularly important – like the local government officers who must collect it, and the civil servants who may be called on to deduct it from state benefits.

If we wanted these workers to withdraw co-operation, they would need the support of other trade unionists. Otherwise they would be vulnerable to victimisation. But our own contacts within the National and Local Government Officers' Association and the Civil and Public Servants Association, said many clerical workers were now on short-term contracts. They risked losing their jobs if they refused to comply. A strike involving so many casual workers was out of the question, as they would get no support from the STUC.

All this is not to say we were the only group advocating non-payment. Dissident MPs like Dick Douglas, George Galloway, John McAllion, Denis Canavan and Maria Fyfe (along with individual STUC leaders like Campbell Christie and Bill Speirs) formed the Committee of 100 after Labour's recall conference. This was intended to be 100 prominent people who'd refuse to pay the tax. The hullaballoo over this pointless élitism was incredible. You could only participate in the campaign if you could afford it. It betrayed eveything I'd been brought up to believe in. The emphasis on individuals was contrary to the principles of the movement. It really grated on me that hardly a paragraph was written about all our meetings in the schemes. But when a group of luminaries launched the committee in the People's Palace they got a front page colour photograph in the *Glasgow Herald*. It stretched across eight columns – but the committee couldn't even stretch to make its 100 quota.

The Scottish National Party voted to back a non-payment campaign the day before Labour's recall conference. This was good in as much as it meant someone – Jim Sillars or Kenny MacAskill – was regularly on the telly telling people not to pay.

But the SNP campaign, in my view, was also elitist. It revolved around the slogan 'Can Pay, Won't Pay' which always seemed illogical to me. Why tell the ones who couldn't afford it to pay and the ones who could afford it not to pay? Activists were to recruit 100,000 non-payers from the middle classes because telling everyone not to pay would simply get the poor into debt.

That was the official line. It was just a balancing act to get the reactionary elements of the party to support the campaign. Scottish nationalists were involved in the grassroots of the federation. When I shared platforms with Jim or Kenny they preached non-payment, the same as me. They spoke the language of socialism. But when we met to discuss our respective strategies in December 1988, Kenny said he had to follow the 'Can Pay Won't Pay' line.

Jim and Kenny's efforts were also undermined by their own people outside the central belt. In Tayside Region, SNP councillors proposed offering a discount to anyone paying their poll tax up front. SNP-controlled Angus was the first District Council to cooperate with the tax even though as a District Council they had no legal obligation to do so. Later, in Grampian, the SNP voted with the Tories and Liberals to deduct the tax directly from DSS benefits.

We were isolated, penniless, and ignored by the media. By the time of Strathclyde Federation's second conference in November 1988, we were alone in calling for mass non-payment. We remained undaunted. Our movement was growing. A Central Region federation of anti-poll tax unions – covering the area around Stirling and Falkirk – was formed late in the year, as were the Lothian and Fife Federations. We were ready to march over the top of the hill. But now a few lone voices in our own ranks began urging retreat. Small left-wing groups like the Socialist Workers Party ridiculed the idea that mass non-payment could defeat the poll tax. The SWP argued: 'Even large numbers organised in a community rather than a workplace basis do not themselves have the strength to win. The state machinery, through fines, arresting of wages and so on, can wear down community resistance.' Democracy has its price and our monthly meetings were constant battles with a few individuals. Unfortunately they included our chairman Drew MacEwan who was shortly to leave the Labour Party to rejoin the SWP.

Sure, we recognised the importance of the trade union movement and making approaches to workplaces. But we reminded them again of the rent strikes. We would ask: Where do the workers live? In their factories? They live in housing schemes, in tower blocks, in run down mining villages, in deck-access tenements. That's where we'll organise. We pointed out that many workers didn't have workplaces. They were unemployed, or worked part-time in non-unionised jobs or stayed at home with children. We would take the union to them. We won the argument because we were closer to the problem. Drew was later voted off his federation post – replaced by Jim Cameron of Strathclyde Nalgo. Often members of the far left live detached from working-class life – just like the Labour councillors and MPs. They could not feel the heat.

In fact, ordinary workers and shop stewards did play a part in our campaign. It was just a matter of getting to speak to them. I remember speaking at a National Union of Public Employees branch meeting in Hamilton. One of our members, Stephen Smellie, held a union position. This meeting took place during a dispute over cleaners' pay. More ordinary women members attended than would normally be the case. I said my piece and the response was really positive. But the full-time NUPE official stood up and said: 'Non-payment is not union policy.'

Not union policy? chorused the audience. When was that decided? They voted overwhelmingly to affiliate to the federation and gave us a donation.

Women workers were always keen to question the wisdom of their full-time officials. One female shop steward campaigned for us inside the Marshall's Chunky Chicken Factory in Cambuslang. She put up federation posters which were torn down by the management. The factory employs 600 workers at the height of the season. The women work in chilling temperatures and have to wear gloves and wellingtons to protect themselves from the cold and wet. The shop steward was herself a process worker who packed chickens after they were plucked.

The hostility of the management meant she spoke against the tax in her lunch break. They don't pay me for that half hour, she said.

Daks in Larkhall was a Lanarkshire clothing factory where the female workforce took the initiative. Two ordinary female workers practically set up their own anti-poll tax union among the machinists. They'd put up posters at the factory and workers would attend meetings of the Larkhall APTU in the Cameronian Hall. Squads of Daks women came to our demos with perfectly sewn banners.

We tried to bypass the leadership as much as possible and speak to shop stewards in their workplaces. It let them know we weren't these two-headed monsters described in the literature from head office. We got a tremendous reception from stewards in Rolls Royce, Yarrows and Govan Shipyards. They were always very warm, promising to support our demos no matter what the STUC circular said.

We actually got to speak to the joint trade union executive representing the thousands of manual workers with Glasgow District Council. Many of the shop stewards were members of the Labour Party. But once they heard us speak they not only agreed to affiliate – they donated £200. I later spoke to some of these workers in the direct labour organisation canteen in Queenslie. They were all very enthusiastic – despite the hate campaign being waged against us by their employers in the district council. (Many younger white collar workers were very receptive – such as Ministry of Defence staff in Glasgow. The Fire Brigades Union in Strathclyde affiliated as did the workers at Albion Motors.)

The federation tried to revive the tradition of factory-gate meetings. We regularly spoke and held collections outside Yarrows and Govan Shipbuilders, Weirs of Cathcart, and many others.

Sometimes the management got stroppy. One lunchtime we went down to the car park of a clothing factory on the southside of Glasgow. Davie Archibald, a young Militant organiser from Govan, went into the canteen and said: 'Come to a meeting outside on the poll tax. Tam Sheridan's speaking.' Within a few minutes we had a crowd of around 100. We were all set to do the same thing for the next canteen sitting when management moved us on.

The management of Cowglen Savings Bank in Glasgow weren't very sympathetic either. They stopped us using the social club for meetings – we actually had an APTU in the bank. Undeterred, we continued to hold our meetings across the street on a grass verge.

The Labour Movement leaders who tried to freeze us out often claimed Militant were jumping on the band wagon of anti-poll tax feeling. But it was Militant who built the band wagon in the first place.

As I've already explained, the federation was largely made up of people who belonged to no political party. But every successful campaign needs a coherent structure and a committed leadership. Militant provided that leadership.

When you look over the history of the twentieth century, think about the times when working people's struggles were to the fore. Think about those powerful sepia photographs of the hunger marchers in the 1930s. Then ask yourself where the moderate leaders of the Labour Party were during those lean years. The people who marched behind the fluttering Fight or Starve banners were raw recruits – just like the members of our anti-poll tax unions. They too were frozen out by the TUC. They too were part of an unofficial movement. Those brave men and women whose faces stare out of the *Picture Post* or the *Daily Worker* – they too were dismissed as lumpen and rowdy. This was because the National Unemployed Workers' Movement which organised the hunger marches was led by Communists.

The parallels between our movement in the late 1980s and the NUWM in the twenties and thirties are very important. Although we learned a lot from older people with experience in trade unions, much of our vitality came from those who were new to political organisation. The low-paid, single parents and young unemployed who supported us were seldom trade union members.

Likewise, the NUWM first organised in the 1920s among soldiers and sailors returning from World War One. These young men had been conscripted to the trenches in their teens. They had never known work or trade union membership. Starvation stared them in the face when they were demobbed. Official unemployment stood at two million in 1919 – yet there was no benefit system.

Wal Hannington, the leader of the NUWM, was a young toolmaker and shop steward who began agitating against unemployment in the engineering shops where he worked on the outskirts of London. The leaders of the trade union movement at that time had co-operated with the war effort. After the war the ruling class no longer *needed* to compromise with the unions. Unemployment was soaring. But the Labour leadership took little action. It was up to ordinary shop stewards to defend their workers against cuts in wages and conditions.

The forty hours strike of 1918–1919 is perhaps the most famous example. It was a general strike which started in Glasgow. This was the strike which provoked the state into arresting the leaders and occupying the city for days, placing guns on top of the city chambers and parking tanks in the streets.

The strike was very dangerous to the ruling class as it quickly spread to England, where Hannington became involved. It united employed and unemployed. A cut in hours would make life easier for workers and hopefully give employment to the returning troops. But the strike collapsed due to the lack of support from the leadership of the engineering union – some things never change. All the radical shop stewards were sacked and had to organise outside the workplace.

These radicals threw their energies into emerging unemployed workers' committees. Unemployed committees emerged in much the same way as anti-poll tax unions more than sixty years later. Some committees were started by Communists, others were a mixed bag. The Liverpool committee was typical. There were three Communists, a syndicalist (who believed that workers should form one big union to overthrow capitalism) a vicar, an ex-royal Navy Petty Officer and a devout Catholic.

The NUWM and the Anti-Poll Tax Federation both grew from strong geographical bases. Glasgow was the starting point for a Strathclyde federation which eventually sent speakers throughout the country to form a Scottish and an All British Federation. Hannington, from Slough, concentrated at first on London, where he brought the committees together. The London District Council which he formed printed a newspaper, *Out of Work* which linked unemployed committees around Great Britain.

The Communist-led NUWM, like the Federation, advocated direct action. They backed strikes by those in work and factory raids, as well as the famous marches. In England they stormed the offices of the local Guardians, the people in charge of adminstering poor relief to the unemployed in the days before the welfare state. These worthies could decide to pay nothing and force families into the workhouse. This was a Victorian institution, a cross between a factory and prison.

In Wandsworth, London, the Guardians refused to give unemployed families money unless they came into the workhouse. In 1921 the local NUWM committee arranged for 1000 people, including many women and children, to line up outside the workhouse. Once 700 were inside, they took over the place, demanding better food and conditions. The Guardians were then forced to pay poor relief to the unemployed in their own homes.

Hannington very much wanted the support of the official movement. But when the Labour Party eventually called a special conference on unemployment, in February 1921, it met in secret. Strike action was rejected. Although there was a short period when the TUC formed a joint committee with the NUWM, it was never a happy marriage and ended after a few years.

So the NUWM fought on alone to raise the level of benefit, give the unemployed a dignified collective voice and to support striking workers. They realised the interests of employed and unemployed were the same. In fact, the TUC actively opposed the hunger marches. It accused the Communist organisers of putting the health of the hunger marchers at risk – just as the Labour Party in the 1980s accused the Federation of throwing the poor into debt. This is a patronising, though persistent tactic. It exploits concern for the working class to stop them doing anything for themselves.

The Labour party was jealous of the growing power of Hannington in England and Harry McShane, the NUWM leader in Scotland. In order to undermine the NUWM success in radicalising the unemployed, it set up alternative committees which attempted to channel energies back into soup-making and away from the Communists.

But after 1931 the Labour leader Ramsay MacDonald tore off this mask of concern and actually joined forces with the Tories to form a National Government. This government introduced the Means Test to further impoverish families hit by unemployment. When the National Hunger March set off in 1932, the government told the police to obstruct the marchers wherever they went. Many of the leaders, including Hannington, were arrested and sent to jail. Many of the marchers were injured with truncheons. The collaboration of Labour regional councillors in introducing the poll tax, then setting sheriff officers on the poor, was a bit like Ramsay MacDonald joining with the Tories to force the Means Test on the unemployed. The loudest voices calling for the police to clamp down on the federation came from Labour politicians.

Reading about Hannington and the men and women of the NUWM was a great inspiration. You are never alone if you know your roots.

We had right – and history – on our side. But we were skint. Campaigns run by the official movement have access to everything you take for granted: office space, telephones, secretarial services, printing and distribution – not to mention hard cash. Being cut off from all that forced us to take to the streets. It meant we had more direct contact with ordinary people than the salaried politicians. We had the courage to put our arguments before people. This was the way our great-grandparents built the labour movement. They had no millionaire supporters. The press was as hostile, if not more so, than today. So was the emerging broadcast media. Lord Reith, the first Director General of the BBC, instructed journalists to ignore the workers' case in radio reports of the General Strike in 1926. But the pioneers of the labour movement overcame these problems with a mixture of commitment, determination and hard work. It was also important to have the right ideas and to communicate them clearly.

Oily-tongued politicians often accuse us of sloganising. But the labour movement was built on slogans. If an idea is relevant to people's lives, it can be encapsulated in a few words. The nineteenth-century Chartists cried Union is Strength when they campaigned for the vote. Socialist temperance followers wanted Scotland to be Sober and Free. In 1926 the call was Strike or Starve. Everybody knows what Coal Not Dole means. All the rent strikes in South Africa had slogans. Workers in the Lenin Shipyard in Gdansk, Poland, shouted, 'There is no Freedom Without Solidarity.'

Slogans can be poignant, poetic and powerful all at once. During the recent Timex dispute in Dundee, pickets nailed a sign outside the factory saying, 'There are none so blind as those who cannot see.' It was aimed directly at the scabs who covered their eyes while being driven past the workers whose jobs they'd taken. It made the point perfectly. People repeat slogans and pass them on. They help build movements. Even before we had one million non-payers in Scotland, people thought there were – it said so on all our badges. Our 'I'm one in a million' sticker was a self-fulfilling prophesy.

We launched the movement with the slogan 'This Far and No Further.' People immediately identified with it. They felt they had been abused for so long, had lost so much, and weren't going to take any more.

Empty slogans, on the other hand, just demoralise. The new look Labour Party stripped itself of the last vestiges of socialism in the late 1980s and bellowed 'Meet the Challenge, Make the Change'. What did it mean? How was it meant to inspire anyone? We had better words, possibly even better tunes. We just lacked glossy packaging.

Access to technology is very important. It's worth remembering that you needed a special licence to have a photocopier in East Germany under the Stalinists. Few people were allowed to own typewriters in Ceasescu's Romania. We don't work under those restrictions in Scotland. But a different kind of censorship operates in the so-called free world.

Newspapers and television companies are controlled by a few very wealthy individuals who do not like challenges to the system which keeps them wealthy. At the start of the campaign we had very little coverage. We had to reach people directly. But bulletins, posters, magazines, all cost money. Your freedom of speech in Britain varies according to your income level.

Community printing presses are relatively cheap and intended for use by small groups. A network of these print shops sprang up in the 1970s and 80s. Then they were taken over by the councils and became increasingly politically restricted. This was particularly the case during the poll tax period, when some of the council-funded printers who helped us were actually raided. Fortunately we found a small printer which was also independent. Our campaign would not have been possible without Clydeside Press. This workers' co-operative was started up ten years ago by Tommy Kayes. He first got the presses running with his redundancy money from Inchinnan Tyre factory, where he worked as a storeman. Tommy describes himself as a freelance subversive and the political orientation of Clydeside is towards class-based anarchism.

Quarter of a million distinctive federation window posters flew off Clydeside's presses in 1988 alone. Each had a big, bold, NO on the front as in NO Poll Tax Here or Castlemilk says NO to the Poll Tax. This was a design pioneered in Govan to great effect. On the back of each poster we printed a list of the questions which came up most at meetings and answered each one. It gave simple facts in simple language:

No one in Scotland can be jailed for non-payment
No one goes to court for non-payment

Non payment does not affect your house – whether it is rented or bought

There are no fines for non-payment, the £50 and £200 fines are for non-registration

The penalty for non payment is a 10% surcharge – £30 in Glasgow.

Gangs of unemployed people from areas like Pollok, Easterhouse and Drumchapel took bundles of the posters in a couple of old cars and would just pile into an area. I remember going into the high flats in the Gorbals. My legs still remember the stairs. But it was worth it because people were so grateful. They were actually thanking us. There was such a thirst for knowledge.

Clydeside Press printed several million items for the federation over the years. Eventually our local groups approached Tommy Kayes directly. He was always good with credit. Sometimes Jack Harvey or myself descended the stairs to their wee basement shop in the High Street at two or three in the morning to find the guys still grafting away. They would often work till 6.00 am to get more stuff out.

Material had to be produced at very short notice – especially once the campaign was underway and the bills came through the doors. Say, for example, Strathclyde Region released inaccurate figures suggesting the non-payment campaign was slipping. People were basically being bullied into paying up. If the television news ran those figures on Thursday we'd be out in the schemes on Friday, setting the record straight with thousands of leaflets printed by Clydeside Press.

The time factor influenced the design. Layouts were functional, with blocks of type, straight lines and no colour – well, very occasionally a splash of socialist scarlet. When we were working towards our first big show of strength on 18th March 1989 the posters just urged people to come to THE DEMO. Folk saw it and said: What demo? Soon everyone was discussing it.

Our material contrasted starkly with that of the Scottish Trades Union Congress. Artists designed their full-colour posters, using powerful woodcut images evoking past struggles and so on. Yet they were totally ineffective as political instruments. When a brutal piece of legislation is attacking your class, you've sometimes got to suspend the love of art for the task in hand. It's often the case that the slicker the medium, the more meaningless the message. Our arguments were so powerful, we did not need to dress them up. Our posters were distinctive and immediately recognisable. The simplicity and clarity was itself artistic.

Because we were shunned by the official media, we had to be very imaginative. Posters and leaflets were not enough. We needed to counter all the nasty medicine about fines and debtors lists being dispensed on telly every night by Dewar, Maxton, Wilson and the rest. Again we looked to the past. The Young Communist League and the Independent Labour Party in the 1920s literally took their message to the streets – armed with chalk and whitewash. Our canvas was the jumble of decay which blights all cities: the railway arches, the facades of demolished warehouses, the walls guarding vast, empty, industrial sites. Reconnaissance teams would first survey the city, identifying suitable backdrops. These had to be prominent, but dilapidated. We didn't want to be accused of wanton vandalism. In fact we performed a service by obliterating the existing sectarian graffiti with revolutionary messages. These were mostly quite stylised and hopefully a good few cuts above Remember 1690 or Up the Ra.

GET MILITANT! PAY NO POLL TAX! was featured on bridges, fences, and motorway embankments. We became quite famous for our paint squads. Our artists were like Michelangelo in the Sistine Chapel – hanging upside down, working painstakingly into the small hours.

One Saturday at 3 am Keith found himself stuck to the road bridge he'd been painting for the previous hour. His predicament went unnoticed by all the cars and taxis coming back from the dancing. They pumped their horns in approval as they sped beneath him.

Such working conditions meant spelling was occasionally mud-dled. A few letters looked a bit Russian. Not everyone approved.

Charlie Gray had our advertisement on the M8 painted over several times because he had to drive past it to the council each day. There was also the big gas works in Provan, which overlooks the motorway to Edinburgh. About thirty people were involved in the major operation to paint a giant slogan on the side. British Gas started talking about charging us £10,000 damages, but we heard nothing from them. We made the front page when the doors of Hampden Park were painted the night before a big international match between Scotland and France. Does Hampden Park constitute a useless building? Is it a legitimate target for the graffiti squads? Scotland fans might argue about that. Some might even say it has a useful function as home of the national team. But what the heck, we scored on the front page.

Admittedly we broke our own rules when we painted Mount Florida station next to the football ground. But football crowds were our ideal audience and it was worth bending the rules. Graffiti squads were very active in the run up to that game, which came shortly before our demo on 18 March 1989. A team of us went down to the station, which is nearest to Hampden. We wanted all the fans to catch details of the demo as they got off the train. Our lookouts got arrested that night, while the vandals had a lucky escape.

After the trains stopped, Jack and Alan were painting the wall which runs beside the railway line at the end of the platform. The letters stretched about ten yards. Alan must have gone through a gallon or two of industrial paint in those forty-five minutes. Jack had started painting the staircases on either side of the platform, while Alan was out of sight finishing off the wall beside the tracks. He had just reached the number eight in March 18 when one of the six lookouts shouted POLIS!

Alan had to decide whether to finish painting and get arrested, or run away leaving the demo date incomplete. With true revolutionary zeal, he finished the number 8 with the cop just ten yards away. Then he dropped the brush and bombed it upstairs with the polis on his tail. He sprinted in the direction of panic, turned a corner, and just kept running. Eventually he found himself in the grounds of a big empty mansion near Queens Park. Like some kind of Colditz escapee, Alan dived into the bushes and curled up like a hedgehog. He lay there for about an hour, listening to the police walkie talkies and praying their torches wouldn't pick out the flash of Brilliant White emulsion in the undergrowth. He looked like a ghost, every inch of his body was covered in paint.

When he finally uncurled himself, he realised he had no money to get home to Govan. So he began to walk in a westerly direction, only to be apprehended by two traffic police. 'Where have you been?' they asked, looking him up and down. He thought they knew who he was and were having a bit of a laugh before arresting him. 'I was painting my granny's house', said Alan, playing along. They went into hysterics. This is it, thought Alan. Any minute now they're going to say, 'Get in the van, you've done well, but you're nicked'. But they just kept kidding him. Have you ever done any painting before? Is your granny paying for the spillage? They were highly amused but totally unaware Alan was a wanted man. He had crossed the border into another police division and they knew nothing of the Mount Florida commotion.

Some people might disapprove of these actions. They might think we were no better than vandals. But I know the Glasgow public differentiated between our paint jobs and real vandalism. In fact, they overwhelmingly supported us.

One time, Jack and Alan were painting the big wall that runs alongside platform 1 of Glasgow Central station. They had borrowed a couple of donkey jackets and orange bibs and strode down the platform nodding to people. Then they jumped onto the roofs of the bothies to paint the wall in big letters. Unfortunately they got their spacing wrong. When they came to the edge of the roof, they had an unfinished slogan which terminated in mid air.

Alan jumped on Jack's shoulders. Then they heard noises inside the wee bothy, 'Would you like a big pasting brush so you can reach?', says the railway worker popping his head out the bothy. They even asked them in for a cup of tea. When a supervisor spotted Alan and Jack, and called the Transport Police, the bothy boys were able to tip them off. Another night, Jack was painting another wall, at a derelict site near the Great Eastern Hotel for the homeless in Duke Street, Glasgow. It's crumbling brick and may have been an old abattoir at one time. He had lookouts posted at either end but it's a big site and they were each a quarter of a mile away.

So he didn't hear them call his name. A crowd of middle-aged women at the bus stop across the road saved his skin. They were coming back from the bingo and began yelling: 'JAACK! JAAACK! It's the polis. C'mon over. Stand wi us and they'll no catch you!' It shows the level of public support. If those women saw someone painting a wall in other circumstances they would normally say: 'Why aren't the polis doing something about that?'

Paint, paste and brushes were one of our biggest expenses in those years. If the polis approached, you had to drop everything and run. So we were always losing our equipment.

We also had to find the £25 per week rent for our office in Renfield Street. We got it in early 1989. It was five flights above the Blue Lagoon fish and chip shop and very small. But it was ours, and that was a great achievement. So we were always thinking of imaginative ways to raise funds.

We sold anti-poll tax Christmas cards by Jim Blair. Jim is a fireman with an amazing talent for caricature. He produced some of the strongest images of the campaign. One of them appeared on the front of 'This far and no further', the booklet which spelt out the federation's strategy. It depicted Thatcher speeding towards an iceberg at the head of the Titanic Poll Tax. The tip of the iceberg has a wee saltire and the words 'Stop It', while underneath, unseen, is the spreading mass of non-payment.

Blair built up a strong following and was a big help to us. But we still raised most of our money on the streets and agitated at the same time. Maclean, it should be remembered, made some of his seditious speeches outside Shettleston Football Ground. So we'd go to football matches with our collecting cans. Modern crowd behaviour meant we never attempted to address them, but we always got a good amount.

We used to head for the bingo halls on the south side. Coaches took the women home to the various schemes afterwards and we'd jump on saying: 'I'm the new caller' and they would say 'Show us your legs eleven then'. It was great crack. A few women would give us part of their winnings and they'd talk about it on the bus all the way home. Guys were a bit scared of collecting on these buses. The women would have a real go at them – revenge in numbers, I suppose. Sometimes our opponents would sneer in both ignorance and envy: Where do they get their money? We got our money from working-class people themselves. That's why we can honestly say it was their campaign. Every weekend we'd raise hundreds of pounds in the pubs.

One Halloween in Pollok we all dressed up and collected. I was a fireman, Keith was a highlander with a Pay No Poll poster under his kilt and Big George was just an exhibitionist in a brown mac and hat. His outfit almost put me off stockings and suspenders for life. When I walked into pubs like *The Cart* dressed in the yellow helmet and fireman's boots, the whole place would freeze and I'd have their immediate attention. 'It's okay, there's no fire. Reach into your pockets and help fight the poll tax'. They always did.

The *Cart* were really generous. They would raffle bottles of whisky for us. The customers would even chip in to pay the fines of local boys who got caught while out with the paint squads. When they had a band like The Unit playing they'd allow us up to the mike to make a short speech. George worked there as a bouncer for a short while – he got taken on because he knew all the trouble makers. We raised around £70–£80 every weekend in local bars like the *Cart*, *Argosy*, *Pines* and *Howdens*.

We didn't just collect on our home patch. Every weekend thirty of us met in the city centre. We'd split into fifteen pairs and work our way round the pubs. You'd always end up in conversations with people. But when you left everyone would be wearing a sticker.

Young office workers in pubs like the *Alhambra* and *Sandowners* were very supportive. Even the much maligned wine bars gave generously. We collected in gay bars as well. DJ's in the disco pubs announced us over the sound system. We'd work our way round the *Horseshoe*, which has the longest bar in the city.

There was a certain invincibility. After the campaign was well-established you'd hear people ridiculing anyone who admitted having paid. It became a bit of a status symbol: 'I've not paid. They're not getting a penny from me!'

We even went into the famous *Saracen's Head*, or *Sarry Heid*, in the Gallowgate. The clientele are a mixture of yuppies slumming it and dossers drinking white tornadoes – a strange concoction sold nowhere else. Truth to tell the old boys did not have many coppers to spare – it was more bags of laughs and loads of support.

When March 18th came round, the day of our first national demo, the whole city must have known. We hired a doubledecker bus a few days beforehand and took it round the city centre. It was open-topped and we all wore Maggie Thatcher masks and shouted through the megaphones about the poll tax being the best thing since sliced bread. Then we went to Drumchapel, Castlemilk and Easterhouse and stirred things up there. We wanted to reach out beyond the worthy activists and we succeeded.

We even managed to get some pipers to lead us. All the usual pipe bands were very expensive and I spotted some young guys busking outside Fraser's in Buchanan Street. Their skirling and drumming verged on the anarchic, but that was all part of the appeal. The Mad Pipers later became closely associated with everything we did. They were unofficial pipers for the unofficial campaign.

The march was taking place two weeks before the tax took effect in Scotland and just as the campaign in England was starting off. The Militant in London arranged a special train to bring a thousand people up. They arrived at Central station at 6am to the sound of torrential rain and a drunken piper playing 'Auld Lang Syne'. We headed up to the Art School for cups of tea.

I arrived early in Glasgow Green where the thing was supposed to start. There was nothing there except mud, me and Jim Cameron, the new chair of the federation. Suddenly it was like one of those speeded-up movies, where all these people appear from nowhere and start building things.

The bus arrived with people on top, singing. A giant banner made by Richie Carroll and a few others at Glasgow University hung down the one side. There were banners from trade unions and countless local anti poll tax unions. There was a big bunch of firefighters from Merseyside, all in uniform, and people playing maracas and banjos.

We wanted ordinary Glaswegians to see us. So we arranged to walk up past The Barras, along Duke Street in the East End and finish at Alexandra Park in Dennistoun where Dick Douglas and Terry Fields would speak. This was part of the Hunger March tradition. They didn't just walk to London. They had marches within Scotland itself, lifting spirits in working-class communities from the thread mills of Renfrewshire to the Fife coalfield. It let the unemployed know that the National Unemployed Workers' Movement cared about them. We were letting the people of Glasgow know the Anti-Poll Tax Federation cared about them. Judging from their reaction, they already knew.

All along the route, people came out of the pubs and shops to cheer us. The folk from England had never seen anything like it. I remember running the length of Duke Street to get to the front of the line. It took me about half an hour. Rain was coming down in sheets when we got to the park. But for once it didn't matter. We were just so pleased we'd pulled it off. This rag and bob tail band of individuals from the schemes, who'd been ignored by the Labour Party and shunned by the STUC, was about to become a massive army. We had mobilised 15,000 people before the bills even appeared. Now they were about to drop through the letterboxes. All that remained was to get one million non-payers on the march.

4 Expulsions

WITCH-HUNTS are not new in Scotland. Pollok is famous for them. Five people were strangled and burnt for the crime in 1677, when the area was still a big country estate outside Glasgow.

Thousands of poor Scottish women died this way in the seventeenth century. The country staged the worst outbreak of hysteria in Northern Europe, largely because the King, James VI, took a close personal interest. But everyone played a part in the macabre dance. Fingers were pointed at neighbours, friends, even relatives. Anyone who felt threatened simply accused someone else. Panic overpowered reason.

When large numbers of people start behaving so theatrically, there is usually a puppet master directing the action. Local landowners, in this case, pulled the strings of power and money. They exploited people's ignorance and superstition and, most of all, the fear of being labelled a witch. Fear kept troublesome tenants under control.

Witches were usually singled out because they did not knuckle under to authority. You could not afford to be deviant if you were a peasant, a carter, a cobbler or a miller. You had to keep your head down. The witch-hunt was a form of social control. Once accused, you could do little to defend yourself.

The landowners got help from those interested in preserving the social order. Church ministers, university professors and lawyers all lent their expertise. In 1699, when twenty-six people from Glasgow, Govan and Paisley were accused of bewitching a landlord's daughter, the Rev. James Hutchison said the crime was confined to poor people who could get their malice and envy satisfied by casting spells.

Men called witchprickers earned money travelling round Scotland accusing and torturing. They would pierce a long brass pin into each part of the woman's body until she slipped into shock and stopped screaming. In triumph, they claimed to have located the Devil's Birthmark, an invisible spot insensitive to pain.

Pollok's witches were Janet Mathie, her children John and Annabel Stewart, Margaret Jackson, Marjory Craig and Bessie Weir. They were accused of casting a spell on their landlord, Sir George Maxwell of Pollok. He claimed they made him ill by sticking pins into his wax effigy. Sir George had a running quarrel with one of the families and had refused to give them work at harvest time. He quickly recruited superstition to this labour relations dispute. As was common, he got others to lead the accusations. A strange dumb girl who was lodged in Pollok house identified the witches.

The confessions of the Pollok witches are kept in the Mitchell Library in Glasgow. None was signed by the accused. All the prosecution witnesses were friends and employees of Sir George. Their accounts are based on gossip and outrageous stories about meetings with the black man, meaning the devil.

Modern witch-hunters might leave their long brass pins at home in the cupboard. Paisley's Gallow Green no longer smells of burning human flesh on a Saturday. But deviants are hunted down in the same way.

When US Senator Joseph McCarthy accused artists, writers and filmstars of being communists in the 1950s, he used the same tactics as seventeenth-century witch-hunters. Hollywood stars lined up to accuse their former friends. Those were the celebrated cases. Dockers and civil servants never worked again after being labelled subversive. Suggest a fairer way of sharing out the USA's immense wealth and you became a non-person in the land of the free.

These methods were also used again in Pollok in 1988. Time had pulled a curtain over the case of Bessie, Janet and Annabel. The fields they toiled were tarmaced over, their rows of earth-floored cottages replaced by our rows of dreary tenements. But the power structures remained much the same. So did the politics of fear.

Vague gossip condemned the seventeenth-century witches. It would not stand up in a court of law today – even under British justice. But the Labour Party's National Executive Committee and National Constitutional Committee would certainly give it a hear-ing. In 1988, an attempt was made to demonise socialists in Pollok. The quality of evidence used to expel us from the Labour Party was much the same then as it was 300 years earlier. Obviously, we live in a more humane times. But with a bit of imagination, the events of the 1980s bear some similarity to the past. For Sir George Maxwell, read Jimmy Dunnachie, MP for Pollok. For the silent accuser – read Joyce Gould, the Labour party's director of organisa-tion. As for Sir George's acolytes – the people who provided the fantastic prosecuting evidence – their 1988 counterparts would be the MP's wife, his paid researcher and the female partner of his paid researcher. My own part was naturally that of the Devil incarnate. Which just left the witches. Here the similarities between the seventeenth and twentieth centuries end. Pollok in 1677 could only boast of six witches. By 1988 the place was crawling with them.

They first appeared in great numbers that summer, when Pollok's anti-poll tax unions took to the streets. The women left their broomsticks at home. But they did carry big banners made of bedsheets and painted with magic markers. We walked from the shopping centre to Bonnyholm Park near my house. It was one of the first housing-scheme-type rallies. Again, we were using the tactics of small local hunger marches of the 1930s – letting people know someone cared. Bedsheets were also draped over the verandas overlooking the route, a strong sense of local solidairty was being forged. We even had the Pollok majorettes twirling their batons at the head of the pack.

I invited Jimmy Dunnachie to come and speak, along with Tony Mulhearn, one of the Liverpool Labour councillors surcharged for refusing to set a rate. Tony was there as an example of a leader who was willing to break the law for his principles.

Jimmy Dunnachie said: 'There's nothing you can do. The Tories are going to introduce this tax whether we like it or not. So you'll just have to work for the return of a Labour government.'

He got a terrible response. The women made their disgust very obvious. After nine years of laws designed to further lower our living standards, all our local MP could do was offer a white flag before the battle had even begun. I think Jimmy was glad to be on the stage and out of reach of those angry women. He has refused to attend any public meetings with us since.

He wrote to Joyce Gould in London almost as soon as he got home. Not to report that party policy on the poll tax was way out of line with the feelings of his constituents. But to request an investigation into the North Pollok branch and my activities as its secretary. Mr Dunnachie was horrified at having to share a platform with Tony Mulhearn. He was alarmed that I publicly criticised Labour policy and encouraged Pollok people to join the party and force it behind non payment. 'I find this particularly alarming in view of the large numbers of new members Mr Sheridan has recruited to Pollok Labour Party recently,' he wrote.

The MP preferred to limit membership of the Labour Party to a select few. When I arrived back from university in 1985, the North Pollok branch was almost moribund. It had a paper membership of thirty, of whom six were active. This was in an area where the working class was traditionally well organised, through trade-union activity in Rolls Royce and the Govan yards. Within two years we had recruited 200 people. As a result of our campaigns on road safety, youth unemployment and the Poll Tax, North Pollok became the biggest branch in the constituency.

We were not going to allow all that work to be scored out by the bureaucrats in Labour Party headquarters. Jimmy Dunnachie left us with no option. North Pollok decided I should challenge him during the reselection procedure the following year. We stood a good chance of ousting him. The MP was to be chosen by a new method based on the number of members. This benefitted us as we had the biggest branch.

It is very difficult for party activists to get rid of a Labour MP. Once in parliament, he or she often moves to the right, while the local party remains committed to socialism. Reselection was introduced in the early 1980s to check this process. It was intended to stop MPs behaving like royalty: taking their salary year after year and doing nothing in return. If the People's Party was worthy of its name, then its MPs should answer to the people who put them there.

Jimmy Dunnachie himself became MP for Glasgow Pollok by default rather than design. He was a regional councillor who made no waves in Strathclyde and so was unlikely to brew up any storms at Westminster. Mediocrity brings its own rewards.

★★★

Double standards are no barrier to a career in the Labour Party. The previous MP for Pollok, Jimmy Whyte, shared his successor's aversion to attending public meetings in the constituency. He ran his own road haulage business.

This is all very sad when you think of Scotland's role in building the Labour movement. Its tradition of great orators like John Wheatly, Jimmy Maxton and John Maclean. Most contemporary Scottish Labour MPs are just time servers. A few stuck their necks out a bit. Ron Brown, Jimmy Wray, John McAllion, George Galloway and Denis Canavan come to mind. But listening to the rest is woeful. If they lived in the south of England they would be Conservatives. Power is their preoccupation. Not the power to change lives, but power for its own sake.

They say Westminster is the most exclusive club in the world. Few Labour MPs are willing to put their membership at risk by bad etiquette. One who was, James Maxton, was censured for the use of 'unparliamentary language.' In the 1920s, he said that Tories who withdrew free school meals from poor children were 'murderers'. He was right.

The right wing of the Labour Party was livid. But Maxton said: 'We the Clydesiders think it is the very worst form, the very worst taste, that it shows very bad breeding, to kick a man who is in the gutter, or to withdraw a crust from a starving child. That is the Glasgow idea of conduct and breeding.'

Sixty years on nothing had changed. In 1988 Labour party whips tried to shout down Denis Canavan for speaking during a debate on the Housing Scotland Act. Sit down and shut up, they yelled. Canavan was speaking against the plan to slowly privatise local authority housing and push up rents. But the Labour whips – the people who enforce party discipline – wanted the Bill to be passed. Why? So MPs could get down to the serious business of debating the televising of the House.

Writing in the *Glasgow Herald* shortly afterwards, Canavan noted: 'Cosy deals seem to be struck between the two front benches to deliver Bills by a certain time. Any backbencher who dares rock the boat will be threatened by some thug from the whips' office or told that disagreement with the party line is self-indulgent.'

Many MPs don't even need such threats. As Canavan frankly admitted; 'It is within the leadership's gift to hand out most shadow ministerial jobs . . . loyalty is often confused with sycophancy by opportunists and careerists, jockeying for position in the Westminster power game.'

That is British parliamentary democracy in action. There is no democracy or social justice within those walls. Just cosy deals between two élite groups of politicians, most of whom come from similar, comfortable backgrounds. Name one Scottish factory which has remained open thanks to the debating skills of Scotland's representatives in Westminster.

Having said that, our society gives working-class people few public platforms. But people listen to MPs. In Militant, we believe in using Westminister as a platform. A means to an end rather than an end in itself.

Anyway, Jimmy Dunnachie was not making much use of his platform. He's a man of few words. He has always refused to debate with me in public. Most of his talking was done by his agent and paid researcher, Stewart Maclennan.

Maclennan has an interesting political background. He encourages the press to vilify Militant as sinister left wingers. But he keeps it quiet that he was once himself a Trotskyite. Unfortunately, our free press has never managed to explain the term or who Trotsky actually was. He fought for freedom and equality before the Russian Revolution of 1917 and paid with his life for continuing that fight under Stalin. He was the Soviet Union's first dissident.

Stewart Maclennan was one of the leaders of the Trotskyite International Marxist Group. Now he pursues witches with a zeal which suggests he would happily reach for the old brass pin if he could get away with it. Most of his criticisms hinged on various complicated references to standing orders and proper procedure at meetings. It didn't exactly win hearts and minds as most people hadn't a clue what he was talking about and didn't care much either.

But locals were angry when they heard about the investigation. Our activists were well known because of involvement in the day-to-day issues affecting them. They knew us as the boys and girls who kicked footballs around the street ten years before. All this nonsense about 'sinister tentacles' and 'burrowing moles' seemed really bizarre to them. It was easy for the *Guardian* newspaper, 400 miles away, to write in its leader columns: 'Militant are trying to revive their flagging fortunes by assiduous meddling in a handful of Scottish constituencies, notably Glasgow Pollok where they are trying to get rid of the sitting Labour member.' How can you meddle in the place you have lived since you were two years old?

We kept local people informed at every stage of the investigation. We presented them with facts they could judge for themselves. This was not easy. As with historic witch trials, you never get to know the case against you. But we circulated a reprint of the letter Jimmy Dunnachie sent to Joyce Gould calling for my investigation. We listed our campaigning record and asked: 'Why the enquiry at all? Why spend all this time and money attacking us, instead of attacking the Tories?'

We faced being thrown out of the party for selling the Militant newspaper and encouraging socialism. Yet Eric Hammond, leader of the Electricians' Union, was still in the party when he signed a deal with Rupert Murdoch, owner of News International. Murdoch was and still is a staunch supporter of the Conservative Party. He owned the *Sun*, the *Times*, the *Sunday Times* and the *News of the World*. Hammond promised never to strike and in return his members were given the jobs of the sacked workers at Murdoch's new printing plant at Wapping in the East End of London. Yet he was warmly welcomed at the Labour Party Conference each year.

So was Bob Maxwell, the multi millionaire socialist who sacked his own workers at Permagon Press for joining a union. He also stole from his workers' pensions to finance his obscenely opulent lifestyle. Membership of the Labour Party was alright for him – so why not platers, welders or unemployed people in Pollok?

We put out a leaflet asking: 'Who's Labour Party Is It?' It carried an appeal from Pollok residents who were not Militants, but who embodied socialism. George Farrell, a sixty-nine year-old retired cabinet-maker who had lived here thirty years; Margaret McPherson, a TGWU shop steward in Rolls Royce who had lived here for over twenty years; Big George's disabled father, Eddie McNeilage, a former shop steward's convenor who had lived here twenty-two years. They all said: 'The Labour Party Belongs to the People of Pollok! Let Us Join!'

As a result, in August 1988 alone, we submitted 128 membership applications. We recruited on doorsteps, at bus stops, in pubs and shops. George McNeilage signed up forty-five people in a week. But Constituency Labour Party officials refused to approve them at the monthly meeting. On the same night, the constituency party accepted membership applications from Shawlands and Pollokshields, the more middle-class parts of the constituency. These people were teachers and lecturers. The message seemed to be: 'Labour Party Membership – Only Professionals need apply'. Ironically, the *Daily Mail* at that time reported that Labour had lost 10,000 members in twelve months. It wasn't full up.

The people we signed up in those few weeks came from families who had been voting Labour for generations. Why shouldn't they have some say in the party after those decades of loyalty? Instead, these stalwart supporters were dismissed with contempt. Crosses on ballot papers, that's all they were good for in the eyes of the constituency commissars.

Stewart Maclennan told the press: 'One wonders whether this represents 100 Labour Party recruits or 100 from the Tommy Sheridan Fan club. Ordinary people who join the party deserve better than to be used in this fashion.'

This comment did not endear him to the voters of Pollok. One woman who supported us told the enquiry she resented suggestions she was being manipulated by men young enough to be her sons.

Chic McPherson would not mind me saying I am young enough to be his son. Chic was a member of North Pollok branch at that time. His history does not correspond with the picture of the young upstarts who were supposed to be taking over. Now in his fifties, he worked on the river all his life, in Barclay Curle Repair, Yarrows, and the Elderslie Dock. He also spent time at Linwood. Chic has arthritis of the spine now. But his diary is full. He campaigns for justice on behalf of people suffering from asbestosis. Older men all over Pollok and Govan are dying from this disease. If it develops into a cancer in the lining of the chest – mesothelioma – it kills within six months. Chic's cousin, Angus, a joiner, died of it at fifty-three. His brother-in-law, William Cook, a pipefitter, died in his forties back in 1976. William was a big muscular man, but towards the end weighed four and a half stone and could not lift his pint of beer. The dangers of asbestos fibres were known in the 1930s, but the owners of the factories did not inform their workers. Women have caught the disease through washing their husband's clothes. A child caught it from playing in a cupboard where his father hung his working gear.

Chic advises sufferers on their compensation rights. Until recently these were time-barred. Lawyers acting for the shipbuilding and engineering employers would spin out the cases until the victim died with his claim. Chic has been at hundreds of funerals since William died twenty years ago. He has comforted breathless, wasted men in Pollok, Govan, Springburn, Rutherglen, Greenock, Port Glasgow . . . he never tires. But there's no room for his type these days in the Labour Party.

Rose McCann, the poll tax campaigner in Cowglen, was refused entry into the party after paying her membership fee. 'I was told I wasn't acceptable. I can't think why. My father was a turner in the yards and used to march me into the polling station at Govan. When I first got married and moved to Tradeston his advice was: Make sure you know the name of the Labour candidate.'

By rejecting older activists, the party turned its back on a rich past. But it also cancelled out its future by ridiculing the young. Jimmy Dunnachie said the Bonnyholm Park audience was made up of kids. We'll never know whether he referred to everyone under thirty, or just the teenagers who came. But to get young people other than student activists along to a political meeting – let alone to join a political party – is an achievement in itself.

We opened the doors and windows of the local party and took the roof off to let young people inside. Black Muslims in America used to say: 'Mobilise the young and it shames the old into action'. Maybe that's unfair on the old. But the injection of youth gave the over-fifties a boost. They could share their experience.

Pollok's Labour Party Young Socialists' branch was the biggest in Scotland, with more than 100 members. When the party tried to reduce Militant's influence by lowering the age limit, we brought in enthusiastic local teenagers like Kirsteen Walker. She took politics to the streets and became the Pollok LPYS Secretary. But Keir Hardie House sent Irene Graham along to investigate. She quizzed them on procedure and waved the rule book a lot. Perhaps she does not mix with young people from the schemes very often, for she found them 'verbally threatening'. Her report to the investigating committee said: 'Few members present seemed to know what was going on or why they were there.'

Certainly they were raw. Our plan was to recruit first, then educate. They weren't taught about socialism in school. We wanted to show them how to direct their anger. We were trying to revive the consciousness-raising street activity of the Independent Labour Party in the 1920s and the Young Communist League in the 1950s.

When I was Militant's youth organiser we would approach teenagers on their turf outside chip shops on street corners, or outside amusement arcades. We would talk about the basics. That YTS schemes were slave labour. That young people were super exploited. That they had little or no facilities for recreation.

Isobel Dunnachie, the MP's wife, seemed also to be dismissive of youth. Mrs Dunnachie was motivated by fear. These Young Turks from Pollok were throwing a boulder in the pond of her uneventful constituency meetings.

They wanted some action. For the MP to stand up for them. They refused to know their place – just like the witches on the Pollok estate all those centuries before. This was why Joyce Gould touched down in Glasgow on 30 August 1988. The national organiser was here to begin an investigation at the behest of the local Labour laird.

As in witch-hunts of old, ignorance was a positive virtue which helped smooth things along. 'How much do you know about Pollok, Mrs Gould?' asked Fiona Ross, Scottish Television's political reporter during an interview on the day she arrived. 'Not a lot,' she replied. 'But I think that's an advantage.'

Why did the Labour Party want rid of Militant? In 1987, Neil Kinnock more or less pronounced socialism dead and decided to modernise the party. He said Labour had to realign itself with the centre of the political spectrum. There was lots of talk about throwing away cloth caps. Speaking as someone who has never worn a cloth cap, I believe Labour's failure had nothing to do with head gear. Labour failed because it did not map out a socialist alternative to the madness of the free market.

Those who mould Labour into a cheap imitation of the Conservative Party believed Britain voted for Thatcher because her policies were popular. She talked about redistributing wealth through share ownership and the sell-off of council houses. So Labour abandoned plans to renationalise British Telecom and British Gas. It made not a cheep about the sale of council houses – the real reason behind the appalling homeless figures. Thatcher talked about giving people more choice. So did Kinnock. But what did it mean?

Under capitalism choice is severely restricted. You can choose the best home for your family, the best education for your kids and the best medical care. But only if you have the big bucks to pay. The choice for working-class families is no choice at all.

Genuine socialism, where resources are pooled together, would allow everyone's quality of life to be raised to the limit. The very best homes, schools and health care would be yours by right. Choice would no longer be the preserve of the better off. Why didn't Kinnock and the Labour Party present this vision, explain this inspiring alternative? Maybe it was because that kind of future would require a fundamental challenge to the power and wealth vested in the city boardrooms. A good few eggs would have to be cracked to make the socialist omelette.

Kinnock was mesmerised by the economic boom of the 1980s which mainly affected the south of England and north of Scotland around Aberdeen. Thatcher claimed in 1988 that the country was in its *eighth* consecutive year of economic growth. A section of society benefited. They were caricatured in the glossy magazines. Clad in designer gear, they lived in penthouse flats on old dockland areas and took three holidays a year. These were the fizzkids of the City's finance houses. They guzzled champagne each night after selling the world to its wife and pocketing the profit.

Satisfying the avarice of these people is the *raison d'être* of the Conservative Government's economic policy. Tory politicians are simply the parliamentary face of capital. Our men in Westminster, if you like. When the Chancellor of the Exchequer sets interest rates, he is thinking of his paymasters in the city – not the young couples with mortgages who have to live with the consequences. That's why parliament begins at 2 pm – to allow the real decisions to be taken in the city boardrooms in the morning and rubber-stamped at Westminster in the afternoon.

It was these Champagne Charlies that John Smith wooed when he covered the prawn-cocktail circuit of the investment houses and banks as Shadow Chancellor. He tried to convince the financiers that Labour could also be their men in Westminster.

It was a long way from 1973, when the Labour Party's election manifesto promised to shift wealth and power towards working people and their families. Kinnock's Labour Party was now more concerned with pleasing the wealthy and powerful. Yet wealth and power had moved even further away from many working people and their families. Labour ignored the hard facts behind the boom years.

★ In 1970 there were 9,000 unemployed people in Glasgow. By 1988 there were 67,000 people out of work. When my parents came to Pollok, 60,000 people worked in Clyde shipyards. By 1988 there were less than 5,000.

★ Since 1979 the top ten per cent of UK earners saw their income rise by twenty-two per cent. The bottom ten per cent – most of Pollok – saw their income drop by ten per cent.

★ Nearly half of the £20 billion tax cuts under Thatcher went to that top ten per cent.

★ While the Government planned to spend £8000 million on Trident nuclear weapons, one child in five lived in poverty.

★ While Britain's rich farmers were paid by the government NOT to grow wheat (in order to keep the price up), 40,000 children in Africa were dying each day of starvation.

Thatcherism exposed the savage nature of capitalism. This is what Labour wanted to emulate under Kinnock and still want to emulate under Smith. This is what they want to manage better. Managing capitalism is like managing a slaughterhouse. No matter how efficient you are, no matter how humane, blood is spilled in the end. Slaughterhouses could not exist without death. Capitalism would not exist without exploitation.

John Smith and Neil Kinnock should have made this point: with every boom the rich get richer. With every slump the weakest fall over the cliff edge. The eighties boom was doomed like all the rest. In many ways it was even worse than previous, brief Golden Ages because it was built on credit. Personal debt rose from £90 million in 1980 to £283 million in 1987.

While the Labour Party wooed the city speculators, it was left to a Tory, Sir Ian Gilmour, to expose the miracle as a clever conjuring trick. Manufacturing, he pointed out in 1989, was devastated in the slump of the early 1980s, and had only just recovered its 1979 level.

It had expanded by just 1% a year between 1979 and 1989 – the slowest growth on record. Real jobs were not being created. Even the sunrise areas – the electronics industries – failed to shine. Between 1976 and 1986, the UK electronics sector actually shed labour by 1.5% a year.

While British firms struggled to keep up, tax cuts were spent on German cars and Japanese CD players. Imports were up by 90% since 1982. In Glasgow, the Labour council gloried in this glut of consumption. They pretended it was some kind of alternative to the old rust bucket days of shipbuilding and engineering.

The city's Lord Provost, Susan Baird, laid the last tile on a big glass pyramid called The Forge in 1988. It was built on the site of the old Parkhead steel works, which once employed 25,000 people. The shopping complex was expected to hire 2,500 mainly low-paid part-time workers. Welcome to the post-industrial age.

They had no solution to unemployment. The only difference, until 1991, between Labour and the Tories economic policy was the former's pledge to take Britain into the European Exchange Rate Mechanism, ERM. When Norman Lamont did just that, the rug was swiped from under Labour's feet. And when the policy proved a disaster, Labour could not seriously criticise it. If they were in power, they too would have kept-interest rates high to maintain the value of the pound within ERM. They too would have spent £5 billion of our money trying to keep the pound in ERM when its value plunged.

Labour's failure to argue for socialism meant they had little to offer the casualties of capitalism. Cambridge, the ultimate eighties boom town, was suffering visible and widespread poverty in 1993, according to a report by the city council: one in six of the city's population was living on the breadline.

'The masses don't want socialism' has been the refrain from a certain section of the Labour Party since it was set up. Squeals about infiltration of the party by extremists are not new. But what are the party's traditions? You could easily argue that an essentially socialist movement has been hijacked by right-wing extremists for most of this century. Marxists have been part of the Labour Party since the first meeting of the Labour Representation Committee in 1900. The committee had a dozen members representing various groups who had loosely come together to promote separate representation of labour in parliament. There were seven trade unionists, two from the Independent Labour Party, one from the Fabian Society, who thought capitalism could be reformed gradually, and two from the Marxist Social Democratic Federation.

Parliamentary candidates under the auspices of the Labour Representation Committee could advocate different policies, as long as they supported the idea of a separate Labour group in Westminster. Revolutionaries could be Labour candidates. Right from the start, Labour politicians and trade union leaders were corrupted by exposure to parliament. They were so desperate for official recognition from the Liberal government that they seldom advocated socialism.

Socialism was not promoted because the Labour parliamentary group of forty-five MPs supported the Liberal Government at every turn. The Independent Labour Party was so frustrated by this that in 1911 they called on the leadership to act independently of the Liberals in the House of Commons. It's interesting that the parliamentary leadership urged caution and opposed this motion. One of them, Philip Snowden, expressed sympathy but said: 'Commonsense, judgement and experience' had led him to vote against it. If ordinary members had listened to such talk then – so similar to the pragmatism of John Smith today – there might not have been a Labour Party.

The party adopted a formal constitution in 1918. This committed Labour – and still does – to ownership of the means of production and an economy planned according to need not greed. Militant still supports what is known as Clause IV. It says the party pledges: 'To secure for the workers by hand or by brain the full fruits of their industry and the most equitable distribution thereof that may be possible, on the basis of common ownership of the means of production, distribution and exchange, and the best obtainable system of popular administration and control of each industry or service.'

Another development in 1918 was to open membership to individuals – as opposed to just socialist societies and trades unions. This lead to an influx of middle-class professionals. The Fabian, Beatrix Webb, wrote that this would turn the party from a group merely representing class interests of the manual workers to a fully constituted political party of a national scope.

Bandwagon jumpers began warming up. Many of these professionals had sussed that the days of the old Liberal party were numbered and Labour was the fastest gravy train for an ambitious young man. This was the start of the long and deadening tradition which we see today in the large number of well-modulated QCs who claim to know what's best for their working-class constituents.

One early example was Craigie Aitchieson, a lawyer who stood for parliament as a Liberal in 1923 and denounced socialism. He lost. The following year he was applying for membership of the Labour Party. He realised the socialists, possessing few lawyers, would need a Lord Advocate. It was a good career move.

Wealthy Aitchieson eventually won the safe seat of Kilmarnock for Labour and became Lord Advocate. The ILP weekly newspaper, *Forward*, asked why, after the work, tears and self-sacrifice of working people, were they now being told only good legal brains could represent them in parliament? Aitchieson eventually joined the Tories in the 1931 National Government.

Aitchieson and his ilk rose on the back of a party which had expanded greatly due to the wartime industrial unrest. Strikes across various industries created a stronger class consciousnes among working people. They began to see their mutual economic interests. Socialists like John Maclean encouraged the process, with his classes in Marxist economics.

Maclean was a member of the British Socialist Party, successors to the Marxists who helped found the Labour Party in 1900. The

BSP were affiliated to the Labour Party in 1918. That year, John Maclean stood as the parliamentary candidate in the Gorbals. He had the backing of the local Labour Party and Glasgow Trades Council despite opposition from the Labour Party executive in London. Anyone but Maclean, they said, but the local activists insisted.

The Labour Party saw its vote grow from 500,000 in 1910, to 2.25 million in 1918, 4.5 million in 1922 and 5.5 million in 1924. This did not happen because of moderation. People did not vote Labour because they wanted a party indistinguishable from the Liberals. They voted because they had been radicalised by workers' agitation, like rent strikes and industrial unrest in the war years.

Many of the people involved in this agitation – like Willie Gallacher and Helen Crawford, a suffragette and left-wing ILP member, set up the Communist Party in 1920. But Communists were not allowed to affiliate to the Labour Party, like the BSP or the ILP, despite the fact that many were already members through their trade unions. In 1924 they were even prevented from joining Labour as individuals. This was absurd. The Labour MP for London Battersea, was Shapurzi Saklatvala, an ILPer and founding Communist.

But the parliamentary leader of the Labour Party, Ramsay MacDonald, was desperate to distance himself from the Russian Revolution. Overawed by the pomp and ceremony of the British parliament, determined to ingratiate himself with the establishment, MacDonald wanted to convince business interests that Labour meant no harm. Just like John Smith sixty years later.

Many local Labour parties were positively enthusiastic about the Bolshevik menace. Communists were comrades they had worked with for years. In Greenock the Labour Party was effectively the local Trades and Labour Council. The council adopted a popular local Communist as their parliamentary candidate three times between 1922 and 1924. The national leadership responded by kicking the Greenock trades council out of the party.

Greenock was not isolated. In 1923, the Communist Aitken Ferguson almost won Glasgow Kelvingrove for Labour. In

Motherwell a Communist called J Walton Newbold won the parliamentary seat in 1924 with the backing of the Trades and Labour Council. Debate over Communist affiliation raged during the 1920s. One year, ten local Labour parties were disbanded by the leadership.

It was not only the Communists who fell foul of the top men. The ILP, which for many people in Scotland *was* the Labour Party was next on the list. The ILP linked many of the movements which made up the Red Clyde. As a result it moved from being a rather intellectual organisation before the war to a vibrant political force afterwards. Scotland was a stronghold. It had 20,000 members here by 1920 and 307 branches five years later. It therefore became a threat. A 1920 report to the cabinet on revolutionaries said; 'The great mass of Labour is steadily shifting to the left. One sign is the increased membership of the ILP, which in Scotland is becoming more left-wing.'

The ILP employed full-time organisers, just as Militant do today. It was their work on the ground which helped to ensure the election of ten Labour MPs in Glasgow in 1922. Many of these were men who had been involved in the Clydeside agitation. When they caught the train to London at St Enoch's station a crowd of 100,000 turned out to see them off. The ILP MP John Wheatley said the experience changed his political life, banishing any doubts he once harboured about the people not being ready for socialism. Another, Emmanuel Shinwell, said the crowd looked at him with eyes which had once again the gleam of hope, where despair had too long held sway.

Neither of Labour's minority governments in 1924 or 1929 gave the ruling class much to worry about. Ramsay MacDonald was anxious to keep the British Empire together. Philip Snowden, Labour Chancellor of the Exchequer, admired market forces and set budgets which were little different from the Conservatives.

MacDonald said he no longer saw the Labour Party as a working-class party, but one which represented all the people – just as Webb had predicted. He said there was no great call for socialism in the country. MacDonald spoke at a time when two per cent of the population owned two thirds of the country's wealth. As late as 1931, one in four Scottish houses was overcrowded. More than half the population of Glasgow lived in houses of one or two rooms. Diseases like TB were part of everyday life. Much of MacDonald's rhetoric resembles the Labour modernisers of today. Yet they, like him, are speaking at a time when the division of wealth is greater than ever and working-class housing is crumbling.

The Clydeside group, lead by Jimmy Maxton, pushed the cause of socialism in parliament even when it meant criticising the Labour leadership. They adopted a socialist programme called A Living Wage, which they thought would transform society. It included provision for a National Health Service, non-contributory pensions, nationalisation of key industries, state control of credit and money, public ownership of the banks, the introduction of family allowances and, of course, a realistic living wage.

Much of this programme was adopted by the Labour Party after 1945. But when Maxton proposed it in the 1920s he was accused of egotism, self-indulgence and acting against the best interests of Labour. Just like the Labour left in the 1980s, he was accused of peddling simplistic dogma. Meanwhile, the national leadership making these accusations went into the 1929 election with a manifesto not mentioning unemployment.

Maxton's socialism was popular in Bridgeton. He had the largest Labour vote in Scotland – in a constituency with a tradition of working-class Conservatism. While his efforts at promoting socialism were endorsed by the folk of Glasgow's East End, he found himself under investigation by the Labour Party's Scottish Executive. He was accused of being a member of a prohibited organisation (The Anti Imperialist League which had Communist links). He was questioned over his views on confiscation (he did not believe capitalists should be compensated when a future socialist government took their factories and banks into public ownership). He was also charged with sponsoring the *Sunday*

Worker, a newspaper which was officially condemned by the party. Selling newspapers has always been a risky business for Labour Party members.

Maxton's popularity ensured no action was taken on these matters. But his crimes paled into insignificance when set against those of the second Labour government. As unemployment grew, it occupied itself with cutting benefit, first to those not genuinely seeking work, then to married women and casual workers.

The Labour chancellor, Philip Snowden, was obsessed with being fiscally prudent and so cut public expenditure (just as Gordon Brown, ironically Maxton's biographer, would now be if a Labour government was elected tomorrow). Moderation only leads you in one direction. MacDonald and Snowden, who had accused Maxton of damaging the cause of socialism, deserted Labour in 1931 for a National Government with the Conservatives. 'Tomorrow every Duchess in London will be wanting to kiss me,' MacDonald told his chancellor as they cemented the deal. They went on to introduce the Means Test, splitting families and starving children at the height of the Great Depression.

Labour suffered for the betrayal and was nearly wiped out in the election that year. Yet the Party leadership's response was to further hammer the very people who had opposed MacDonald and Snowden all along. The new Labour Leader, George Lansbury, offered Maxton a front bench position if his ILP group stopped being a party within a party. This abandoning of socialism in our time Maxton refused. Within a year the ILP had disaffiliated from the Labour Party.

Autocratic Labour leaders continued to expel those with whom they disagreed, whether Marxists or Christian socialists. Labour members who worked with Communists to fight fascism in the 1930s found themselves hounded out of the party. These included the left-wing MP Nye Bevan who was expelled in 1939. Within a few years he was back in the fold. He remains famous as the man who gave us the National Health Service. Yet he was nearly expelled again in the 1950s when he opposed the leadership's backing of the nuclear bomb. Ironically, Neil Kinnock, at an earlier stage in his career, was a great admirer of Bevan.

History was carefully laid aside in 1988–89, when Labour vowed to extirpate Militant from the map of Glasgow. The witch-hunt moved beyond Pollok. There was talk of twenty activists being expelled, most of them hard-working people in poor areas like Castlemilk, Drumchapel and Springburn. Most were active in the poll tax campaign. HQ calculated that if it killed them off, it could scupper the campaign. Glasgow Labour councillors like Stuart Bates and Margaret Dick were to be investigated after years of service.

Just as the leadership in the 1920s was blind to the radicalism of its local members, so the national organisers of the late 80s ignored grassroots opinion. The Scottish National Party overturned a Labour majority of 23,000 when Jim Sillars won the Govan by-election in November 1988. No Poll Tax was beside Jim's name on the ballot paper and his support for non-payment was at the forefront of the SNP message.

Many Labour activists were so demoralised by the party's failure to fight the tax they did not come out for the Labour candidate, Bob Gillespie. Sillars could even claim to have received goodwill messages from Labour party members. He evoked the rhetoric of the Red Clyde. But while his socialist speeches and fighting talk won over Govan voters, Labour perversely turned on the socialists in its own ranks.

When Joyce Gould's investigation of Pollok was finally leaked to us, it was as vague as any of the documents in an old-fashioned witch trial. Around eighty per cent of the evidence against us came from Mrs Dunnachie and Carol Thompson. It was detailed and tedious, full of innuendo like: 'At this point I saw David Churchley lean over and speak to Kirsteen Walker and both got up and left the meeting' or 'Tommy Sheridan attended the GMC Executive meeting in June 1988 wearing a Militant sticker on his jacket.'

The verdict of Ms Gould in March 1989 was that all the activists in Pollok be banned from holding party positions. The entire North Pollok Branch was suspended. I was to be recommended for expulsion for bringing the party into disrepute. By demonising me, making an example of a well-known person, they hoped to frighten others.

My 'trial' in October 1989 was an anti-climax. I had been a member of the Labour Party for eight years, since I was seventeen, so it should have been a traumatic occasion. But I had plenty of time to prepare myself for what was a *fait accompli*. Chic McPherson came to Keir Hardie House with me as a silent friend. When you've got someone like Chic at your side, it doesn't matter what the spivs throw at you. 'They can wear all the red rose badges they want,' he said. 'But it's better to wear the badge of courage than the badge of respectability'.

5   People power in 1990

There was a lot of con going on in 1990. This was the year Glasgow was on the world's stage – or so the PR men told us – as European City of Culture. It was the culmination of a decade when Glasgow's socialist council tried to bury the city's working-class roots. Glasgow Action, a faceless private-sector led organisation with power over our future, actually suggested building a walled city in the central area. That would have kept the plebs from messing up the pedestrian walkways.

The idea was to market the city centre – with a little help from the Tories' advertising agency Saatchi & Saatchi – as a rich person's playground. They said this was the only way to attract inward investment and create jobs. 'We'll make Glasgow a Florence on the Clyde', said the council leader, Pat Lally, unconvincingly. In fact it was just one big junket for the city fathers, who were desperate to smooch up to the money men. At one point in 1990, Mr Lally tried to sell part of Glasgow Green to private speculators. It was the oldest piece of common land in the city – but he wanted to turn it into a

Florida-style fun park which would cost families a fortune to visit. A huge campaign by people from the East End forced him to back down.

During this year the much-loved curator of the People's Palace, Elspeth King, was effectively forced out of her job. She and her assistant, Michael Donnelly, devoted sixteen years to uncovering the history of working people. She was regarded as an expert in her field. But she did not see her job as packaging the past for the marketing men. So the council created the new post of Keeper of Social History, Elspeth's job, and gave it to someone else. There was uproar. Especially as the council lost £4.6 million on a disastrous showpiece exhibition for 1990 called 'Glasgow's Glasgow', a sanitised version of the city's history. This audio-visual extravaganza breached the principle that museums were educational and ought to be free. It was priced too high for the punters. Those who did go heard little about Calton weavers, striking apprentices or squatters movements. But there was lots about the tobacco lords and iron masters who bought and sold our predecessors.

The council spent £50 million on culture that year. This money belonged to Glasgow people, but it was used to subsidise events which they could not afford to see. Pavarotti, Frank Sinatra and the Bolshoi Opera were heavily subsidised. But ticket prices were £20 upwards, more than unemployed Glaswegians were given to feed and clothe their children. John Heron, one of our supporters, sold T-shirts from his stall in the Barras saying: 'Not A Lot of Pavarotti for the Poveratti.'

Our printers, Clydeside Press, were closely associated with Workers' City, a cultural militia of artists and writers based in *The Scotia,* a writers' pub. They challenged the council on matters artistic and won the argument. Farquhar McLay, who edited the book *The Reckoning*, summed up their position when he wrote:

'For the people without a hope, the Year of Culture is the final proof, if proof were needed, of Labour's abject collusion with the forces of monopoly capitalism against the social and cultural aspirations and creative spirit of the working class – the final relinquishment of even the pretence of socialist principles.'

But something big *was* Glas-going on in 1990, to pinch the Saatchi-devised slogan. Bigger, even, than Pavarotti. By April of that year nearly half the city's population had joined our campaign. They refused to pay their poll tax.

We had posters printed with the slogan 'Glasgow 1990: City of Defiance'. We tapped into the resentment many Glaswegians felt at the culture city junketing. We were the real story – the biggest campaign of civil disobedience this century and it started in Glasgow. Elspeth King recognised it – she had anti-poll tax banners displayed in the People's Palace. They quickly disappeared when she left.

Jack, Alan and Gerry McGuire even got the message relayed from the city chambers. Disguised as window cleaners, they sauntered through the marble corridors with a big banner stuffed in their bucket. The City of Defiance slogan was quickly draped over a balcony looking onto George Square. City shoppers, office workers and down-and-outs were giving it the thumbs up. Had the council suddenly remembered its roots? Meanwhile officials were running about like headless chickens trying to find a way to open the balcony doors.

By this time non-payment in Scotland had become a deluge. It was like water seeping through the wall of a dam. Just a trickle at first. Then more rapid splashes through the hairline crack. These became a stream. The crack burst open and you had a flood.

We worked hard. In January of 1990 we ordered one million information bulletins from the printers. We even started a newspaper called *The Anti-Poll Tax News* – a bit like the way Wal Hannington's paper helped forge the national unemployed movement back in the 1930s.

Average bills of £300 were announced back in January 1989. The Scottish Secretary, Malcolm Rifkind, had introduced a financial cushion in the first year – probably fearing the message a mass non-payment campaign would send to England and Wales, who were due to get hit in April 1990. He congratulated Strathclyde Region for making his job easier by keeping bills low. But the tax for most people was still higher than rates. A couple in Glasgow would pay £612, in Edinburgh £784, in Dundee £648 and in Aberdeen £608. Bills were burnt publicly in April 1989. A learning process took place.

Summertime was quiet. Then, in September 1989, it was revealed that a fifth of adults in Strathclyde – 350,000 people – had paid nothing. In Central Region, covering Stirling and Falkirk, non-payment was also twenty per cent before 1989 was out. In Tayside, including Dundee, one in seven had not paid up.

By the end of the tax's first year in Scotland, April 1990, the newspapers revealed more than half a million people had paid not a penny. Non-payment was running at six times the level of defaulting on rates. Strathclyde had 400,000 in arrears, owing a total of £101 million. We knew this was an underestimate. We had acquired confidential figures which included those who had been paying but stopped – the true extent of the rebellion. Our sources from within finance departments always proved correct. I remember meeting people in anonymous little cafes to pore over computer printouts.

The poll tax was unworkable all over Scotland. But instead of calling it a day and leaving the government to do its own dirty paper work, Labour councils insisted they would meet their targets. Lothian announced the tax was costing three times more to administer than the old rates. On the same day they approved £250,000 expenditure to employ more collecting staff. Strathclyde prepared a quarter of a million warrants in January 1990 after people had ignored their final warning letters.

Threatening noises were already being made about warrant sales. But at the same time, a survey by Glasgow University showed eighty per cent of those withholding payment lived in poverty. Strathclyde Business School said low-income households fared worse and would be crippled when Malcolm Rifkind eventually swiped the financial cushion from under them, sending the poll tax sky high.

We began to stop sheriff officers entering homes very early in the campaign – on the Fourth of July 1989. Americans had the Boston Tea Party, we had a garden party at Janette McGinn's house in Rutherglen. Janette was the widow of the folk singer, Matt

McGinn, and was to be poinded to recover fines for non-registration. Around 300 people arrived thoughout the day. Given that the garden of her council house is covered in a few paces, it was pretty cramped.

Loads of musicians came along. Janette's friend, Andy Dick, met a guy who was supposed to be in hospital that day having tests for a serious illness. 'Nothing was going to make me miss this,' he said, accordian under one arm. Janette had a banner hanging from the bedroom window, identical to the one used during the 1915 rent strikes: God Help the sheriff officer who enters this house. They got the message and did not come near. A crowd went up to lobby the sheriffs, William Kay and Co in Hope Street. It was a dress rehearsal for the years ahead.

There was a great cross-fertilisation happening. The campaign was the making of lots of people who got involved at the early stages and were now able to address meetings. People like Craig Beaton, a young guy of nineteen who got involved in Militant through the Dumbarton anti-poll tax campaign and ended up speaking all over the country. We were moving further afield by this time, to country areas like Shetland and the Highlands. My job was often to chart the virgin territory, especially England and Wales. Jim Cameron used to joke that I was double booked so often he never had a problem opening a meeting. It was always: 'Unfortunately Tommy Sheridan cannot be with you this evening. . .'

Meanwhile I'd be speeding through the night on an Intercity train, trying to sleep in the stale white light of the second-class compartment. I spent half my life in transit in those pioneering days. I'd get through all the newspapers, the *New Statesman* and the *Economist*, then start rapping my fingers on the formica table in frustration. A girlfriend bought me an electronic chess set to ease the boredom. I've always liked chess but it made the frustration worse – I always ended up cheating the computer.

Candlelight processions in Leeds would be followed by radio interviews in Bradford before shooting off to Kent or Blackpool or Bristol to speak at their anti-poll tax federation meetings. Then a rally in Liverpool. I was really being stretched. But people were so encouraged to hear what was happening in Scotland.

The meetings were not that different from the ones back home. One of the most memorable was in Birkenhead on Merseyside. People were hanging over the balcony of the town hall – it was the biggest indoor meeting in the town since the 1940s. Birkenhead, dominated for many years by the Cammell Laird shipyard, is one of the first areas of Trotskyite activity in the country. There were riots there in 1932 when the police attacked a demonstration of the unemployed. Barricades went up in the streets and the disturbances lasted three days.

Our meeting was held when the local Labour MP, Frank Field – a man who recently wrote a paper urging the privatisation of all pensions – was trying to expel local Militants. The theme was, Fight the Poll Tax Not Militant. I met a pensioner that night who'd walked twelve miles from Elsmere Port just to attend.

On another occasion we went to Belfast when there were rumours that the tax might be introduced in Northern Ireland. I'd gone to a sports centre in the morning before a local radio interview in the afternoon. But there was a bomb scare and we had to evacuate the place. I managed to grab my clothes and get outside only to discover the road was closed. We risked missing our interview. The guy I was with took me on an incredibly complicated route where we had to scramble across pipes and over a canal to get to the studio.

The best day was in November 25, 1989, when we formed the All Britain Federation. Two thousand delegates met in Manchester Free Trade Hall. Hundreds came down from Scotland. The hall is built on St Peter's Fields where 250,000 Chartists pledged to pay no taxes back in 1832. They forced the government to pass the Great Reform Bill – which allowed people outside the landed gentry to vote for the first time.

The big difference between England and Scotland at that time was the focus on town hall protests. We had invaded regional council chambers in Strathclyde and Lothian when the poll tax was being set. Cameras came along, there was lots of singing, and everyone left after a few hours. We had a right to occupy the public gallery like anyone else. Once, Lothian's Labour group ordered their workers to remove chairs in the public gallery, in a bid to prevent more than sixteen protestors sitting in. But there were no truncheons. The regional councils who set our Poll Tax were big, remote bodies. Few people in Glasgow could tell you their regional councillor or what they did – let alone where they do it. So people did not automatically descend on the regional council. Our protests had to be pre-planned.

England was different. Town councils were smaller and more accessible to voters. So demonstrations were bigger, more spontaneous and more volatile. But it was the intervention of the police in England which made the biggest difference. Unlike Scotland, they did not seem to respect the right to make a protest. They waded in, truncheons flexed. Confrontation between cops and demonstrators took over from the real business of embarrassing councillors.

Violence, after a year and a half of peaceful protest, was suddenly at the top of every news editor's schedule. I was even flown to Germany to take part in a Europe-wide discussion show called *Europalava*. Tony Benn couldn't make it and my name was suggested by someone from the *Guardian*. It was a real culture shock. One morning I was at a demo in Dumbarton. By teatime I was speeding along the autobahn from Frankfurt to Baaden Baaden.

The television company booked me into a five-star hotel and picked up the tab. I'd never been anywhere like it before and probably never will again. You opened the door, expecting to find a bedroom, but you were in a hallway. It was like a luxury apartment with a jacuzzi through one door, a bedroom through another and a dining room somewhere else. I remember being so nervous I even bought a shirt and tie and wore trousers instead of jeans. The working-class respectability factor must have got to me. The programme was transmitted live to fourteen countries and I wanted to make a good impression for the sake of the people I represented. So it was especially disastrous when, sitting in the studio five minutes before the cameras were due to roll, I noticed the seam of the trousers had burst all the way up the inside leg. They had been a great buy – reduced from £40 to a tenner in a shop in Renfield Street. Now I knew why. Should I cross my legs for the entire two hours? Here I was, all nervous about international television, and I'm sitting with this big rip in my trousers. Fortunately I caught someone's eye and they sent the wardrobe girl over to stitch them on the spot. Two minutes later, we were on.

Germany couldn't understand the Poll Tax. They had a local income tax and the gross unfairness of our system was a bit too much to grasp. So was the idea of the poor doing something. I went for easily-translatable sound bytes. 'We're going to melt down the iron lady'. I could see a smile coming across the presenter's face. Thatcher was a world leader and here's this wee guy from God-knows-where saying he's going to finish her off! But the very fact the Europeans were interested indicated she really was in trouble. And from our point of view the exercise was beneficial. The Fed got £400 for my appearance.

Scotland must have been the only place the satellite did not reach. But it somehow beamed into the psyche of the media in Glasgow. I was invited on Radio Clyde for the first time ever while in Germany. That was rich. Clyde is the most listened to radio station in the West of Scotland and one of the most successful commercial stations in Britain. They ignored us for over a year. Their presenters would call Edinburgh to speak to Kenny MacAskill while myself or Jim Cameron would be addressing meetings in Duntocher or Drumchapel just up the road from their Clydebank studios. Disturbances in England suddenly made us news in Scotland. Now we were on Margo MacDonald's popular morning talk show. 'Now we go over to Baaden Baaden and our special linkline to Tommy Sheridan'. . .

It was back to breid and porridge in Pollok next day. I had a Restart interview at the DSS. When you are unemployed, the social security call you for these interviews to push training schemes or low-paid work. Your benefit can be docked if you don't co-operate.

Fortunately I was quite well-known by this time. I always got an easy grilling from sympathetic workers, most of whom are low-paid and unable to afford the poll tax themselves.

'What do you want to do?'

'Well, do you have any places for investigative journalists in Nicaragua?'

'Sorry, Tommy. Nothing as yet. You can go.'

The town hall riots meant five or six newspapers now turned up at our Glasgow conferences instead of one or two. Mark Douglas Home, then of the *Independent*, interviewed me in the Blue Lagoon chip shop downstairs from our rooms. He seemed genuinely interested in the way the campaign had been built. For once, a journalist wasn't banging on about Militant infiltration and threats of violence.

At last we were getting a little recognition. Credibility was built by tapping into the power networks which the media acknowledged. We held All Britain Federation press conferences in the House of Commons. Reporters turned up. We met the left-wing Campaign Group of MPs. It made the papers. No spoiler campaigns like 'Stop It' were mounted in England. The Federation *was* the opposition to the Poll Tax. No one else was doing anything.

We launched Artists Against the Poll Tax in parliament, with Gary Kemp from Spandau Ballet and the Wee Papa Girl Rappers. Fraser Wishart, President of the Professional Footballers Assocation, helped get Footballers Against the Poll Tax off the ground in Scotland. My mate, Billy Davies, then playing with St Mirren, was a supporter along with his brother, John Davies, and Alan Moore who both played with St Johnstone. This all helped publicise the two very ambitious demonstrations we planned in March 1990. One was in London for the introduction of the tax, the other was in Glasgow to celebrate one year of people power and mass non-payment.

House of Commons press conferences can get to you. You have to be a bit reckless now and again. Like the time we got a tip off from the media that Thatcher was touring the Volvo plant in Irvine, Ayrshire. She could flaunt herself all over Poland, but daren't announce she was coming to Scotland. Her visits were always kept secret. A whole bunch of us decided to combine a day trip doon the watter to Ayrshire with an impromptu debate on the merits of the Poll Tax. Our problem, as usual, was lack of funds. We were completely brassic when we got on the train. We made a class appeal to the ticket collector to let us travel for free. When he heard the nature of our mission he was only too happy to pass us by. 'Just give her all the best from me!'

We passed a market on the way to Volvo and Jack said, 'C'mon, we'll take some rotten fruit.' Someone else suggested eggs and I ended up with one in each pocket. When we got to the plant and saw the battalions of police, it was clear we'd get arrested for blowing our noses. But Jack hurled his egg and solidarity bid me follow. Unfortunately, I missed and only hit her car, but they still nabbed me. I was shoved onto the floor of the meat wagon, face down with my arms up my back. All I could think of was this other egg in my pocket. What if they frisked me and the evidence smashed? When they finally allowed me to sit up, I made a contorted effort to dispose of the thing without being seen. I hid it in the folds of a polis raincoat stuffed down the back of the seat. Fortunately it was dry when we got out and the guy left his coat behind. I wonder what happened to that hidden egg. . .

All the police in the station were really positive. They were fuming about the Poll Tax because their rates had previously been paid for them. Anyway, Thatcher provoked a special vitriol in Scotland, even among some polis. It was sickening to see her in person – to see that breathtaking hypocrisy. The brutality delivered with a gracious smile.

I don't think the sheriff in Kilmarnock had much time for her either. When the egg case came to court I was refused legal aid and played at being a lawyer by defending myself. After listening patiently to my cross examination and summing up, he said he did not wish to question the sincerity of my case or my witnesses. But he had no alternative than to find me guilty. He fined me £100 for aiming an egg at the Prime Minister of the day. It was a pretty good deal.

At least the sheriff kept things in perspective. We were smashing eggs, not heads.

'The police have taken a match to a tinder box,' I confidently told the television journalist as the missiles rained around our heads. 'They have used a water cannon to extinguish a match.' The film crew had stopped Steve Nally and I as we tried to escape the mayhem of Trafalgar Square.

A few moments earlier, we stood on the podium at the foot of Nelson's Column and watched in disbelief as a running battle unfolded around us. People were moving. Police were moving. There was screaming. People were being dragged along the flagstones. It was awesome in a way. This had been the biggest political march since the days of the Chartists. We were 200,000 strong. Looking down from the platform, parts of you felt powerful because of the massive crowd. Other parts felt really helpless because of the violence.

Lines of demonstrators shouting 'No Poll Tax! No Poll Tax!' faced grim walls of police riot shields. It was like the Roman army marching into battle. It appeared really disciplined though it was in fact spontaneous. The nearest thing I can compare it to is gang fighting in the Glasgow schemes. Much of it is theatre. Your mob chases another mob. You get to a certain point and stop. Then the other mob chases you. In between, there are a couple of skirmishes, but never mass confrontation.

The day had started so well. Our rally in Glasgow was the biggest unofficial demonstration in Scotland since the Upper Clyde Shipbuilders work-in in 1971. The Mad Pipers (or the Hot Chocolate Pipers since they change their name for every demo) skirled from George Square to Queens Park. Forty thousand people followed, with balloons and banners and kids on their shoulders.

Through Glasgow Cross, Bridgeton and the Gorbals, locals turned out to cheer us. There was so much good feeling. I remember one of our stewards – Jack Harvey – was approached by a lanky guy backstage who said he wanted to sing a song. I don't know about that, says Jack, thinking he had a chancer on his hands. It turned out the skinny guy was Ricky Ross from Deacon Blue. He had heard about the rally from his pal Michael Marra, who was playing piano. So Ricky and Lorraine McIntosh were so keen to take part they just turned up in anti-poll tax t-shirts on the day.

After speaking beside Jim Sillars and Dick Douglas I was whipped away to the airport, leaving the crowd to Deacon Blue, Hue and Cry and the Wildcat band.

I'd begged friends and comrades for money to fly to the London rally. British Airways even held up the plane, though that was probably due to my desperate pleading with the girl at the departure desk. When I got on the plane the stewardess looking at her watch was a girl I'd been at school with, Gail Healy. 'This is the guy who's been keeping you all back,' she announced to the other passengers. We then chatted on the way down. I didn't know then we would become much closer. We began seeing one another when I came out of prison in 1992 and have been together ever since.

Our press officer, John Rathbone, met me in Heathrow. John had worked hard to make the day a success, staging stunts with London bands like Big Audio Dynamite, the Wee Papa Girl Rappers and the Stereo MCs.

We were pressed up close on the tube from the airport. It was a warm day, and the underground had that smell it always has, of grime and burnt rubber and sweat all mixed together. But John was in high spirits. It's looking really good, he said. We got off at Charing Cross and elbowed through the crowd, eyes squinting against the sunshine. Make way for the child, we shouted, as the only way to make a passage. We'd pass a guy playing banjo, another on the tin whistle.

Eventually we reached Nelson's Column. I was on after Tony Benn. My first inkling that there was something wrong came as I began to address the crowd. 'I bring the solidarity of 1 million non-payers in Scotland,' I shouted through the inadequate PA. 'It's not enough to talk about the Poll Tax being unfair and unjust. We have to act against it I hope our brothers and sisters in England and Wales will join us in a mass campaign of non payment. . . .'

For those who were listening, it went down well. But I gradually noticed that no one was looking or listening anymore. All eyes were fixed to a point somewhere behind my left shoulder. It was like a tennis match where the ball goes over the net and all heads turn in unison.

I looked round and saw hordes of policemen on horseback, charging into the Square. Police cars and vans appeared from nowhere, driving like maniacs into the crowd. Loudhailers screamed for people to move back. But there was nowhere to go, we were boxed in.

George Galloway stood beside me with his young daughter. He was really worried about getting the wee girl out before things got too wild. By this time, riot police appeared from beneath the South African Embassy. The individual instances of violence will stay with me forever. Most vividly, I remember a few people setting a portacabin alight on the scaffolding at the far end of the square. Further up the scaffolding a long-haired guy in a green flak jacket held a fire-extinguisher in outstretched arms above his head. I thought: surely not. But yes, he flung it over the edge and it somersaulted, almost in slow motion, into the crowd below. My heart sank. This had been a real family occasion. There were a lot of kids on the march.

Anarchists who defended such actions said they were aiming at the police. But these idiots were 100 feet up. It was crass stupidity. The same people later began throwing bricks at firemen who came to put out the flames. I was sickened by that. The Fire Brigades Union had been 100% behind non-payment and the Federation.

Things were getting out of control. Our chief steward – one of 2000 on duty that day – instructed everyone to get out of the square. That included Steve and myself, who was secretary of the All Britain Federation.

We may have been the leaders, but we had to adhere to the instructions. On occasions like this, everyone returns to their allocated role, otherwise you just get chaos. The fire-extinguisher incident was still in my mind when the television crew nabbed us. I don't mind co-operating with the media, even on the battlefield. But this time the bandits caught me out. The director manoeuvred me, left a bit, right a bit, until I was directly in front of the blazing portakabin. While I was speaking, these flames were shooting out of my head. Even better for them, I was talking about matches and tinderboxes. It was great TV. I looked like the arsonist.

Media presentation was the last thing on our minds at that moment. We were figuring how to reach the waiting transit van without sustaining serious head injuries. Once inside we sat for a long time – the driver couldn't move and we couldn't see out the back. We heard the sound of screaming and smashing glass, but could only guess at who or what was being hit.

Eventually, in the late afternoon, we got to Steve's flat. He lives on the 17th floor of a council hi-rise in Lambeth, south of the Thames. It epitomises my experience of London. From one window you've got a view of the Oval Cricket Ground. From the other you look right over the river to the Houses of Parliament and Big Ben. But the place where you're standing is falling to bits. The lifts never work. The water is always being disconnected and the heating cuts on and off at the wrong times. You'd wake up either shivering or running with sweat.

I'd slept on Steve's couch many times on trips to London for meetings of the All Britain Federation. I would slag him about his wee black-and-white portable telly. You could never watch the football properly.

Now we were fixed to the flickering screen, watching the day's events unfold and getting more depressed. The numbers on the march, the success of the rally, all forgotten and irrelevant. The atmosphere in the flat was a mixture of exhilaration, exhaustion and bitter disappointment.

I was running on nervous energy, having eaten only two slices of toast all day. We just sat drinking tea, listening to the radio, answering the phone; trying to piece together what happened while all the time the telly buzzed in the background.

Wally Kennedy, a Hillingdon councillor and a senior steward, appeared at the door. He was able to give us an eye-witness account of events beyond Nelson's Column. He told us a small group of anarchists had sat down in the road just outside Downing Street around 1.15pm. They had caused a bit of trouble, refusing to accept the discipline of the demo, marching in side streets behind black flags. They were hurling verbal abuse and beer cans at our stewards – one of whom, a woman, was punched. Another, Mike Waddington, was confronted by a wild-eyed guy waving a broken bottle. All the stewards were wearing fluorescent orange bibs. 'This guy came up and started accusing me of being an orangeman, ranting about Northern Ireland and being totally incoherent. He had others around him and I had to get away pretty quick,' said Mike. The stewards told marchers just to walk around the people who were sitting down. This solution was working well. Then the Metropolitan Police used a mallet to crack a peanut.

Wally's story was supplemented by others who called the flat that afternoon, gradually completing the picture we were trying to build up.

Mickey Neill, a twenty-four year-old shelf packer, was in the thick of it all. He came to the demo with his flatmate after seeing posters near his house. Mickey remembers the crowd being divided outside Downing Street. A wedge of police pushed half the march south towards the Embankment and the rest north into the Square. Mickey and his flatmate were on opposite sides of the divide.

'Coppers were just grabbing people and throwing them into each section of the crowd for no reason. Families who'd been sitting on the grass embankment eating their sandwiches were manhandled into line.' Mickey, still by himself, was pushed into Trafalgar Square, along with the troublemakers our stewards had tried to isolate.

'All of a sudden this mass of coppers rushed towards me. There were more at the back. I was thrown over a barrier. I got up and saw four or five coppers standing over one guy on the ground and just beating him with their truncheons. A woman who argued with them got a riot shield pushed hard into her face. I was pretty angry and a bit excited. I was still by myself and just got caught up in things. I ran into the square and joined the crowd throwing things at the police horses. It lasted a long time. I was later arrested in my bed by five police who had a photograph of me with a scaffolding clip in my hand.'

The experience politicised Mickey, who served six months in Pentonville and later joined Militant. Guys like him did not set out to cause trouble. They were were so incensed by the truncheons and riot shields that they fought back.

It was very different from Glasgow that day, or indeed all the other demonstrations, occupations and illegal activity involving the Scottish Anti-Poll Tax Federation. Given the concentration of the working class in Scotland, the police knew strongarm tactics would be well out of step with public opinion. There was even a mutual respect. You lost count of the individual polis on Scottish demos who'd say they weren't paying their Poll Tax.

The police are doing a job I wouldn't do. I wouldn't encourage anyone to do it. But most families, if their house is broken into or their son is knifed in the street, will call the police. We do need some form of social control. The police become the enemy when they are used to enforce *political* control. At the end of the day, they are bodies of men and women who will be used against working-class movements. Occasionally, the weight of the movement means they come over to our side. Maryhill Barracks were locked in 1919 during the forty-hours strike and troops were brought from other parts of the country. They feared local soldiers might refuse to turn their guns on the strikers.

That was not a consideration in Trafalgar Square in 1990, where the Met. went completely over the top. It shouldn't surprise anyone. The London force was already notorious for its behaviour at Orgreave during the miners' strike and on the Wapping picket line.

As the stories reached Lambeth, we began to suspect the police may have started the trouble deliberately. They broke so many agreements – like not letting us sort out any sit-down protests. At the last moment, they changed the dropping-off points for coaches. When we realised how big the turnout was going to be, we asked if we could change the destination for reasons of safety. We suggested Hyde Park instead of the square. That request was refused. All their decisions were designed to increase the likelihood of trouble and give them an excuse to charge.

I think they were *told* to intervene. The run-up to the demo saw a spate of Red Smear stories in the national papers. 'The commuter seated in second class on the 2.40pm Intercity train from Bristol to Paddington had revolution on his mind,' began one *Sunday Times* piece accusing Steve Nally of co-ordinating bloody insurrection.

By March 1990 we had 1,500 Anti Poll Tax Unions operating in Britain. These unions organised 6,000 lobbies, demonstrations and public meetings in the two months before the introduction of the tax. Feelings were even running high in the shires. Former Tory voters were repenting the error of their ways. News programmes every night carried footage of town-hall protests when councils were setting their poll tax level. So the ruling class panicked. They were watching a mass revolt. The Met. in my opinion, were under instruction to provoke aggression in order to discredit our movement. They thought they could contain the resulting violence and win the day. But they underestimated the strength of feeling, the size of the crowd. That's why senior officers were forced to admit afterwards: 'We lost it, we lost it.'

There is nothing new in this. You will find historical precedents on the very pavements showered by glass in 1990. Charing Cross Road and the Strand were wrecked on Bloody Sunday in 1887. Four demonstrators were killed and 200 people were hospitalised when armed police and a regiment of guards with fixed bayonets tried to stop the unemployed as they marched down St Martin's Lane. The last full-scale riot in the West End of London took place in 1932, when special constables tried to stop Hunger Marchers taking their banners into the square.

The group named by the national press as the co-ordinators of the 1990 Trafalgar Square riot was Class War. The *Sunday Times* claimed their members made up an indigent, criminal underclass with tattoed faces and mongrel dogs on strings. But Class War had a membership of a couple of hundred across the UK. Around 3,000 people got caught up in the violence that day.

As Martin Kettle remarked in the *Guardian* at the time: 'There hasn't been a riot in British history that has not been blamed on a conspiracy by a minority. But they are never found.' We accepted a small band of troublemakers had acted stupidly. But there was no pre-planned conspiracy on their part. They were just a bunch of idiots. And the skirmish could have been contained by our own stewards if the police had not broken agreements. The people in uniforms were to blame, not the people in denims.

Both the BBC and ITN then called asking Steve and I to appear on their main evening news bulletins. They each dispatched cars to take us into the city centre.

It wasn't until I got into the BBC taxi that I saw the real extent of the devastation. London looked like Beirut. Even as we drove through town at 7 pm, small bands of demonstrators were looting. Restaurants were smashed, cars burnt out. You could feel the danger. Police in full riot gear were still patrolling the streets. Guys with head wounds were being treated in the corner of the BBC studio. Journalists and cameramen had been attacked. I arrived two hours early for the broadcast and spent the time looking at the day's film footage. It became glaringly clear how horrific the whole thing was. I was overcome with revulsion at what a few people purporting to be demonstrators were doing. But I was even more repelled by the behaviour of the police. They deployed men who simply lost control. I will never forget the scene of the woman being brutally trampled by the police horse.

During the interview, which was live, I condemned police tactics along with those acting irresponsibly, like the maniacs who threw the fire-extinguishers or attacked journalists.

Steve's interview with ITN was pre-recorded. He was being pressed about the violence, which he condemned. He said we wanted a Labour movement inquiry into the trouble. If it found groups who deliberately came to cause trouble, they would be barred from future demos. He said these groups should be named.

I also went out of my way to say that Thatcher had created the conditions which caused this violence. If she hadn't introduced the Poll Tax there would not have been a riot. There is some truth in the saying that a riot is the voice of the unheard. These people were scarred by her legacy. London is the place where this legacy is most glaring. It draws together the extremes of capitalism. There are the excesses of wealth in the West End, and the City – like the Lloyds building.

Then there's the homelessness. Shelter says there are 130,000 single homeless people in the city. There are now, in 1994, some 6,000 people sleeping rough in central London. Ten years ago the number was negligible; they didn't bother to count. Plenty of the genuinely dispossessed were on the demonstration. They smashed the windows of Porsches. They overturned BMW's. Thatcher's Children, products of an uncaring society which sees no place for love and co-operation, were taking their revenge.

The rampage was not entirely indiscriminate. Not that I think smashing Porsches will change the world. But it can be partially explained. I didn't hear about too many Ladas being torched. Stringfellows, the upper-crust nightclub, was wrecked but the pub next door was untouched.

Fast-food chains were also singled out for repeated attack. By this time, McDonald's had become one of London's five largest employers. It spearheaded the shining new service sector, replacing those manufacturing jobs which disappeared in the 1980s. Three quarters of their workers are under twenty-one. They earn less than £2 an hour but still have to smile. Most officially work less than sixteen hours so they have no holiday or sickness pay, nor any employment rights. But often they find themselves called in for twelve-hour shifts, adding up to eighty-six hours a week. McDonald's pay no overtime rate. The company made $958.6 million net profit worldwide in 1992.

Nobody set out to smash McDonald's that morning. But when order broke down, is it any wonder young people decided to show what they thought of the low-wage future being mapped out for them?

Nor did anyone go to demonstrate against the Poll tax saying: I'll get three personal hi-fis and two colour tellys. Just like in LA the opportunity arose. Our society worships consumption like a new religion. By 1990, spending money had become a fervent cult. But as with many cults, you had to pay for the privilege of taking part. The people who looted that day had been exposed to all the rantings and ravings of this amoral creed.

Looting was counter-productive from the point of view of our movement. But there are worse things than opportunistically reaching into a smashed shop window for a video or personal hi-fi. Who commits the biggest crimes? An anonymous ploughman poet from the eighteenth century summed it up when he said:

> The law locks up the man or woman
> Who steals the goose from off the common
> But leaves the greater felon loose
> Who steals the common from the goose.

I wouldn't even rule out looting as a form of political action. John Maclean considered it when unemployed ex-servicemen were starving in 1919. Food riots have been organised more recently in Peru and Brazil. Rather than starve to death, I'd loot.

Fortunately we haven't got to that stage in this country. But if the Tories get their way with social security changes, if compulsory workfare is introduced, then I'm not going to condemn penniless people taking meat from Safeway. I would support it. I might even organise it. When you're trying to change society you've got one bow with several arrows. There are different arrows for different times. Trafalgar Square, 1990, was not the right time for looting to be used as a political weapon.

Admittedly, there is no way we would have got those headlines, or the massive international coverage, if there hadn't been a riot. By the morning of 1 April, 339 people had been arrested. Of the 2,189 police on duty that day, 374 were reported injured, fifty-eight requiring hospital treatment. Eighty-six demonstrators also reported injuries. Millions of pounds worth of damage had been inflicted in London's heartland.

The foreign press described it as the death crisis of Thatcherism. 'The Iron Lady is seeing the beginning of the end,' wrote the columnist Alberto Cavallari in Italy's *La Repubblica*. 'The Poll Tax revolt is only the most vivid manifestation of a deep-rooted social crisis.'

Money men were nervous. Shares fell by twenty-six points. The pound plunged. The government tried to pin the blame on Labour MPs like Tony Benn and Dave Nellist who told people not to pay their poll tax. But an opinion poll in the *Sunday Correspondent* newspaper the following week showed three times as many people blamed the Tories as blamed the Labour Party for the riot. That was the worrying feature for Thatcher. The whole kudos of her party was law and order: stability. Now this stable country was ripping apart at the seams. Dave Nellist, in particular, brilliantly championed our cause in parliament and delivered this message in their most exclusive club.

It might not have been as significant as George Bush having to send troops into central Los Angeles. But Thatcher was also a world leader, and a standard bearer of capitalism, jetting across continents proclaiming the triumph of free market values. Yet a few feet from where she eats breakfast she's got riots she can't control. It really undermined her.

The international press were already there in force because of the massive opposition to the tax. Imagine not one bottle had been thrown and every scrap of loose masonry in the Borough of Westminster had remained on the ground. People would simply have gone home to Coventry, Glasgow or Leicester, and got on with the job of organising a mass non-payment campaign, stopping the sheriffs, chasing the bailiffs and holding street meetings and rallies.

Thatcher quit in November that year. The Poll Tax made her an electoral liability for her party. They feared that non-payment in England would follow the Scottish pattern and double in the second year. The whole thing was a disaster and she was the architect. She had to go.

Our Scottish campaign dug her political grave. What happened in Trafalgar Square was the lowering of the coffin. Eighteen million non-payers in Britain threw the clay on top.

There is one sad postscript to all this: something that never became an issue in Scotland, but began to tear at the movement in parts of England and Wales. The pretext was Steve's ITN interview. When he talked about having an inquiry, he said it should name names. His remarks were taken out of context by some anarchist groups. They accused us of grassing people to the police. Anyone who knows Steve knows he would never nark to the authorities. It would be a contradiction in terms. The Federation has been involved in numerous forms of illegal activity. Our members were the first to go to jail for non-payment of the tax.

I escaped the worst of the harrassment. I was out of sight in Scotland. I was heckled at some meetings, called a grass and even a brat. Sometimes they even threw beer cans and other missiles. I usually approached them afterwards – they always shut up when confronted on their own, face-to-face.

Most of these people would describe themselves as anarchists. One of the first anarchists, the Russian Bakunin, said violence is a creative act. But he didn't mean it should be directed against people who were organising the working class. Why attack those who have already put their head on the chopping block?

We knew anarchists in the Scottish Anti-Poll Tax Federation. They were socialists who became cynical about the ability of political parties to achieve change. They were good, sincere people.

There's a long tradition of class-based anarchism in Glasgow, going back to Guy Aldred. Anarcho-syndicalists, who believed industrial action rather than political activity would change society were very influential on the Clyde before the First World War. Willie Gallacher was a prominent anarcho-syndicalist before he met Lenin and founded the Communist Party in Britain.

Some of the most inspiring socialists in America's history were anarcho-syndicalists. They were the men and women behind the International Workers of the World or Wobblies, who wanted to create one big union. Clydeside Press and Workers City are both anarchist. We wouldn't have beaten the poll tax without them in Scotland because they let us use their printing press when we had no money to pay.

In England anarchy appears to differ from this. The interesting feature about a number of the arrests of the so-called anarchists involved in the Trafalgar Square trouble was the number whose parents were so upset. Daddy was a stockbroker and mummy was a head teacher. You'll find many of these groups contain people from privileged backgrounds whose grudge against society is from a middle-class point of view. Perhaps they rebel against their parents' materialism. It's a pampered and privileged rebellion. People from that background see it as a bit of fun.

We don't get much of that kind of thing in Glasgow. It's difficult to drop out if you're already at the bottom. There are all different kinds of oppression. Economic oppression is by far the worst.

Certainly some young working-class people will be attracted to anti-establishment groups which allow them to vent their anger and frustration. Just look at the number of Glasgow teenagers who join sectarian outfits. It's a way of belonging and rebelling at the same time. Nihilistic groups like Class War have something of the same appeal. Their full frontal criticism of the state – the way they attack the police, pillory the Royal Family, organise Stop the City and Bash the Rich events – that will strike a chord with some people. In an Acab Press pamphlet 'Poll Tax Riot: ten hours that shook Trafalgar Square' the anarcho element who attended the march speak approvingly of: 'The frenzy of ecstatic smashing and looting.' One describes the attack on a sunglasses shop in Covent Garden and boasts of acquiring a pair of £150 Giorgio Armani specs. 'Rioters not only furious but now cool,' he writes.

What do we make of this? Do you judge the success of your campaign by the number of sunglasses you steal? If so, how many pairs of sunglasses would you need to bring down the state? It's easy to have a go at obscene wealth but offer no alternative except to attack. It's all very macho. But they don't talk about another way of organising your life, or of organising society.

In places like London and Bristol there's a big layer of anarchists like that, who have as much hatred even for democratically-elected people like me as they have for Thatcher or Major. They hate the idea of leaders. We're supposed to change society by, well, what? Things just happening? Nobody's supposed to organise it or provide direction.

Anyway, the whole thing rumbled on for the rest of the year. Meetings in England became a real drag because this anarchist element kept shouting about it. At the All Britain Federation AGM in Manchester in November 1990, two of these groups put up resolutions condemning Steve and myself. They were overwhelmingly defeated and Steve and I were re-elected with massive majorities.

I remember Alan McCombes making the point that if they had even a remote understanding of life in working-class communities, they would not have made that condemnation. You never call someone a grass unless you've got very good evidence. That's how potent it is. The consequences are physically serious. He invited these marble-mouthed intellectuals to come to Pollok or Easterhouse and call me a grass. Just to see what would happen. Of course we never saw them in our communities. Getting drunk at a demo and attacking stewards was a good laugh for them. But it's a lot harder to turn out on a cold January morning when the sheriff officers are coming to old Mrs Wright's door.

6   The jaws of victory 1991

The worst moment for Jean McGahey came when the photographer lunged forward. Her feet were not touching the ground at the time. Two polis grabbed each arm, hoisting Jean through the crowd which stood between her front door and the waiting bus. It was November and bitter cold. Both cops swung round just before bundling her into the coach. A white flash blinded Jean at that moment. Maybe she twisted away from the light, her face screwed up against the cold and the public humiliation. Maybe she stared straight into the lens, dull and defeated. All she can remember is being thrown inside the bus with the others. It was difficult to think straight in the confusion. Screams pierced the chatter of the walkie-talkies. The helicopter was still droning in the grey Greenock sky overhead. It appeared from behind the moors and descended on her council house like something from a drugs swoop in Los Angeles.

She asked the young policeman what would happen to the grandchildren if their mothers were arrested, as was being threatened. He smirked and said they'd be taken into care.

As things turned out, the young mothers kept their liberty and their children. The only human gesture in a day of carefully-planned intimidation. Sparing the women was probably motivated by self-interest. They were crammed in the house like everyone else. Being in the house was the only grounds for arrest. But snatching children in morning raids causes outcry even when abuse is suspected. Could the authorities honestly defend splitting a family on the grounds that granny hadn't paid her poll tax?

Eleven people were dragged from Jean's house. They were all friends and neighbours who came to stop the local sheriff officer, Bob McIntyre, poinding her furniture. He arrived with a crowbar and loads of polis. At first he yelled abuse through the front letter-box. Some of the guys yelled back. They weren't moving. Then he moved round the back. Jean heard a terrible splintering sound as he smashed the crowbar through the wooden door. Still they wouldn't let him in.

The voice of the commanding officer boomed through the letter-box. He sounded like a civil man. She knew a few local polis from the Greenock amusement arcade where she worked. The arcade was beside the bus stops in the centre of town. Jean got to know lots of people who sheltered from the incessant rain by heading for the one-armed bandits. The polis would pop in on dreich nights for a cup of tea and a gab.

Now the big chief wanted into Jean's home for a chat. She let him in. He said his piece in the living room. How this was not a job the police enjoyed, but the law was the law. Nothing would happen to her if she just opened the door to Mr McIntyre. She thanked him but said it was her house and she would decide who was invited in. She opened the door to let him out and his men stormed the place. His word was worthless.

The sergeant at the station stumbled over the charge sheet. 'Let me get this right,' he mumbled. The charge was deforcement. It was used to put peasants off their land during the nineteenth-century Highland clearances. The last time it saw the light of day was the rent strikes in 1922. It means stopping a sheriff officer in his line of duty and carries a maximum penalty of death.

Jean had never been in trouble before. Here she was being criminalised by a tax no one wanted, but a regional council was determined to enforce. This was the people's party's justice. She was held in the police cell overnight and the enforced isolation and imprisonment persuaded her to say she would go to the building society and draw out savings to pay her arrears. But we were waiting on the steps of the court. When she saw everyone clapping and cheering she changed her mind. She remembered she wasn't on her own. And she had beaten the sheriff officer. The poinding was void because the police had intervened.

McIntyre did not give up. Out of all the thousands of non-payers in Greenock, he poinded Jean McGahey a second time – getting access to the house while she was out.

The Trafalgar Square violence was immortalised by the media. Little attention was paid to the forced removal of a middle-aged women from her home because she could not afford to pay the Poll Tax. The *Greenock Telegraph* covered the story, but other papers just gave it a paragraph, if that. What an indictment of our free press.

Jean was not targetted by mistake. She was a typical victim. Although regional councillors hinted that they would only turn the screw on wealthy non-payers, it was the vulnerable who got kicked in the teeth.

Betty Cunningham from Bellshill in Lanarkshire doesn't fit the rich refusenik category either. Betty has severe spondylitis – inflamation of the joints in her spine. She is classed as severely disabled. Yet Betty was one of the first people in Strathclyde to be visited by sheriff officers.

She was in her usual seat when they arrived. It's in the corner facing the front window of her living room. Everything she needs is arranged on the aluminium-legged table across her lap – newspapers, magazines, and her long cigarette holder. She can reach for videos in the wall unit next to the chair without difficulty. Getting up is a different matter.

Betty was a school cleaner for thirteen years. It was heavy work. During the summer she had to scrub the walls and scour the desks with steel wool that leaves your fingers raw. The newsagent down the road joked that he knew she was coming because of the waft of carbolic soap. By 1990 she could hardly make it to his shop. Just walking 100 yards up the road to buy a newspaper made her feet swell up. Years of scrubbing crippled her. She has a hole in her knee and her hip is wearing away.

'It's just the wear and tear,' she'll say in a rich Welsh accent which has survived her move from Abergavenny thirty years ago. She's a very dignified and resourceful woman. She made wedding dresses for each of her three daughters, now aged thirty-one, twenty-nine and twenty-five.

One of Betty's daughters – pregnant at the time – was in the house when the sheriff officers came in 1990. They gave no notice. They just battered the door of the terraced council house in Community Road one summer day, waving what they claimed was a warrant. Jack Cunningham, Betty's husband, told them to send it to Maggie Thatcher. They returned with four policeman who told the Cunninghams to open their door. It was the law. If they noticed Betty's disability, it didn't move them. They strode through the house, valuing the wall units and the television cabinet which helped make Betty's life a wee bit more pleasant. Ann Curran and her sisters, all from Bellshill Anti-Poll Tax Union, ran from Liberty Road round the corner. They asked the sheriffs to leave Community Road. Couldn't they see this woman was disabled? Why give no notice? The younger guy turned round to one of the pregnant Curran women and sneered: Do you know the father of that wean?

These animals respected neither health nor age: Betty Cunningham was forty-nine when they came. Margaret Wilson was sixty. But vulnerability seems to attract these bullies. Margaret is a widow who stays in a multistorey in Drumchapel. She is five feet tall and weighs six stone ten pounds. Since her heart attack three years ago she has taken daily medication. Margaret's life story is worth repeating because it so closely follows the path of the working class in the West of Scotland since the last war. You might be happy and comfortable in the good years, when the economy demands your skills. Then the economy fails, or your body fails through illness. You have no skills to sell. Down you tumble into the safety net a few inches from the hard rock bottom. Rich people also hit recession. Rich people also get sick. But somehow they never fall as far as you. There's always a well-placed friend to catch them before the halfway mark.

Margaret was one of the first tenants in Drumchapel. The scheme didn't have tarmac roads when she took her five-apartment tenement flat. Rents were high and Margaret discovered she could not be evicted because her husband was in the army. So she did not pay. That was a legacy of the First World War rent strikes – you cannot put a soldier's family on the street.

She did not need to challenge the law when her husband came home. William Wilson was a cooper to trade. Distilleries and bonded warehouses around Glasgow and Dumbarton were desperate for his barrel-making skills. Margaret and her children never knew debt. They were the comfortable working class. On a good week Margaret's man came through the door and handed her £70.

Then he got diabetes. The managers of the distilleries and the bonded warehouses said their insurance would no longer cover him. Poor health priced him out of the labour market. Margaret's life changed dramatically. William was idle for eight years before he died. She went out to work as a cleaner in the local health centre. Then her health also failed. Now she lives on a pension of sixty pounds a week.

Margaret Wilson tried to pay her poll tax. But after a few months, the extra cost was showing up in rent arrears. Winter arrived, along with bigger electricity bills. So she stopped paying. Given her health and age, she didn't have a choice. The district council's own figures show more than half their tenants believe they are spending too much on heating, even though they can only afford to heat one room in winter. The average tenant spends less than a tenner a week on heating. Damp houses suffer condensation and are hard to heat. These account for thirty-seven per cent of the council's housing stock – while another 13,000 are so damp they are 'Below Tolerable Standard'.

None of that was taken into account by Rutherford and McPherson, the sheriff officers who sent letters to Margaret warning that her goods would be poinded. Since Labour politicians at this time were telling those in financial difficulty to come and explain things, she took the bus into the sheriffs' Bath Street office in Glasgow's commercial district, and offered £20. 'That's no good,' they said: 'We want £50.' She explained she did not have £50. 'We'll go to court and get a warrant to poind your household goods,' they replied.

A few days later she received a letter saying they were coming. She was terrified. 'I wanted to go into the drying cupboard and hide. I was worried about the angina, worried I might have another attack.'

She contacted Ann Lynch from the Drumchapel Anti-Poll Tax Union. We assembled a crowd at the entrance to the flats. But Rutherford and McPherson never showed. It simply had the effect of frightening an old lady.

Sheriff officers have always been hated in Scotland. That's why the founding manifesto of the Scottish Labour Party in 1888 called for a change in the way debt was collected. A century later, the successors to Keir Hardie were making good use of the legislation he wanted abolished.

In 1989 the Labour Party in Scotland was still saying it hoped to avoid using poindings and warrant sales to recover money from people who had not paid the poll tax – although they were already setting the sheriffs on those who had not registered. Then their position shifted to saying only the wealthy 'Can Pay, Won't Pay' would be targetted for brutal methods of recovery.

Here is how it works: people do not pay their Poll Tax so, the creditor, in this case the Labour run local authority, goes to a sheriff court to obtain a summary warrant. The warrant is passed to an officer of the court – the sheriff officer – who is instructed to wring the cash out of the debtor, some would say by fair means or foul. He can use the warrant to arrest wages or bank accounts or he may start the process which is supposed to end in the public auction of a person's goods: a warrant sale.

The sheriff officer and a witness first go to the debtor's house to poind the goods. Poind is a Scots word meaning to identify and value goods for a future sale. (It's so degrading, these strangers deciding what your most precious possessions are worth.) The sheriff officer can come back within a year and take the poinded goods away to an auction room. He must give you notice. But if you are out he is legally allowed to break down the door and lift your things.

Strathclyde Report, the regional council's own newspaper, published the results of a survey they commissioned in 1990 called 'Community Charge and Poverty' by Dr Angus Erskine of Strathclyde University. Dr Erskine spoke to 312 low-income families and discovered most were already in debt. This new burden, he noticed, was beginning to harm their physical and mental well being. He advised the council there was little hope of the region recovering the Poll Tax from these people.

Armed with this information, what did the regional councils do? Why, they tried to force out the money anyway. Compare it to trying to get juice from an orange which has already been squeezed. To get a few drops, you twist and grind and pound at the fruit until it is bruised and limp. By the time *Strathclyde Report* printed Dr Erskine's results, in Autumn 1990, the Region had already given the sheriffs *carte blanche* to attempt warrant sales.

'We have taken legal opinion and have no powers to interfere with the poll tax on the grounds of hardship,' said John Mullin, the chair of finance. He added: 'We are cast in the role of agonised spectators.'

In other words, he had been dragged, kicking and screaming, to the front row of an arena where the poor were thrown into the gaping jaws of the debt collectors. Presumably the rest of the coliseum crowd were also horrified Labour politicians.

Except it wasn't quite like that. Mr Mullin was in fact the lion tamer for Strathclyde. His instructions allowed the beasts to maul the poor. He fed the lions when he paid the sheriff officers – and they were well paid for collecting the Poll Tax.

The Federation promised from the outset to protect anyone threatened by the sheriff officers. Many of the people who were poinded in 1990 had not told us the sheriffs were coming. Some were like Betty Cunningham and had been given no prior notice. We wanted to give these brylcreemed barbarians a taste of their own medicine. Maybe they would then think twice before heading for the schemes in their business saloons.

But while sheriff officers used shoulders and crow bars to break down the council house doors, we were more subtle when it came to invading their space. We used our brains. We occupied the premises of dozens of sheriff officers throughout 1990 and 1991. Sometimes we would be protesting on behalf of a particular individual. We also made general demands. We usually asked them to give four days' notice of any poinding. Then we could organise to stop them.

There is no law of trespass in Scotland. You can only be charged for *forcibly* entering someone's property (unless, of course, you're a sheriff officer). This leaves the way open for imaginative protests.

Scottish crofters took advantage of this with occupations during the nineteenth-century Highland Land War. The Gaels regarded land as a common resource to be shared collectively; their landlords considered it a commodity to be bought and sold for profit.

In 1888 around 100 local men from Park on the island of Lewis occupied a sporting estate belonging to Lady Matheson. They had been pushed on to tiny coastal strips of land so that the ruling class could shoot a few stags. And Lady Matheson didn't just exploit Scottish people. Her Glasgow-based family firm, Jardine Matheson, made a fortune selling opium to the Chinese.

The local men shot a large number of deer and fed the venison to their families. They couldn't be charged with trespass. But the law protects property and they were tried for mobbing and rioting. A sympathetic jury in Edinburgh acquitted the Park men who were so encouraged they raided a sheep farm. Several thousand people and a piper came along this time. The land raids continued into the 1920s. The government eventually gave the Highlanders security of tenure and fixed rents. But huge swathes of Scotland remain in a few jewelled hands to this day, despite a succession of Labour governments.

Occupations have also been used in urban settings. Wal Hannington led factory raids by the National Unemployed Workers' Movement in the 1920s. Scores of unemployed people marched into factories where low-paid workers grafted long shifts. They then demanded a cut in hours and a rise in wages to benefit both the employed and the unemployed. During the 1984 miners' strike, a group of Glasgow anarchists occupied the offices of Price Waterhouse, the accountants who sequestrated the NUM funds. They got in by timing when the concierge went to buy his newspaper. Then they chained the doors of the newsagents while he was inside. Twelve of them entered the Price Waterhouse building and nailed steel sheets over the doors of the lifts. They had earlier sent a couple of guys round posing as elevator engineers to measure the thing up. In the end all twelve were led out hand-cuffed together and charged with damaging the property.

We did not want to be accused of vandalism as that detracts from the political point. But we also saw the value of subterfuge. The first invasion – of Gray Scott & Co in Glasgow's Jamaica Street – was a carefully-planned operation. The sheriff officers had illegally poinded a Paisley woman by valuing goods which did not belong to her.

There had to be a way of getting into the building, while forcing out the staff. Obviously we couldn't physically eject them. But we hatched a plan to get them out and get a laugh at the same time. The most important thing was to plant people inside the office to hold open the two sets of security doors.

Jack Harvey telephoned Gray Scott, pretending to be a Mr Chubb from the factor's office. 'We hear there's a problem with draughty windows,' said Mr Chubb. Naturally they replied: 'We've been saying for ages that our windows are terrible! It's about time something was done!' Nine out of ten office workers you speak to will say their windows are draughty. Mr Chubb, who had nothing whatsoever to do with locks, security etc, said: 'I thought as much. I'm going to send Mr Frame, the joiner, round tomorrow morning to inspect them – will 9.30 – 9.45 be okay?'

Mr Swann from the caretakers telephoned next. He explained the fire alarm was being tested the following day and they must evacuate the building. They didn't make the connection with the matches. Being conscientious types, we also told the fire brigade it was a drill.

The morning of the raid arrived. Keith Baldassarra called at the Jamaica street office, pretending to be the husband of the woman threatened with a poinding. He was accompanied by a sober-suited Alan McCombes, masquerading as Councillor Con from Paisley. Alan was shouting through the glass partition, demanding to be allowed inside to plead his constituent's case.

Jack Harvey – Mr Frame the joiner – was already inside. So was his mate, Gerry McGuire. Fortunately Jack is a joiner to trade and looked as though he knew what to do with the tools. Gerry just fumbled. The windows were metal, which threw them a bit but Jack bluffed as usual. As he started measuring he gave a thumbs up to the rest of us, waiting in various doorways across the street. Somebody immediately dived over and set off the fire alarm. Then we moved.

As soon as the first secretary opened the door, Councillor Con leapt into action. He held it open to let the staff out. 'Fire drill! You'll have to go!' said the senior sheriff officer. But Alan and Keith just stood firm with their backs against the door. By this time the guy knew it was a fix. But he was astounded when the two joiners flew across the room and grabbed the other door. 'Not you as well!' he cried in disbelief.

We passed the departing staff on the stairs and sailed into the empty office. Two sheriff officers refused to leave. We gave them a final chance then barricaded the door with desks, hung banners out the windows and demanded the poinding be withdrawn. At first the firm refused to negotiate – they just kept telling us to come out. But only a court interdict would remove us and the police were anxious for a settlement. So the head man in Gray Scott signed the Anti-Poll Tax Federation's dotted line after a few hours. The illegal poinding was rescinded. We had won. We left peacefully, feeling well pleased with ourselves. Only Jack Harvey was disappointed. Fearing arrest, he passed his joiner's tools to a couple of genuine workmen on the scaffolding outside. He never saw them again. Gray Scott then poinded a seventy-three year old woman in Macduff, a fishing village near Aberdeen. Again it was illegal – they had valued furniture which was exempt from the poinding process.

I was on one of my all-too-frequent visits to England at the time. But Alan, Jack and the rest organised mini-buses from Glasgow, Dundee, Edinburgh and Stirling. They arrived in Aberdeen about 5 am and slept on the floor of an anarchist bookshop in the main street.

Once-bitten Gray Scott had by then installed extra security measures. We needed another ruse. By freak chance, one of our guys in Aberdeen collected hats. Two of our people got peaked caps looking like those from Security Express, the private delivery firm. Then they parcelled up a box the size of a large refrigerator. Enormous letters on the front said 'To Gray Scott and Co.' They wanted the parcel to wedge open the door.

It all went to plan, though there was a bit of wrestling between the sheriff officers and the postmen before our cavalry – average age seventy – charged up the stairs.

The whole of the north-east was alive with news of the occupation. Our gang got the letter they wanted and headed back to the bookshop in time for the Grampian Television news. The pensioner at the centre of it all was interviewed. I think she was a Scottish nationalist. Anyway, they were all really keen to hear her reaction.

She spoke in broad Doric, a dialect from that part of the country. Nobody could understand a word – but *she* looked pleased.

A few weeks later Alan McCombes met a guy from the south of England who had relatives in a wee village near Aberdeen. They were convinced that a team from the central belt had kidnapped the sheriff officers and taken them to Glasgow. It was a really big thing up there. Grampian Police were furious. Their Glasgow counterparts tended to be more laidback about occupations. In fact, two of our people were charged with breach of the peace for the Aberdeen incident. They had given their names in good faith on the day, to assure the police that no vandalism had taken place. Warrants for their arrest went out weeks later despite promises that no action would be taken.

Some sheriff officers tried to sweat us out. We spent thirty hours in George Walker and Co. in Mitchell Lane, Glasgow protesting at their ignoring the legal requirement to give four days' notice of poindings.

Unfortunately, we had not reckoned on an overnight stay and brought no food. Subterfuge had failed on this occasion and we were left growling at them through the glass. Then one of the Pollok young team noticed the suspended ceiling. I have to say they have never employed some of their former criminal skills towards a better cause. Somebody was hoisted onto a pair of shoulders. Within seconds, wiry wee guys were crawling like mice between the lowered panels and the roof, and you'd have thought they *were* mice the way the clerks reacted. They almost jumped on their chairs when these Adidas-clad youths began dropping on top of their desks. But there was no violence. The boys just sauntered over, opened the doors, and we walked in shouting: 'This is a peaceful occupation. We're asking you to take your personal belongings and vacate the building.'

The police sealed off the entrance to the lane. But several shops backed onto it. The manager of a Chinese restaurant allowed our supporters to smuggle food through his kitchen and the security guard in *Superdrug* turned a blind eye to people running another supply line through their back shop. Alan McCombes threw us a rope from the office window opposite. Then he sent poly bags of crisps and sandwiches down the makeshift winch. The TV pictures that night really paid tribute to our ingenuity. We refused to be starved out. We walked free without arrest the next night, having secured some commitments on the four-day notice.

Once we just had to break in. This was when Stirling Park sheriffs descended without notice on Betty Cunningham, the disabled woman from Bellshill. It was a spontaneous protest which meant the security doors blocked our way. So it gave way under a size ten Reebok.

Stirling Park was another overnighter. For lack of anything else to do, we went exploring in the attic. An old appointments diary noted a golf date with Archibald Gillespie, the director of finance at Strathclyde Regional Council. So much for the sheriff officers acting independently of the council. There were also piles of golf ties which we knotted together to hoist up food. Inexplicably, we found a pair of handcuffs in the drawer, 'So this is what these kinky sheriffs get up to!' we shouted to the press, waving the evidence.

We heard a terrifying noise at around 3 am. It was the buzz of an electric saw, followed by a mallet shattering the plate glass. A squat guy, a police joiner, was mowing down the door. Then the polis charged in and arrested us all. The subsequent trial was very significant. It became clear that the police were working from photographs of anti-poll tax activists kept on record at the station. The constables who identified us in the dock were not the arresting officers. Our solicitor Alan Miller ran rings around them in court. It became quite clear they had been told who was who.

Alan was angry when we all got community service orders. This is the punishment below a custodial sentence. The press uncritically accepted that we had wrecked a sheriff officer's premises and caused damage of £15,000. That exaggerated figure referred to the fittings destroyed by their own joiner's mallet and saw.

During the Stirling Park occupation, we found minutes of the Society of Messengers at Arms. They complained that the police were not being brutal enough. They were thoroughly scunnered with us that summer. Not only were we blocking poindings, we were hounding them in their own territory. We'd occupied premises, not just in the big cities, but places like Dumfries, Hamilton, Dumbarton, Ayr, and Greenock.

Sheriff officers are shady creatures who prefer to lurk in the cracks and crevices of public life. Our impromptu visits were like switching on a light and watching cockroaches scuttle for cover. Every occupation put these pests under the glare of publicity. Eventually they got so fed up that they crawled before the cameras voluntarily. For the first time in their sixty-eight year history, the Society of Sheriff Officers and Messengers-at-Arms held a press conference to explain the nature of their work.

So the public had it all wrong. They were really good guys who loved their kids and helped old ladies across the road (before swinging crowbars through their doors). Michael Kelly Associates, a PR company, was hired to transform their rottweiler image into that of friendly cocker spaniels. Michael Kelly is a former Labour Lord Provost of Glasgow. The very man who used the smiling Mister Man in the Glasgow's Miles Better campaign in the 1980s. He started all the hot air which ballooned in 1990. It was an appropriate PR choice. But not even Michael Kelly could transform the average sheriff officer into Mr Happy.

A journalist tipped us off about the press conference in the Hospitality Inn, in July 1990. Sixty of us arrived to find the room empty – they knew we were on their tail and switched the venue at the last minute. A *Daily Record* journalist was speaking into his portable phone in the corner of the room. We could hear him getting instructions from his desk. The guy raced out of the building with our mob tearing behind. He disappeared into a waiting car. I jumped the first taxi in the rank and uttered the immortal instruction: 'Follow that car!' The driver thought he was in *Miami Vice* and screeched into action. The team followed in a convoy of assorted cars, taxis and the mini bus we'd parked round the corner. The reporter's car stopped outside the Kelvin Park Lorne Hotel a mile away. We headed straight for the meeting. The sheriffs were starting their television interviews when they heard the distant sound of NO! NO WARRANT SALES, NO WARRANT SALES IN SCOTLAND! They looked terrified when we appeared. Here they were sipping filter coffee and munching chocolate fingers in a well-upholstered conference room. Their victims had caught them with their pants down. 'These people are animals,' I shouted. 'How dare they try to justify breaking into the homes of the poor and stealing their possessions!' They dropped their biscuits and left. But the press were not disappointed. We immediately occupied their vacant seats and held our own impromptu conference. It was our first and last in such plush surroundings.

Again I must emphasise how our campaign came into conflict with the law. The philosopher Edmund Burke said that bad laws are the worst sort of tyranny. So breaking a bad law is like a slave breaking his bonds. When your chains are invisible it's sometimes harder to throw them off. If you believe law is a good thing, a neutral instrument serving all the people, then you are psychologically shackled.

Initially our opponents argued that the law must be obeyed because breaking it led to anarchy. It really annoyed them when, with the help of a couple of sympathetic lawyers, we turned the law against them! It was like wounding the enemy with his own sword.

It all began in Stranraer. A young solicitor called Gordon Dangerfield discovered that bad laws, like tyrants, can also be incompetent. I remembered Gordon from the Labour Party Young Socialists when I was at university. We did not always see eye to eye on political matters. He claims he won his place on the Scottish executive because Militant forgot to put up a candidate. Gordon inherited a real class anger from his grandfathers who were both shop stewards – one, from Bridgeton, was a pattern maker in the shipyards, the other, from Anderston, an electrical engineer.

Gordon was a trainee solicitor in Greenock when the miners' strike brought his politics into focus. He saw how the state used the whole apparatus of law and order to break a group of workers, whether on the picket line or in their pockets, by freezing their union's money and denying benefit to their families.

He could do little about this as a lawyer until the day a middle-aged man called Tom Ronald walked through his door. Tom lived by himself on income support in one of the poorer areas of Stranraer. He had just been poinded for not registering for the Poll Tax. 'Here's my case,' he said. 'See what you can get out of it. They can do what they like to me, I'm not paying.'

Gordon was a criminal lawyer and this was a civil matter. Tom had approached him because he was the Prospective Parliamentary Labour Candidate for Galloway and Upper Nithsdale. More importantly, he had spoken out for non-payment. Gordon leapt at the chance to take up the case – for nothing, because Tom was not entitled to legal aid.

'Up until then I really could not use all my skills in the service of what I believed,' said Gordon. 'Here at last was something I could do. I could offer a legal training 99% of people didn't have. It's been the most satisfying work of my career to date.'

Gordon appealed against the poinding, arguing Mr Ronald's three-piece suite was exempt because it was reasonably required for the use of the debtor. Dumfries and Galloway Regional Council said a single man did not reasonably require a three-piece suite. One chair was enough. Even the sheriff, who was not noted for his liberal views, threw out that one. Gordon then successfully argued the poinding was invalid because the value of the remaining goods poinded would not meet the debt.

After that, Gordon offered the federation his services. There was a lot of scope for the law to be challenged. The Abolition of Domestic Rates Scotland Act contradicted the Debtors Scotland Act which came out in the same year, 1987. The first piece of legislation was designed to hammer the poor. The second was the brainchild of the Scottish Law Commission, a fairly liberal body who wanted to make Scotland's debt-recovery procedures a little more humane.

The Debtors Act established all sorts of rules about how to conduct a poinding. Lots of items were exempt: clothes, toys, anything needed for work, heaters, essential furniture, anything needed for storage, including wardrobes. Of course, everything on HP or hire was out, which covered most televisions and videos.

I remember rhyming off this list at a meeting in Drumchapel which was crowded with people clutching sheriff's letters. A wee voice at the back shouted: 'Well, there's bugger all in my house they can take!' The woman was typical – the whole purpose of the Debtors Act was to stop the sheriffs hitting people who had nothing. Gordon often says the local authorities could have used this Act to justify not pursuing the poor for the poll tax. They never did. They wanted the money and lacked the bottle.

Gordon once nullified every one of Dumfries and Galloway's warrants after a woman taperecorded a poinding of her house. Her cassette was full of comments like: 'On you go and watch Playbus, I've got to attend to these gentlemen.' But after dealing with the kids, Mrs Rankin could be heard saying: 'Now why does this piece of paper say petition when it's supposed to be a warrant?' Gordon was playing the tape in the car and nearly drove off the road. The document was totally illegal. The council hired Gerry Marr, an advocate who had written books on this kind of thing, which is called diligence. But for all Marr's eloquence, Gordon won the day. Sheriff Smith said the petition was hopelessly incompetent. All eighty-six poindings carried out by the region were invalid – along with every previous benefit deduction and wage arrestment, 5000 in all.

Lots of these cases made the legal journals. In fact, Gordon never lost a poinding appeal. He once got a guy's car taken off the schedule on the grounds that being in the driveway, it did not come under household contents. No legal aid was given for any of these cases and Gordon did all the work for nothing.

He trained our activists to represent victims in court and wrote a briefing paper. It contained sample court forms applying for the release of poinded articles. These were in the name of Margaret

Thatcher, a retired politician of 10 Dulwich Street, Stranraer. Mrs Thatcher was applying for the release of a number of poinded articles, including a Hitachi television, a Panasonic Genius microwave oven, a sideboard (natural pine) and a boxed set of the works of Karl Marx.

The sideboard (natural pine) was reasonably required for storing crockery. The Panasonic Genius microwave oven was essential because Mrs Thatcher was a busy single parent whose children came home at different times and ate at short notice. The television was exempt because it was a vital educational item for her children as well as the only available entertainment in a rural area. The boxed set of Karl Marx was reasonably required by the debtor in her business. She earns a modest income by writing political articles for newspapers and journals. She often requires to make reference to the works of Karl Marx in the course of her writing.

Lots of ordinary people became Perry Masons thanks to Gordon's briefing. Hundreds of victims had their goods released by our people. They included Betty Cunningham, the Bellshill woman.

Kenny McGuigan, a former policeman from Airdrie, organised the Coatbridge Anti-Poll Tax Union along with Margaret Macy. He found himself being led to the cells by one of his old workmates after a passionate outburst on behalf of a woman he was representing. She had been traumatised when she called him. There was a young baby in the house and they had poinded the unit where the mother kept nappies and children's clothes. The father had a collection of 200 video tapes which he built up over the years. These were all valued at £50. Kenny managed to release most items but snapped when the sheriff refused to exempt a stereo which belonged to someone else. The old boy was basically calling the family liars.

Kenny is a big imposing guy who really cares about the people he is trying to help. A few of them lived in his housing scheme, Craigneuk, which was once a pit village. All the houses still have fireplaces and he says some people have burned their garden fences and bedroom doors to keep warm in the winter.

He also hates sheriff officers. When Kenny was about ten he came home early from school one day to collect his football boots. 'My mum was in an awful state. My dad wasn't at work. And there were these two men in the house. Really imposing men with very shiny shoes. Apparently my mum had taken a part-time job to earn extra money and there was a misunderstanding over the amount of tax owed. These sheriff officers were round demanding documentation. She was frantic and all the drawers were pulled out, the contents spilled over the carpet. People really were terrified of them.' Maybe all this was on Kenny's mind when he turned on the sheriff.

'How dare you question the integrity of these people!' he said. 'They have no previous convictions. They are honest people who have been victimised and hounded.'

The sheriff began to move his wig around. He warned Kenny to be quiet or he'd be arrested for contempt of court. But Kenny was in mid flow: 'You are a corrupt old man! A protector of a regime that allows this to go on daily.'

The police were called and Kenny was led to the cells. The entire public gallery was on his side. Supportive cheers accompanied his exit. The sheriff knew he'd cause an outcry if he took the matter any further. Kenny was released without charge after a few hours.

For all our successes, we have kept the court work in perspective. It embarrassed the authorities. It gave people practical help. It also clogged up the collection process, which was all to the good. But Gordon Dangerfield himself stressed the political struggle was more important. Once you enter a court, you are allowing matters to be decided by experts and so shutting the doors on the people outside.

Allowing courts alone to decide issues affecting workers is often the death knell of a campaign. Political issues get side tracked. Ultimately it's more important to get a hundred people outside a house to stop a poinding than to challenge it legally after the event. Just like it's important for workers to occupy factories and go on strike rather than trusting solely in the legal process which steals away the time, and their jobs. Too many trade union leaders allow disputes to be side-tracked into hostile courts.

7   They shall not pass

There are certain types of cars it is particularly foolhardy to drive into parts of Glasgow and Lanarkshire. Vauxhall Carltons and Peugeot 405s often end up with deflated tyres and eggs scrambled on the windscreen. One Peugeot owner went for a pub lunch in Bellshill and returned to find his vehicle treated to a generous helping of chips with tomato ketchup.

Porsches might provoke resentment. Citroën 2CVs might inspire hilarity. But Carltons and Peugeot 405s generate a very specific contempt. They are the fleet cars used by several firms of sheriff officers.

When a woman in Craigneuk, Airdrie ran up catalogue debts recently the sheriff officers could not get near her house. Angry neighbours recognised their car and spontaneously assembled to send them packing.

Women in Lanarkshire towns keep lists of vehicle registration numbers in their kitchens. The bush telegraph begins to sing if the cars are spotted. Friends and neighbours are called. Children on bikes run to the families who don't have phones. Before long a crowd has assembled to welcome the sheriffs. Ann Curran in Bellshill has been known to chase cars along the street and corner them at traffic lights. 'See that! That's just a communist agitator!' the sheriff once shouted at her in Holytown. 'They threw away the wrong bit when you were born, ' she replied.

Ann, a single parent in her thirties, is the secretary of the Bellshill Anti-Poll Tax Union. Sheriffs' officers put their feet on the gas pedal when they see her coming. Women like Ann spent five days a week standing outside houses threatened with poindings at the height of the campaign. The county has the biggest phone tree in Scotland. If someone in Bellshill gets notice of a poinding, they call Ann, who calls all her sisters plus Ian who calls Mary who calls Betty and Dave . . . and so it goes on till you have a picket. Since 1990 the Scottish Anti-Poll Tax Federation has prevented more than 4,000 homes being poinded in this way.

Ann's mother, Agnes Allan, is also fearless. She had a growth removed from her brain but was stopping poindings a few weeks after the operation. Disability was turned into defence in Holytown, in the middle of Lanarkshire's deindustrialised sprawl. A guy blocked the sheriffs' path with his wheelchair giving the people inside the house time to pass the television out of the window and hide it in next door's dustbin.

Attempted poindings rallied people who didn't go to the initial meetings and demonstrations. Mary McQuaid, from Birkenshaw in Lanarkshire, was a part-time worker in a biscuit factory then a busy mother with little time for politics. But when her husband handed her money to pay the poll tax she bought shoes for their daughter, Bernadette. She never told him.

Once, a neighbour asked Mary to help prevent the poinding of a local single parent. When she arrived at 7am, a girl called Fiona Pupkiss was hanging posters from lampposts down the street. Fiona's partner is Ian McDonald, the Militant organiser for Lanarkshire. The three became friends and Mary spent thousands of hours camped outside houses all over Lanarkshire – Viewpark,

Preparing to stop the warrant sale in Turnbull Street, Glasgow (1/10/1991)
(Courtesy of the *Rutherglen Informer*)

Celebrating the end of the poll tax, George Square, Glasgow (22/3/1991)
(Courtesy of the *Evening Times*)

The first press conference from jail: prisoner 2/92 speaks out.

Tommy Sheridan addresses friends and neighbours in
Pollok, Glasgow (1/7/1992)

Bothwell, Motherwell, Uddingston, Holytown, Cambuslang, Shotts, Wishaw – all towns devastated by the murder of the steel industry.

Sometimes poindings were like gala days, with barbecues in summer and rolls and sausage in winter. Soup was compulsory. Some pots became legendary, like the broth made by a Cambuslang man who emptied in a bottle of whisky after his wife instructed him to add a glass of wine. Everybody comes with a loaf, cheese or ham to help feed the masses. Local shops donated food, as did the mobile grocers who supply the villages in Lanarkshire or the big housing schemes. In winter we made a brazier from an oil drum and the local coalman often threw us a sack of fuel.

The sheriffs can call at any time during daylight hours: we usually covered a poinding from 8am to 8pm. Even if you wear three pairs of socks and giant moon boots, the cold gets you in the end. Mary McQuaid remembers a makeshift polythene tent in a Bellshill garden collapsing on top of her during torrential rain. Betty Curry, from Cambuslang, will never forget the winter day when she collapsed with exhaustion. The snow was four inches thick. Betty, a woman in her fifties, stood outside a house for fourteen hours while the icy blast from the field opposite seeped through her body.

Lanarkshire seemed to be targeted for action by the sheriff officers because it is a network of urban villages. Maybe they thought we would find it hard to organise. They made a big mistake. Lanarkshire's anything but parochial. The National Unemployed Workers' Union were strong there in the 1920s when they had Hunger Marches through the mining villages. They had a branch which used to meet in Hastie's farm hut in Blantyre, an old mill town best known as the birthplace of David Livingstone. Blantyre had a Communist councillor at one point.

Sixty years later, Terry Donnelly, a research chemist who was secretary of Blantyre Anti-Poll Tax Union, divided the town into nine areas. When Terry got a call about a poinding in Devlin Grove one Sunday night, he'd gathered fifty people outside the house by the following morning.

One of Hamilton Anti-Poll Tax Union's first fundraising efforts was an answering machine for the secretary, Stevie Smellie. Places like Lesmahagow, Coalburn, Rigside and Cumnock, former mining villages many miles from Glasgow, would phone him for squads of Poll Tax Busters.

Cambuslang was the worst hit town. Rutherford and McPherson attempted to carry out 1500 poindings there over eighteen months. Maybe they thought they could stretch us. But Cambuslang responded by building the strongest anti-poll tax union in Britain. It was once the largest village in Scotland, and remains a close community even though it now falls within Glasgow city boundries. Mining was the main industry in the nineteenth century but by the Second World War the pits were in decline. Men still went to work in mines like Blantyreferme No 3 at Newton but most went to the steel foundries like Colville's Clydebridge works. Others worked in metal-bashing jobs at places like the Clyde Nail Company.

Cambuslang has changed. There are now no mines and no steelworks. In Halfway, below where the Loanhead pit used to be, fifty per cent of the school children receive clothing grant because their parents are on Income Support. On the Circuit estate that figure rises to almost eighty per cent.

Some things have not changed – like the radicalism of Davie and Betty Curry. Both are stalwarts of the campaign, along with John and Jean Evans. Davie was a machine tool storeman in Rolls Royce before moving to Cambuslang. He and Betty were involved in community politics. They ran a food co-operative and unemployed workers' centre in Cambuslang but quickly became disillusioned when the Labour Party authorities told them to remove the words 'Jobs, Peace and Socialism' from their banner.

The first person poinded in Cambuslang was a van driver called Barry Wilson. He couldn't take the day off work and trusted Betty and Davie to organise the crowd. Davie used methods he's employed for every poinding since that day. He went round the schemes with a loudhailer, repeating the address where the sheriff officers were due. The local ice cream van displayed posters so customers could read the time and dates of poinding while waiting for their double nougat.

When Davie arrived at 7 am no one was around. Then locals appeared from doorways and side streets. Dozens of young people filled the street. That's when the Currys first met George and Betty Lindsay who then became heavily involved in the Cambuslang anti-poll tax union. George is a soft-spoken guy who worked in the Clydebridge Steelworks for over twenty-nine years. He loaded the steel into a furnace which brought it up to temperature before it was rolled into slab form. They gauged the temperature of the white hot metal with their naked eye. You could always tell the guys who worked there because they had no eyelashes.

George was made redundant in 1977. For years he was involved in the tenants' association, football clubs and summer playschemes. He spent summer days taking local kids down to Prestwick airport to watch the planes. He sees the anti-poll tax union as an extension of his community activities.

Working-class activists like Dave and Betty Curry, George Lindsay, Mary McQuaid and Ann Curran know what it's like to struggle on a budget. But even they were shocked by the living conditions of some families who called them for help. Ann remembers a young mother who *borrowed* a three-piece suite for the anti-poll tax people coming to see her. The house was just bare boards and she had got hold of a secondhand carpet for our people arriving.

Dave Curry has reassured hundreds of people being threatened by the sheriffs in Cambuslang. But one case stays with him: 'There was a young lassie I just couldnae calm down. She kept greetin' cause of the letter. She couldn't afford to turn on her heaters or give the weans baths, she was payin' that much in hire purchase for their claes. I said, 'C'mon, they're only sheriff officers, they're only guys wi suits on . . .' But she was terrified. The thing was, she didn't even have anything for them to take.'

The worst case Betty came across was an elderly couple in a Hamilton tenement: 'You sat on the settee and your backside was hitting the floor. She hadnae two cups in the hoose. There was a black-and-white telly and a wee coffee table held up, believe it or not, wi books. It only had three legs on . . .'

While villages in Lanarkshire were poinded, housing schemes in the big cities were hardly touched. Easterhouse, with its thirteen Anti-Poll Tax Unions, has never been threatened with a poinding. Pollok was also left unmolested. By this time we had recruited activists all over the constituency. One was Matt Smith, a local character who describes himself as once being a 'cardboard gangster'. He's now in his thirties with a kid. But he used to drink cheap wine down by the shops in South Nitshill and spent a bit of time in jail. He got involved in Militant through the anti-poll tax union and was eventually addressing crowds of 250 about sheriffs' letters. So many people gathered outside the shops on one occasion that Matt had to beg some crates from the milkman so he could be seen.

Attempted poindings for non-payment began in dribs and drabs at the beginning of 1990. The first concerted effort in a big housing scheme was in Foxbar, Paisley, in May. We had told the papers about our flying squads of poll-tax busters. Now we had to prove ourselves. One hundred federation members joined local people in blocking the streets leading into Foxbar.

We had four checkpoints asking drivers their business. Two women were threatened with poindings and we turned away the sheriff officers from both houses. The police attempted to escort them in, but they didn't pass us. I remember being really impressed with the discipline of our pickets. It would become our trademark. The press made a meal of our road blocks. They claimed we had created no go areas for members of the public going about their lawful business. We didn't think sheriff officers were doing moral or lawful business. Big exercises like Foxbar were easier to organise when we moved into our new premises in June 1990. It was in London Road, in the Barras and cost £325 a month to rent. But it gave us access to crowds of working-class people who came to the market at weekends. It had been a butcher's shop and needed new fittings.

Charlie Chuckles, the fancy dress shop across the street, came to our rescue by donating a big glass counter. Having the shop increased our workload. It meant people knew where to come for help and this was always given by volunteers like Ann Campbell, Agnes Brown, Raymond Kelly, Marion McNally, Brian Lewis, and Hannah McArthur. Hannah remembers an old man appearing on the doorstep who said, 'I wish I had some money to give you but I've nothing'. Then he dropped penny caramels into everyone's hands!

The flying squads were kept busy all year. But it was not until November 1990 that they tried to hit another housing scheme. Ann Lynch, secretary of the Drumchapel Anti-Poll Tax Union, came home one night to find a neighbour waiting on her doorstep. The woman's daughter in nearby Cally Avenue was being poinded. She was in a real state. Anne visited Cally Avenue and discovered seven people in the same position. All were terrified their children's things would be taken, although it's illegal to do so.

Ann had two days to organise. She hand wrote a poster saying 'Come and Defend Your Neighbour!' which she stuck up in the bookies, the post office and the pub. Then she phoned every anti-poll tax union in Glasgow.

This was the first Glasgow housing scheme to be targeted. 'I was really anxious, terrified that I might break the chain!' said Ann.

On the morning of the poinding, we put up our banners in the pitch darkness and the pouring rain. Nearly every window in the street had a poster. But it was all quiet. Then vehicles arrived from different APTUs, and students' unions. Labourers from Dumbarton appeared in their working gear. We were able to put about thirty people outside each close.

It was Drumchapel's busiest day because the market was at the shopping centre. Women appeared at different stages with bags of messages. One of the neighbours made her own sandwich board telling the rottweilers where to go.

Ann said it was the young ones who stopped it. We were standing around and almost didn't notice the car draw into the street. Someone shouted, 'There's the sheriff officers!' and it all happened

quickly. Two young boys jumped on the bonnet. The car swerved
and ran over Corinne Dowd's foot. Then it reversed really fast and
speeded out of the scheme.

It was eleven in the morning and Cally Avenue was bursting at
the seams. School kids had come along to celebrate beating the
sheriffs. Then two cops appeared and spoke to Ann. They said the
sheriff officers had been down at the station asking for an escort into
the houses: 'But we told them we wouldn't touch it. It's a civil
matter as far as we're concerned. We're here for real crime.'

There were loads of occasions when cars screeched away the
minute they saw us. Often they never turned up, they simply didn't
have the manpower. By midday we would usually go to their offices
and get a letter saying the poinding was cancelled. But you always
had a few people at the threatened house just in case.

During the Drumchapel picket, the boys spotted two guys with
short hair, briefcases and suits going up a close. They cornered them
and chased them down the street. One of the brief cases opened up
and all these big books which looked like bibles fell out. It turned
out they were Mormons!

Most poindings were attempted on poor people. But they also
tried to make examples of public figures who supported the campaign. Dick Douglas was the most serious case. They actually broke
into his home in Fife. They also tried to poind Jim McVicar, a
Glasgow Militant councillor, who was still in the Labour Party at
that time.

Early in 1991 I got home from a meeting one night and began
playing the usual dozen or so messages on my ansaphone. Three
increasingly frantic calls from George Galloway, the Labour MP for
Glasgow Hillhead, stood out. The first was reasonably calm – of the
'Comrade, I need you to phone me' variety. A couple of beeps later
it was 'Comrade, it's George again . . . see if you can phone me, will
you.' The final one abandoned any pretence at being cool. 'Hey
Tommy! Can you phone me as soon as possible.'

When I caught him later on that night it turned out he was on
his way to the Labour Party Conference when he discovered there

was to be a poinding at his house the next day. George is in an unhealthy environment down at the Commons. But I can't dislike him the way I dislike most MPs. He's a maverick. George was still supporting the non-payment campaign, so it was important that we supported him.

Many commentators questioned our strategy of encouraging middle-class people, as well as the poor, not to pay. But the larger the shield, the better the protection. While they were attempting to enter a house like George Galloway's, they obviously weren't entering the home of an old-age pensioner or single parent.

Despite the short notice, we got 200 people to protect George's wee flat down beside the Mitchell Library. Most of the young ones hadn't been in that part of the city before. It was a simple flat. But I couldn't help noticing the contrast between the nearby leafy Georgian terraces and the youth from Pollok, blasting the place with their rave music and munching bacon rolls and drinking coffee.

After we saw off the sheriffs, George made a speech in front of the TV cameras thanking everyone for coming. 'When I got this letter I did what everyone else should do – I called Tommy Sheridan.' Given that I was the *bête noire* of the Labour Party at the time, it was quite a brave speech.

We didn't get much television coverage for poindings. Helping George showed the whole of Scotland our strength. Sometimes people who did not know what we could do were willing to take desperate measures to ward off the debt collectors.

At the very beginning of the defence campaign, Jack Harvey gave a rousing speech about poindings in the basement of a block of flats in a particularly notorious part of Glasgow. After the meeting a guy with a pit bull-dog on a string approached him. His face was slightly lopsided. He had scars dating back to the time of the Krays. Jack could see uneasy people backing away from this guy through the audience. He was obviously notorious. 'I hear what you're saying, big man,' snarled the bloke with the dog. 'Here's a wee bit of advice. See these sheriff officers, if you get any bother fae them, call this number.' He put a friendly arm round Jack's shoulder and said under his breath: 'Your name won't be mentioned, pal.'

We accept all offers of help. Jack didn't think it wise to get into an argument. But he threw the paper in the bin when he got home. By calling the Anti-Poll Tax Federation on 041 552 1179 you could get your own protection squad, with no strings attached. You don't need a sawn-off shotgun when there's thirty angry people blocking your front door.

When they couldn't set the sheriffs on the poor, Labour turned to the sharp-toothed Tory bureaucracy. Duplicity is a vice people have almost come to expect of their politicians. Saying one thing and doing another is par for the parliamentary course. Weasel words usually paper over the contradictions. But the Labour establishment in Scotland hold their voters in such contempt they hardly bother to hide their hypocrisy.

I've already referred to Strathclyde's finance convenor, John Mullin. That very same day, the 4th of July 1990, he revealed that the council – on its own initiative – had sent the names of 50,000 non payers to the social security offices. Claimants would have the tax directly deducted from their income support. At the time of writing (1993), 128,000 people have had their benefits arrested. We are talking here about the poorest people in the poorest area in Western Europe. In 1990 a fifth of Strathclyde's entire population depended on benefit. In Glasgow, that rose to almost one in three. But instead of the weak being attacked in the last resort, they were the first to be hit.

Everyone on benefit was supposed to pay twenty per cent of the Poll Tax. The region was allowed to deduct five per cent off their Giro. If an MP lost five per cent of his income he'd have to part with a couple of thousand pounds and sacrifice a luxurious family holiday. If a person on benefit lost five per cent of her income she'd have to part with £2.30 a week and sacrifice a basic family meal.

We drew up a shopping list: two pints of milk, a loaf of bread, a tin of beans or half a pound of cheap sausages. Most people can't even make their benefit last a fortnight, even without deductions.

Those last few days are spent borrowing from relatives. In 1992, a study by the National Children's Homes identified 69,850 Scottish families who said their child had not had enough to eat at some time in the past month. Almost as many parents in the survey – 66,040 – said they had gone without food in order to ensure their children were properly fed.

Our first line of attack was to appeal against the deductions. Every appeal cost the authorities £120 so we made the tax more uneconomic to collect even if we lost. The appeals were always on technical grounds. Two welfare rights officers, Frank Dawson and Chris Orr, discovered a loophole in the process and trained our supporters, particularly Ann Campbell and my mother Alice, to represent claimants at tribunals. We ran them ragged. Lots of people got their money back until the government closed the loop hole.

Around this time I officially met Jean McFadden, who was then President of the Labour-dominated Convention of Scottish Local Authorities. I remember being struck by her lack of knowledge about basic things like the level of income support. She was cool and aloof and said the law dictated they must use every possible means of recovery. But no government minister forced Labour councils to deduct benefit. It was their own idea.

Anyway, we suggested they take a typical single parent family living on the breadline and refuse to deduct their benefit. They could cite the principle enshrined in the Debtor's Scotland Act that there is no point in pursuing a debtor if the cost of collection outstrips the amount of money recovered. 'Force the government to take you to court,' we said. 'Even if you lose you'll be able to highlight the callousness of the system.'

But they did not have the moral backbone to take even this action. In fact, the larger the Labour majority, the more congealed were their spines. Secret statistics passed to us in 1990 showed Grampian Region had deducted one person's benefit. Tayside had docked twenty-nine claimants, Lothian sixty-seven and Central 2215. But Strathclyde, that bastion of socialism, had blasted the benefits of 13,950 people.

Bland statistics are easily ignored. It is more difficult when people are invoked. Jack Harvey decided to confront John Mullin with the consequences of his actions when he took a bunch of people into his local surgery. Jack said the women began steaming into him. John began shaking and perspiring: 'I can't speak to you now. I have an appointment. Do you hear? I have an appointment at 2 o'clock.'

It was a Saturday morning and these women were saying: 'John, you are going nowhere until you state categorically that you are opposed to this tax and any attempts to withdraw money from people who can't afford it.'

'I agree! I agree!' he said. He was confused, shuffling papers and dropping things. Quite unable to cope. Beads of sweat glistened on his forehead. He just kept gibbering: 'I can't miss my appointment!'

We later discovered the nature of his very important 2 pm appointment. He was spotted at Parkhead that afternoon, hiding among the crowd in the Celtic end.

Meeting Jean McFadden behind the scenes was ineffectual. Watching John Mullin squirm was enjoyable, but ultimately ineffectual. We needed a big gesture to draw attention to the benefits robbery, so we planned our most ambitious raid to date. We would occupy the Scottish Office in Edinburgh. It would hammer home the political point about the Tories being responsible for this burden on the poor and appeal to popular feeling which views the building as a kind of colonial outpost.

We planned to climb on to the roof. The aerial press photographs were pre-printed in our imaginations. We'd stay a week, waving to our assembled supporters while horrifying the mandarins and infuriating their masters. Our burly postmen were to be pressed into service again. And we even had an insider who'd explained the route up to the roof. How could we fail?

We travelled to Edinburgh at midnight, equipped with sleeping bags, thermos flasks, card games and enough food to last a fortnight. We assembled in a hall around 2 am, sending out reconnaissance teams at 4 am. There was no way we could have got in the place. It was completely surrounded by police. For the next 18 hours we stayed in Edinburgh looking for some opportunity to gain access. But to no avail.

How did they know? In a bizarre twist all our activities at that time were being shadowed by an independent film crew under the guidance of Malcolm Wilson, a former Scottish Television journalist. They may have been guilty of careless talk. More likely our phones were tapped. Press reports around this time told of death threats against sheriff officers: complete nonsense, of course. But these hoax calls allowed the state to sanction the telephone surveillance of myself and others in the federation. It should not surprise anyone. I suppose at that time we were the biggest threat to the Government. We headed back to Glasgow in low spirits. Weeks of eating tinned spaghetti stretched before us. Then some bright spark had an idea. Why not occupy the Tory Party HQ in Glasgow? We could make the same point. It meant breaking in, of course, but we were in a nothing-more-to-lose-mood. We voted 40/20 in favour of this somewhat reckless action. We split up when we got into Glasgow's Buchanan Street Station. It was the middle of the night and each group was instructed to head for the dark lane beside the Victorian office block where the Tories leased rooms.

Someone borrowed a mallet from a nearby building site which cracked the door open with little effort. Our people filed in from the lane and headed upstairs like worker ants. The Tories were on the fourth floor. It was pitch black, but in the darkness something white and gleaming caught my eye. A big delivery of photocopying paper was sitting at the bottom of the stairs. We began jamming the packets of paper between the stair and the main door, effectively barricading ourselves in. Then I bounded upstairs.

I'd passed the 25th in line when I heard this loud, panicking voice from the top floor: 'They've moved! Get Back Down! Get Back Down!' But by this time our A4 barricade was almost complete. We were tumbling over each other in the dark, trying to get the paper away from the door. Imagine sixty anti-poll tax people getting arrested for breaking and entering what was now some nondescript office selling insurance or whatever? I'd have some explaining to do.

Despite shouts of panic and hopelessly-stifled laughter, we managed to disperse before any police appeared.

Among the paraphernalia we took to Edinburgh for the thwarted Scottish Office raid was a big banner saying BENEFIT ARRESTMENTS = FORCED HUNGER. We continued to discuss how best to highlight these disgusting deductions. How better to illustrate the point than holding a hunger strike in the middle of Glasgow?

Not everyone agreed. Big Jack thought it was stupid for already badly-fed people to starve for a full seven days. But that was just the point. The undernourished were the ones suffering; it was their plight we wanted to highlight.

It was June 1990. Apart from myself there was Keith Baldassara, Hugh Carroll, Tam McGee, Alan McCombes, Paul Couchman, Andy Lynch and Linda Thompson from Castlemilk who celebrated her twenty-first birthday during the hunger strike.

Jack's fears that we'd flake out were almost realised before we began. We figured we should eat less and less in the run up to the fast, so we wouldn't notice the hunger pangs. Fortunately I had the savvy to call John Dale, a militant doctor from Derbyshire. 'That's the *last* thing you should do,' said the horrified doc. 'Cram in as much food as you can before day one.' He strongly suggested we take multi-vitamins and drink Rehydrat, a green powder you dilute with water when you have diarrhoea. These contain salts and minerals. At first they tasted like iron filings with added saccharine. After a few days they were nectar.

Permission to camp in George Square was never going to be forthcoming. So we just turned up and began pitching tents. The polis on duty that day was fizzin'. I took him aside for a long involved conversation about how we fully expected the action to be approved by the parks boss that afternoon. Councillor John Maclean was bringing it up at committee. I even produced his glowing letter of recommendation from the notable councillor. By the time the constable returned with a po-faced Director of Parks and Recreation, a little tent city had sprung up in Glasgow's most sober civic space. In fact, a couple of French students saw us and decided to set up camp as well.

Hunger faded after the first two days, though cravings returned at the end of the week. Mornings were the worst. That's when the girl from Gregg's bakery wheeled a big trolley across the square bound for some boardroom. It was brimming with cakes, donuts with the sugar still hot, fresh scones, creamy meringues and empire biscuits. It was unbearable. We'd beg her to take a different route, but she couldn't.

Even the Salvation Army put temptation in our way. They have a soup kitchen for the homeless each night in the square. A big bag of soft white rolls was sent to us one night which we returned, of course. You saw a different side of the city after dark when the skippers came out. There are more homeless people in Glasgow than anywhere else in Scotland. In 1991 the district council's housing department had 8,500 homeless applicants – one in every three aged between eighteen and twenty-four.

Homeless people would come over to the tents and chat. Keith remembers one guy in a shabby suit and a Crombie with worn cuffs. He looked like an underworld caricature. But instead of being a shadowy figure, he was a shadow of his former self. He'd recite poetry he'd written. All the people he'd ever known were turned into verse: his old teachers, his criminal friends, the turn-key in the jail.

On Friday and Saturday night we got no sleep at all. People coming back from the dancing meant the place was still jumping at dawn. George Square is the departure point for the late-night buses back to the schemes. Because we were the official European City of Culture, the pubs were allowed to open till 4 am. It's a pity we didn't repeat a hunger strike three years later when the licensing board imposed a stupid and unnecessary curfew on the city. Then we could have got our heads down before midnight as the place has become so dead. Back in 1990 there was something wild and unreal about it. Thirty women from a hen night formed a chain and danced a conga round the square singing: 'We're No Payin' the Poll Tax! Na, Na, Na, Na!'

Sometimes we had to amuse ourselves. It was World Cup year and we watched Scotland play on a wee portable telly rigged up to a car battery.

Volunteers ran a twenty-four hour stall outside the tents to collect signatures for a petition against benefit deductions and to raise money for the campaign. By the end of the week, 15,000 people had signed and donated the remarkable amount of £2000. The boys from the Special Unit in Barlinnie Prison sent us a sculpture. The unit is famous around the world for giving life prisoners their self-respect and helping them develop into worthwhile human beings. The sculpture was a stooped woman with a heavy load on her back – 'The Burden Of The Poll Tax.' It was made by John Steele, then a prisoner. He wanted us to have it.

There were a few hairy moments. On Saturday a group of fascists from the British National Party surrounded the stall shouting 'Where's Sheridan, we're going to get him!' All the hunger strikers, including myself, were quite weak. The only other people there were the older women on the stall. This turned out to be an advantage. My mother grabbed the megaphone and shouted; 'I'm Sheridan, are you coming to get me?' They looked very sheepish. Then she shouted to the Glasgow crowd: 'These people are fascists!' At that the scumbags ran. This wasn't the first or last time that the vermin from the BNP attacked our campaign. They have harassed our volunteers several times and even threatened the older women with physical violence. Their empty and cowardly threats only took place when they were team-handed and our volunteers were alone.

This incident exposed our vulnerability. Gangs of young people from all over Glasgow travelled to George Square that night – suitably equipped – in case the BNP returned. We had a big football match. There must have been twenty to a side. Strangers were joining in or spectating, as we fired the ball over the upturned benches we'd made into goals. I wish my feet had been as light as my head felt that night.

At last the fast ended on a wet, Wednesday morning. Gregg's sent the same girl out with a trolley of bridies, pies and cakes – this time just for us. Carol Cooper and the Jeelie Piece Club from Castlemilk arrived with a big pot of soup. It had been our intention to march with our 250 supporters who turned up. But we were so exhausted and the weather was so unforgiving, that we just went home after making speeches and taking the tents down. I celebrated with a beef curry and slept for twelve hours.

That Friday Babbity Bowster's pub laid on a big meal and a drink. Then it was up to the Special Unit to return John Steele's statue. The Unit also laid on food but by this time we realised how much our stomachs had shrunk. Most people on the hunger strike lost between 10 – 12lbs.

Despite this goodwill, our stunt received little publicity. Lots of the 15,000 punters who signed our petition said: Why haven't we seen this on telly?

We all know the media is easily bored by the poor. But a good story is a good story. I cannot think of any other occasion in modern British politics when people have publicly fasted for a week. The *Scotsman*, the *Herald*, and the Glasgow *Evening Times* came along when George Galloway and the pop singer, Pat Kane, joined us for twenty-four hours. But the electronic media completely blanked us.

Radio Clyde turned up in the square one day to cover a council press call. I asked why this stage-managed event merited coverage while an unprecedented hunger strike was ignored. They mumbled excuses and scurried off.

If the radio and television journalists had covered the story Labour authorities would have to justify deducting money from people struggling to feed their kids. No one can justify that. So perhaps they didn't want to ask the awkward question. The Scottish media is often praised for refusing to be the government's poodle. This is right – they are different from the Tory-supporting rags down south. But the downside of this is their unquestioning backing of the Scottish Labour establishment.

I learned early on not to give stories to specialist political correspondents. Printing something favourable about us might cause their titbits from Donald Dewar and Brian Wilson to dry up. They just weren't interested. General reporters were better. Some were sympathetic and did their best to treat the Federation with fairness. But they were often working to an agenda dictated by their news editor who asks 'Who are these anti-poll tax people? Why should we give them free publicity?'

Why should they? Well, many journalists are happy handing out free publicity to public relations consultants hired to promote the interests of big firms. You can almost smell the poached salmon buffet in stories which try to inject a spark of life into the opening of a new hotel or the launch of British Cognac Week. This isn't news. At best, it's information. At worst, it's cheap advertising.

Journalists will cover the most inane stories if someone deemed important is on site. John Smith opening a railway station, the Lord Provost planting a tree – both make the telly. We were a bunch of nobodies from the schemes. But we represented another 100,000 nobodies – the seven out of ten Glasgow council tenants who were officially in poverty in 1990. They didn't have company Visa cards to take the press for weird-sounding meals of crayfish bisque with créme brûlée to follow. The people we represented couldn't provide a spread of filter coffee and biscuits at the Albany Hotel to get their point across. We were all they had – a bunch of representative nobodies who starved themselves to highlight suffering. It wasn't enough.

What news values were the media working to? Every good journalist knows news is something somebody doesn't want publicised. Judged by that criteria, our hunger strike was more newsworthy than a whole year of irrelevant VIPs opening new shopping developments. The one exception was the Glasgow *Evening Times* which broke the silence on numerous occasions.

The hunger strike came halfway through the most testing year of the campaign. In March 1990, we predicted the tax and its instigator would be effectively dead within a year. Our 'Glasgow: City Of Defiance' poster featured a Jim Blair cartoon of Thatcher sitting in front of a huge wave saying Mass Non-Payment. Her arms were outstretched to halt the wall of water. In November it finally crashed to the shore and swept her away. A million and a quarter people in Scotland had stopped paying.

Thatcher was deposed before her hated tax. We were counting the days until celebration time. Michael Heseltine featured the poll tax prominently while campaigning against her leadership. It was funny to discover towards the end of 1990 all these ex-cabinet ministers who said they'd never supported the community charge. We were making jokes like, 'How did they ever get it through cabinet!'

We scented victory yet our English supporters by this time were being sent to jail. We had mounted the People's March Against the Poll Tax (organised by former soldier Gerry McGuire) from Scotland to London that year to demonstrate the solidarity of non-payers north and south of the border. Debtors can be put inside in England, unlike Scotland. This caused a big debate in Militant at the time. There were discussions about whether Militants in union positions, who could be sacked for being sent to jail, should pay the tax to keep the jobs and union posts.

Andy Walsh's case caused a lot of concern. He worked for a bank and was on the executive of Bifu, the Banking and Finance Union. Clauses in his contract of employment indicated he could lose his job if successfully prosecuted. Andy had it all. A nice house, a solid job and a season ticket for Manchester United. Obviously it was easy for me to tell a guy like that to go to jail. But we put it to him: if the worst happened and he lost his job, we'd build a massive campaign around it. We'd encourage industrial action. We'd organise a consumer boycott of the bank, disrupting its trade by telling customers how they were victimising someone for his beliefs. Andy agreed. He was jailed. But no disciplinary action was taken and he gained huge respect in his union and in the local Trafford area.

Back in Scotland, non-payers held on to their jobs, but not their wages. The actress, Elaine C. Smith, had her BBC salary frozen. It was probably meant as a warning to everyone else. 'As if she didn't have enough to worry about,' wrote Susan Dean in the *Scotsman*.

She wasn't talking about Elaine, but her television persona, Mary Nesbitt, the hard-pressed Govan housewife. There was something appropriate about it. Wages arrestments, like poindings and benefit deductions, mainly hit the poor.

Elaine was well-known and easily traced. Few people advertised where they worked on telly, so sheriff officers could not touch them. Unless they worked for Strathclyde Regional council. The region arrested the wages of 15,000 of their employees. (By 1993 the figure was 87,000.) Most were low-paid workers like home helps, cleaners and school-dinner ladies.

Shift-workers fared no better. Jim Collins of Easterhouse drives a school bus. After his wages were arrested he worked extra overtime to earn anything near a living. But the more shifts he worked, the more they deducted. Some weeks he lost as much as £50. The maximum he came home with for a 50-hour week was £120. He must pay £30 rent for his damp council flat, as well as big heating bills, his telephone and the insurance.

Fiona Donaghue, a home help from Maryhill, paid £7 out of her £65 weekly wage to meet poll tax debt. Another home help, Mary Constant, had her small wage arrested more than once to pay her husband's poll tax. James Constant fell behind in his payments after illness forced him to quit work.

Gordon Dangerfield helped us successfully challenge the region through the courts. Jim Cameron, chairman of the Strathclyde Anti-Poll Tax Federation, had his social worker salary arrested. Gordon proved the warrant was invalid. We believed this made all the others void. Gordon had won a similar case in Stranraer which forced Dumfries and Galloway Regional Council to withdraw warrants from its employees. But Strathclyde said: 'The rest of them will just have to come to court and prove it.' Sadly, this is not an option open to many home helps on £65 a week. The law was only recognised and applied if it was in Strathclyde's favour.

Our only other tactic was embarrassment. We occupied the finance office administering Strathclyde's wage deductions on 21 March 1991. It should have been a simple matter. But this was a high security operation because there was an Army Careers Office downstairs in Glasgow's Queen Street. Having already experienced the 3 am chain saw in Stirling Park, we didn't fancy being stormed by the SAS.

We sneaked in one at a time until there was a big crowd to disrupt the day's business with songs and chants. I recognised the shop steward from our marches: 'You surely can't expect your workers to continue in conditions like this?' I said. He agreed to phone the Nalgo office for advice, knowing that Jim Cameron – our chairman and a Nalgo official – was bound to answer and say: 'Disgraceful – walk out immediately.' By one of those quirks of fate Jim was out and a right-winger answered the phone. He advised them to continue working and keep him informed.

So we were kind of stuck. We knew Michael Heseltine was making his big speech in parliament that day announcing the death of the poll tax. The BBC had arranged to come over to the Fed. office for some reaction. People coming to pay poll tax in Queen Street that day were getting unexpected advice at the counter: 'It's finished! Forget It! Away and buy a new hat! You deserve a holiday! Here's our number if there's any problem!'

We left after three hours to keep the BBC appointment. They wanted to film us watching Heseltine's announcement in the shop. I remember worrying all day about what I was going to say. I wanted to make it clear it was the people, not the politicians, who beat the tax. We were celebrating a victory, certainly. But there was no announcement about any amnesty. I needed to emphasise the fight would contine as long as the poor were being hounded.

I don't think I've ever got such satisfaction in a television studio as I did that night. After the BBC interview I went along to Scottish Television's studios for a special *Question Time*-type show on the poll tax. A studio audience of Tories, SNP, Labour, trade unionists and I raked over the ashes. I was sandwiched between Allan Hogarth, a 'No Turning Back Young Tory' I knew from Stirling University Labour Club, and an Eastwood woman who turned out to be Allan Stewart's election agent.

Talk about rubbing it in. 'It was the punters, not the pin-stripe politicians who beat the tax,' I said. 'People organising together. Now we'd proved those methods still worked, despite the bad faith of the Labour leaders, why not organise together for an amnesty?'

Campbell Christie from the Scottish Trades Union Congress made lots of sympathetic noises. Few people even realised the STUC still had a campaign. He said something like: 'We should discuss the possiblity with COSLA, we would have to identify those too poor to pay'. I suggested they start with the European decency threshhold which then stood at £108 a week. But we never heard much more when the lights went down.

The camera crew, the lighting people and technicians were coming up afterwards and congratulating me. 'Your lot must be feeling good tonight, Tommy! Well done!' Christie and the paying, law abiding opponents of the tax were ignored. For all the imbalance of coverage, the people who mattered, the workers, knew the Fed. was responsible for beating the tax. We celebrated the next day by letting off hundreds of red balloons in George Square: one for every Tory MP in parliament. They said 'Poll Tax dead Amnesty now!' All the other politicians spent the day claiming credit for killing the tax. But we had to call short our celebrations. We left the square early to stop an attempted poinding over in Bridgeton on the edge of Glasgow Green. Maybe this is why the day seemed like an anti-climax. The Neil Kinnocks and Donald Dewars were saying the tax was dead and buried. But we were still out there fighting the misery it caused. It was the zombie tax – it haunted the poor from its grave.

There were sixty people outside a woman's close in Bridgeton. All the regulars piled out of the pub next door to join in the singing. Usually we maintain a strict ban on alcohol at poindings. But this was a very special day and people were jubilant. Naturally the sheriffs called it off.

We had to turn folk away at midnight that night when the buses took Scots to the big 'End of poll tax' demo in London. Ironically, this was also the day an SNP special conference was called for a different reason but which took the decision to abandon the poor.

The setting, Govan Town Hall, was ironic. The Labour Party had fatally rejected non-payment there in September 1988. Jim Sillars reaped the benefit two months later when he strode forward on that same stage, the new MP for Govan.

I was not surprised that Alex Salmond, the new SNP leader, had wanted to abandon the campaign. Alex is the nationalist Neil Kinnock. He talked a good socialist game until becoming leader. Suddenly he's a new realist. Politics is a stage for people like him.

Impressing the middle-class listeners of Radio Four becomes more important than what the voters in Govan think. Alex used to be an oil economist and I think he was flattered by all these experts who complimented his blue print for an independent Scottish economy. Metropolitan commentators were saying what a smart guy he was, how eloquent, how reasonable. These people were telling him the illegality of this non-payment campaign spoiled the whole slick picture. It damaged his plausibility score on *Question Time.*

But I couldn't get over Jim Sillars speaking in favour of winding up the campaign. I always liked Jim. But there he was, comparing the whole thing to a strike. 'You have to know when to walk out,' he said, 'but you also have to know when to go back'. 'You have to recognise victory.' What trade unionist goes back to work when nearly half the factory is still locked outside the gates?

Kenny MacAskill, who led the SNP campaign, was really upset when I met him a few days later. I knew how much work he had put into the campaign. We had shared platforms in tenants' halls, community centres and at massive rallies over the years. He did not speak at the Govan conference and was feeling very guilty about allowing that to happen. He still vowed not to pay the tax along with many of the SNP's young central belt activists.

The SNP had sold the jerseys. That decision sealed their electoral fate in the schemes. For our immediate purposes, it meant no major party supported non-payment. Yet the tax had two years to run. Non-payment was bound to soar. Would it be two more years of poindings, harassments and jailings? Whatever happened, the Fed. was now officially on its own.

8 The Battle of Turnbull Street

I've never seen a warrant sale. But my grandparents told me about the heartbreak and fear they inflicted on working-class families in the past. I don't want a repeat of that kind of cruelty.

For my mother's family, the Camerons from Govan, warrant sales were acts of establishment barbarism. They had to be resisted.

I remember a story told by my Gran Rose. A neighbour returned from his work and saw the contents of his home piled up in the street. He ran up the close, panicking, thinking there had been a fire and someone might be hurt. He found his wife in tears. Sheriff officers had forced their way into the tiny room and kitchen. They didn't take long to drag out the few pieces of furniture this couple had accumulated over the years. But their pain didn't end there. The chipped chairs, the only table, the prized sideboard, all bundled up into a mountain on the pavement. It stood there overnight. A pathetic display which lasted until the hawkers arrived to start bidding the next morning.

There's a very old joke which goes something like, 'If you see a table with an umbrella on it in Edinburgh you call it a bistro. In

Glasgow it's a warrant sale . . .' That kind of humour in adversity shows how working-class people refuse to be intimidated. You see, the wee bits of furniture out there in the rain are really meant as a warning. Warrant sales are not about recovering debt. They are about public humiliation. The methods of the medieval witchtrials are used again. What mattered most was not to inflict pain on the poor woman being burned or drowned. It was to warn everyone else to keep in line. That's why it's so important for people to organise together. A warrant sale is an attack on the whole community, not the individual who's been picked out for ridicule.

Again and again during our campaign we returned to the Clydeside rent strikes. Every poinding we stopped was inspired by those wartime women. They would hang out the windows, banging their pots and pans when they saw the sheriffs coming. Our eyes and ears had proved just as keen. We had succeeded in reviving that tradition of struggle. We had physically prevented thousands of poindings by 1991.

In fact, one of the attempted poindings in Govan visibly linked the campaigns across the decades. The flat, a tenement in Hutton Drive, had been targetted by the sheriffs during the original rent strikes. I later met the granddaughter of Mary Barbour, the Govan woman who led the First World War campaign. She lived in Drumoyne and was an active member of Govan Against the Poll Tax.

We also stopped two threats by the sheriffs to uplift the goods they had poinded. Joe McEneany, an unemployed twenty-nine year-old from Hamilton, had been caught out by the sheriffs who got into his house and poinded a hi-fi and two portable televisions, one of which did not belong to him. Under the law the goods must be uplifted a year from the date of the poinding. George Walker and Co were planning to swoop on the last day. But when they saw the 150-strong crowd of friends, neighbours and federation troops, they changed their minds. They actually admitted being scared of the crowd.

Another threatened uplift of goods against Linda Vallely, an unemployed mother from Douglas in Lanarkshire was cancelled at the last minute. We had arranged to take hundreds of people down to the village in a massive operation.

Our successes annoyed Charles Gray, the leader of Strathclyde Region. He wanted blood. He said the sheriffs weren't trying hard enough. There had to be warrant sales. In a report by the *Scotsman's* local government editor, David Scott, on 7 July 1991, he was quoted as saying: 'It is high time they started delivering. This is the first time, in a sense, that I have been mildly critical of the system. Sheriff officers should be advising us why there haven't been warrant sales . . . and I'm talking specifically about people we reckon can pay but won't.' This seemed to contradict what John Mullin said earlier about the council being helpless to intervene in poindings and warrant sales.

Anyway, by September that year they decided to move. It all started with a tip off from a journalist on the *Greenock Telegraph*. He heard a warrant sale notification would be displayed in the local sheriff court. There was a week to prepare for battle. We knew the street, but not the family name. Before we could defend the person we had to find them! So about eight of us headed down the M8 and started chapping doors.

We worked our way along the road, which was in a bleak scheme at the top of Port Glasgow. If you had a head for heights you could look down at deserted shipyards and docks. Living on a hill with the wind beating down must be bad enough at the best of times. When you're unemployed with no prospects, it's desperate.

At one time the yards here employed 10,000. Then the government sold Scott Lithgow to their city pals Trafalgar House, who promptly closed it down. Male unemployment in Inverclyde at that time was officially eighteen per cent. In Port Glasgow, one of the poorest areas of the district, it was much higher. The Port is still a close community. But in the past five years it's been torn apart in drug wars, a sadly typical West of Scotland town.

After knocking on dozens of doors, we finally pinpointed the Brennan family. Anne Brennan came home one day to discover the notorious local Bob McIntyre of Abernethy McIntyre, had burst the lock on the front door. The display cabinet, the wall unit, the coffee table and the portable television were all piled into a removal van and driven away.

The Brennans were victims because their name came at the beginning of the alphabet. But the aim of the sheriff officers – to shame the family and scare everyone else – was very nearly successful. Anne and Jim wanted nothing to do with us.

They were terrified of having their names in the papers. Anne was a very nervous woman. When her house was to be poinded nearly a year before she never told anyone – if she had, we could have stopped it. She should have forewarned us. But she never really thought the sheriffs would come. She was so ashamed and embarrassed by the whole thing, she went away to stay with relatives in England at the time of the sale.

Those were a desperate few days. I had an intense series of telephone conversations with Jim Brennan the weekend before the planned sale on Tuesday.

I told him I could understand his fear and trepidation. But this whole thing, it wasn't about him. It was about more than a million people in Scotland who were threatened with warrant sales. I appealed to him to look beyond his own life to the unemployed, the elderly, the single parents who were terrified that they'd be next.

I felt bad about it from a number of angles. Was I exploiting him? Exploitation usually implies self gain. My intention was to get this guy to co-operate in order to defend other people. I didn't like pressurising him. But I was really worried. I thought: What's going to happen here? By this time the *Greenock Telegraph* was carrying front page stories with Bob McIntyre boasting how he was inundated with people coming to pay their poll tax.

We couldn't allow that to continue. Even if Jim Brennan said, 'Get out of my life, I don't want that rosewood unit back, anyway,' we'd still have turned up to stop the sale. In the end, he came round. He was fed up with the hassle from the media and was resigned to the fact that his name would appear in print no matter what he did. No doubt he'd also been speaking to his friends and neighbours, who urged him to fight it. When I phoned on Sunday he said: 'Do what you have to do.'

While all this was happening, we had to tackle McIntyre's intimidation. The organisers of the Inverclyde Anti Poll Tax Union, Davie Landels and Jim Watson, knew him to be a vindictive character – even more zealous than your average sheriff officer. He seemed to enjoy his job. It was McIntyre who later used the crow bar to smash Jean McGahey's door – the grandmother arrested in her own home.

The thing that disgusts me about sheriff officers is that they made a good living before the Poll Tax came along. They don't need it. All the run-of-the-mill things like serving divorce papers meant they were very comfortable. When the poll tax arrived, all normal people thought it was unjust and unfair. Sheriff officers thought Christmas had come early.

So in the days leading up to the sale, sixty of us occupied Abernethy McIntyre's office in Greenock. Eight people came to pay their Poll Tax. Their stories were familiar – someone had lost his job, another had just got a new job, one had left the house. We told them they weren't the only ones. They were in a big, big boat. Once people realise that, they stop jumping overboard. As long as they had our phone number, they felt reassured. After speaking to us, seven of the eight remained non-payers.

We owed it to these people, and millions like them, to stop the Tuesday sale. It was scheduled to take place at 11 am in the police holding centre in Turnbull Street. We couldn't believe our luck. It's about 300 yards from the Fed office in London Road, in The Barras area of Glasgow.

Apparently McIntyre got a knock back from every sale room in Greenock. The region came to his rescue. It was incredible. Not content with allowing him a licence to harass and intimidate, they also provided a place for this act of barbarism. They owned the building where the deed was to be perpetrated.

Monday was hectic. I had several meetings at my house in Pollok, planning strategy for the next day. I was rushing out to speak at yet another meeting at 3 pm when I noticed a brown envelope sticking through the letter box.

It was an interim interdict obtained by Abernethy McIntyre. I was banned from attending the sale or from impeding sheriff officers. It should really have been served by hand. But given the atmosphere in Pollok at that time, maybe it's not surprising that the sheriff delivering it crept up the stairs and put it through the door without so much as ringing the bell.

I later discovered Davie Landels had received an identical interdict. Davie was unemployed for eight years after serving his time as an engineer. He has two young kids and in 1991 was living on benefit in Branchton, another run down scheme stuck on a moor at the back of Greenock. When you look at his situation, it brings the whole interdict system into question. Rich people use the courts like a monopoly board. Poor people are the victims of them. We don't get using the courts like that. We don't have the money or the advice or the wherewithal.

I had no time to challenge the interdict, with the sale due in less than 24 hours. I couldn't even contact our lawyers, Alan Miller or Gordon Dangerfield. They were both in court that afternoon. I was so angry. The interdict banned me from taking part in a legitimate protest. I would ignore it. There was no doubt in my mind.

I tore it up publicly during the protest the next day because I had contempt for what it said and the way it was served. But I would have been jailed whether or not I did that, because they wanted to make an example of me.

I got very little sleep that night. Not because I expected to go to prison. I didn't. But because we were up at 4 am to go to the Fed shop. Some people had been there all night, manning the phones and making reconnaissance missions to Turnbull Street, chatting to the police posted there – asking if they wanted a cup of coffee.

You can see the entrance to the yard from the Fed shop – just across St Andrew's Square, past a big derelict warehouse and the old tannery building. You get to the inside courtyard – or the pen, as the older people called it, through a narrow, tiled close. Several storeys of blank, barred windows look down on you from high red brick walls. Part of the building used to be the old district court, so it had an elaborate Coat of Arms with the motto Let Glasgow Flourish above the door. Two red sandstone statues lean out from the roof: a stern Victorian capitalist with a beard and a tailcoat and an angel with a sword to dispense justice – presumably on his behalf.

Crowds began arriving from early on – 100 people had amassed by 7.30 am. There were vehicles from Stirling, Edinburgh, Coatbridge and Hamiliton.

The Federation phone trees had linked up to form one big Scottish network.

We also had a list of lawyers' telephone numbers pinned to the wall. People in the crowd were designated as runners. If anyone was arrested, the runner would hop it back to the shop and the folk operating the phones called the solicitor right away.

The shop is the size of the average council house bedroom. It was freezing, and there was only a little fan heater to keep warm. But I remember sitting back and thinking how great it was that everyone who came got hot soup and a cup of tea. Someone brought in a wee Belling cooker, someone else brought an urn. There were tins of biscuits and pots of chilli. People had pulled together. It reminded me of the miners' strike. We started with nothing, but we had built this great organisation.

There was a lot of discussion as to the best way to go about stopping the sale. Would we have a better chance if a small group got in early using guerrilla-type tactics? Or should we wait until more people arrived and stop it through mass action?

Someone suggested parking an old car in front of the gates to the yard and then setting it on fire. I was having to be as polite as possible in dealing with these type of suggestions.

The plan we decided on was that several older women, including my mother Alice, would chain themselves to the gates of the yard. It had echoes of the suffragettes. The crowd would form a human barricade in front. When the van with the goods in it arrived, the police would have to arrest a lot of people before arresting the women. The fire brigade would take hours cutting them free. They even wore incontinence pads. By then we hoped the warrant sale would be abandoned.

These women hardly fit the description of rioters. But they are the backbone of our movement. Betty McEachin, a seventy-two year-old from Govan, is typical of the older people who were there that day. She only got involved in community politics after her husband died ten years ago. She was secretary of her tenants' association before joining the anti-poll tax movement. Betty has been at scores of poindings and always stays behind to tidy up any dropped papers or placards: 'So they can't say we're louts.'

One of her earliest memories is of an attempted warrant sale near the Gorbals tenement where she was born. 'I was about eight years old. I remember the windows of this single end were criss-crossed with pieces of planking. There was a crowd of adults pressed together at the entrance to the close, waiting for the sheriffs to come. I thought: 'Is that a communist?'' They're very ordinary looking! Nearly sixty years on, Betty, a very ordinary-looking Glasgow pensioner, was the communist trying to stop the warrant sale. It was still happening.

We set off from the shop at 9.30 am, by which time there were 300 of us with more arriving all the time. Several photographers were positioned on the scaffolding encasing the buildings which lined the route. We had only to cover 400 yards, but we marched all the same, waving banners and singing songs. I fully expected to be arrested that day. Not being a lawyer, I didn't know then that the police couldn't arrest you for breaking an interdict. It's a civil offence.

Davie Landels got the train up from Greenock, even though his friends said he didn't have to go. 'I'd spent months telling people there would be no warrant sales,' he said. It was a point of principle. The funny thing is, when you're in a big crowd, all singing like that, you don't feel scared. You think: 'Stuff their interdict!'

I suppose it was a bit of an anti-climax when we got to the gates and discovered there were only two police. We thought there would be squads of them, trying to stop us gaining an advantage. Anyway, we went ahead with our masterplan. The women chained themselves. We surrounded them. We waited.

About five minutes passed before a policeman said to someone: 'You do realise the gates aren't locked?' We were stunned. There followed a frantic wrestling with chains and unlocking padlocks to free the women. The gates opened. We flooded through the tiled close. Just to the left of the entrance sat an Arnold Clark van containing two sheriff officers – McIntyre and his partner, Freda Reilly. The Brennan's furniture was locked in the back. How did we miss them? No one noticed the van drive in at 6 am. They sneaked the wrong way up a one way street – under police escort, of course. Crash barriers surrounded the van. So the place looked like a cattle market. You could stand at the barriers to bid for things – though if anyone had turned up looking for a bargain at the sale, they certainly didn't identify themselves.

That sight, in 1991, enraged the demonstrators. The sheriffs were not going to get away with it. Everyone made a beeline for the van. There were a lot of angry people kicking it, shaking it, letting down the tyres. But at that point McIntyre started moving the van back and forwards against the crash barriers, pumping his horn frantically.

Dozens of police poured through the gates. They were parked round the corner in black marias. They started to grab people, pulling them away from the van. Everything was hampered by the barriers. People were being crushed.

I was looking straight at the windscreen, shouting at McIntyre: 'Where's your crowbar now?' Finally, he was experiencing some of the fear he seemed to enjoy inflicting on the vulnerable.

Because I expected to be arrested, I was surrounded by a group of burly guys. George McNeilage is quite big and convincing. You wouldn't mess with him unless you had to. On the other side was Ian MacDonald, Militant's Lanarkshire organiser and a former Welsh Rugby player. That didn't deter the police, who leapt in and grabbed me by the neck and arm. George and Ian were pulling me from the other side. It became a tug of war. I was very, very frightened. My leather jacket began compressing my throat. I started to choke. My mother was watching all this with horror. She said later I had turned white and she thought, 'That's it!'

Fortunately, the police let go first. But I was still concerned about the crush – and for the safety of older people like my mother and Betty. I was also very worried that the police would try to take the furniture out of the back of the van. The law says you only have to display the goods and the warrant sale has taken place. You don't need to take any bids.

I made a speech saying: If the police display these goods, they'll be inciting this crowd. They will be taking part in an attempt to humiliate a woman who can't afford to pay a rich man's tax. Do the police know they are getting involved in politics? I was addressing the crowd, but I was speaking to the police as well.

Fortunately, it didn't come to that. There was a lot of singing and chanting as the demonstrators faced the line of police – including the memorable cry 'We've all had our Weetabix!' A man with a waxed jacket and a loudhailer appeared at ten to eleven. He was Hugh Dougherty, a press officer from Strathclyde Region. He announced that the warrant sale had been cancelled.

We had done it. We stood up to authority in the name of justice and won. What a victory for the underdog! They had everything on their side – the law, the police, the courts, the resources. But we had the guts, determination and the will to win. The crowd became ecstatic. We really felt empowered. I was hoisted onto Big George's shoulders. The police asked us to make a space for the van to escape. It was a pathetic yet wonderful sight. It limped out, battered and bruised, like the pride of the sheriff officers inside. There was a football atmosphere – we were the anti-poll tax team and we'd just won the cup. My mother was leading her usual singing – trying to get the crowds to remember the words of 'The International'. 'Sing something we can dance to,' said a teenage guy beside her. There was a lot of laughter. But a few tears as well. It was a very emotionally-charged experience. It could have got out of hand. I could have got out of hand.

There were sixty police and 300 demonstrators. If they had tried to take the goods out of the van, I have to say I'd have jumped the barrier. I would have been furious. And I couldn't have stopped anyone else from doing the same thing.

I am often asked if violence is justified in such circumstances. I abhor violence. It's too prevalent in our society. The good things about human beings – solidarity, co-operation and love – are often put on the shelf in favour of confrontation and aggression. But I'd draw a line between violence and physical anger. There's a big difference between taking a blade out of your pocket to slash someone's face and jumping a crash barrier to stop furniture being stolen to humiliate someone publicly. The first is a premeditated act of malice. The second is anger being physically expressed.

Some people might think that's a bit of a sociological distinction. But you have to ask: What violence is worse? There is the violence of poverty. There is the fear and terror caused by the Poll Tax and the threat of warrant sales. That's a form of acute mental violence. Sometimes mental violence is the worst kind.

I was sick the next day when Charlie Gray said the police were not strong enough. He even said if they had stopped the pickets during the miners' strike, why couldn't they stop mob rule in Turnbull Street? To me, that was effectively saying: 'Why did you not use your truncheons? Why did you not bash a few heads together?'

The dispossessed fighting for their rights have been referred to throughout history as the Mob or the Rabble. But working-class people can only change things when they come together.

The pensioners, the students, the young unemployed and low paid workers who stopped the sale at Turnbull Street on 1 October 1991 – they were no more unruly or mobbish than the Partick housewives who sent the factors packing seventy odd years ago.

The real disgrace is that the region let it get to this stage. During the rent strikes, it was the Labour members on Glasgow Corporation who argued for controls on the slum landlords and sheriff officers who collaborated to terrorise the poor. Changed days. Now Labour politicians act like Uncle Toms, displaying an enthusiastic vigour in carrying out policy they're supposed to oppose. Of course, everybody says they are against warrant sales. The STUC, the SNP, the Liberals, Civil Liberties groups, all condemned them. None of them, but none of them, had organised to stop this one – or any other for that matter. Everybody was talking but nobody was acting. Sometimes you have to make a stand that involves a wee bit more than rhetoric. If we had not taken that action in Turnbull Street, the whole of Scotland would have been shamed.

Our campaign got people off their knees. At the beginning, in 1988/89, I must have spoken at thousands of public meetings. Ten years of Thatcher had knocked the stuffing out of working-class people. She had fought an ideological war against socialism and the idea of society. She thought she'd won. We rekindled the idea of community spirit, of achieving things through solidarity. Ordinary people had broken the law and won. Sometimes there's a higher law.

For days after Turnbull Street, Glaswegians would come up to me at bus stops or in shopping centres where I was selling *Militant* and say: 'Well done, son, that was a victory for us all.'

The scenes had touched a lot of people who were previously sceptical or defeatist. While we were celebrating in the afternoon, there was a call to the Fed shop from Jim Brennan, the man who had been so reluctant to approve us stopping the sale of his furniture. He told Jim Watson of the Inverclyde Anti Poll Tax Union that he had been watching the scenes on TV.

'I just wanted to say you done brilliant,' he said, to Jim's amazement. 'I never thought you could do it. I underestimated the strength of feeling.' He no longer felt scared or humiliated. Nor did anyone else. That was almost three years ago. There still hasn't been a warrant sale in Scotland.

Labour never gave up trying to inject a bit of life into the zombie tax despite our Turnbull Street victory. They came out with a lot of scare stories about services being cut due to non-payment. Instead of blaming the tax, they blamed the people who were too poor to pay it.

Charlie Gray's flea continued to bite the ears of the sheriffs in the coming months. Two weeks before Christmas of 1991, one firm reponded to Labour taunts. At Turnbull Street one individual had been singled out. Now they would try the scorched earth approach. Springburn was blitzed with letters from Gray Scott & Co, giving notice of poindings on 10 December.

Springburn used to be one of the most thriving and active working-class communities in Glasgow. By 1991 it was the third poorest constituency in Britain. It was once the powerhouse of the railway industry. The St Rollox works – later known as British Rail Engineering (BREL) – covered 190 acres. You also had Cowlairs which closed in 1966, the Eastfield Engine Sheds and the Atlas, which is now an estate with twenty-one light industrial units. Another works, Hydepark, employed 8000 at its peak and built 600 locomotives a year.

Workers in Springburn were at the forefront of the co-operative movement in the nineteenth and early twentieth centuries. Miners formed the first co-operatives in Petershill and Keppochhill, which were villages still separate from Glasgow. The Cowlairs Co-operative Society was formed by a group of workers who met in the North British Railway canteen. Jealous local traders tried to get the railway company to sack anyone they found involved in it.

The radical weavers, John Baird and Andrew Hardie, are buried in Sighthill Cemetry, Springburn. They led a march from Glasgow Green to Falkirk in 1820 to seize the Carron Ironworks for the people. Soldiers mowed them down after they were grassed by government agents. Hardie and Baird were hanged and beheaded while another sixteen were transported to Australia.

Springburn used to have row upon row of red sandstone tenements, like you see in the middle-class west end of Glasgow today. It had five cinemas, elaborately corniced public halls and swimming baths. It had its own Winter Gardens. They've all gone along with the jobs. Cowlairs ward now has the highest unemployment in Glasgow, with thirty per cent of the population officially unemployed. The actual figure is much higher. In Germiston, one of the areas targeted for mass poindings in 1991, eighty per cent of the school roll was dependent on clothing grants – the highest percentage of children in Strathclyde.

Early this century, 30,000 people lived in central Springburn. Now the figure is 8000 – with the rest dumped in places like the Red Road flats. These shot up from the site where the Petershill Miners formed their co-operatives all those years ago. The eight blocks of 26, 27 and 31 storeys were built between 1962 and 1969 and were then the highest in Europe. They didn't have fire escapes till recently. You could only get down the stairs by going through the flats. If the lift broke you were stranded. Sighthill now also consists of 10 blocks of 20 storeys – along with the cemetery of course.

This was the area Strathclyde chose to target two weeks before Christmas. Not the Bearsdens or Milngavies or even the West End, but a place containing some of the most concentrated poverty in northern Europe.

We had no idea of the scale of the operation at first. Hannah McArthur, one of our volunteers, came into the Federation shop on 2 December with a letter. Hannah, was then in her late thirties and living in a high rise block in Germiston. She spent ten years working in the kitchens of the nearby Royal Infirmary. Now she spends a lot of her time doing voluntary work for Alcoholics Anonymous. She has been sober for eight years.

Hannah asked her neighbours if they had had similar letters. Gradually they trickled into her front room. One old woman sat and cried. Within three days we had delivered 1000 leaflets and booked a local school for a public meeting. We now knew of thirty poindings. Apart from Germiston, calls were coming into the Fed office from the other four parts of Springburn: Barmulloch, Balornock, Royston and Keppochhill Road. Something big was happening.

That Saturday Hannah noticed the local Labour MP, Michael Martin, in the shopping centre. She told him she was worried about a letter from the sheriffs. 'Then you should pay your poll tax,' he snapped.

Michael Martin has proved particularly adept at playing on the area's crushing poverty. It once had the highest number of Irish in Glasgow. Martin is often endorsed from the pulpit.

Recently I was campaigning in his constituency during a district council by election in Dennistoun. A lively wee woman with red hair and a Labour sticker was standing next to me outside the polling station. She knew absolutely everybody who went into vote. And the punters were all being incredibly nice to her: 'You're looking great! Haven't seen you in ages, where have you been?' Somebody told me she used to run the pub down the road and I heard her say she now had a wee hotel up in the Highlands. Had she been brought here specially for polling day? I turned to her and said: This has been a great day for you – all these people telling you how well you're looking!

'Aye,' she replied. 'It's cause they all owe me money!'

That's politics, Springburn style. Placemen masquerade as community activists. One woman in Germiston had a reputation for being able to get people council houses. Whether it was true or not, it shows the perception in the housing schemes of Labour as corrupt and self-seeking. This woman was loathed. When her name was mentioned at one of our meetings, one member of the audience shouted, 'Where's the noose'.

During the run-up to the poindings, Michael Martin demanded we be barred from the local school. He was backed by Ian Davidson, then Strathclyde's education convenor and now the Labour MP for Govan. He demanded £260 million for the let, the amount he claimed the Fed owed the council in unpaid poll tax.

Five days after Hannah got that first letter, we'd delivered 6000 leaflets. We now knew of sixty poindings in the five different areas. But how could we speak to people when we were banned from using a local education college? December is not the best time to hold street meetings in Glasgow. But they left us no alternative. Kenny Weir, the Militant organiser, and Willie Campbell, Secretary of Springburn Against Warrant Sales, went round all the areas in an old Yugo and a megaphone.

The first meeting was at a bus stop in Barmulloch on 8 December, two days before the planned blitz. Thirty people stood in the cold, waving poinding letters. All were worried about their weans' Christmas presents – which we explained the sheriffs couldn't touch. By the time of the next meeting it was freezing cold and dark, but seventy people appeared. We eventually got a classroom in a school in Germiston on 9 December, the night before the attempted invasion. It was packed with angry people. One of those targeted was a woman in a wheelchair.

We planned it like a military operation. We allocated a different anti-poll tax group to each of the five areas. Every group was told a local meeting place and each area had someone in charge. So Govan's team went to Germiston, where my mother and Hannah were in charge. Cambuslang went to Barmulloch, where Willie Campbell and another local, Tam Hickey, himself the subject of a poinding, were organising things. Sheila McDonald, the woman who had organised those massive 1989 Royston meetings with myself and Jim Sillars, had received a poinding letter. So she was in charge of Royston, conducting resistance from her own targeted flat.

Our activists carried sheets of paper with lists of poinding addresses. We were adding to them hour by hour so they are scrawled in a variety of writing styles. The lists named the organiser, the defence team and gave contact numbers. Poinded houses with phones were to be used to liaise with the Fed office. All poinded houses were to have window posters.

The Pollok posse were assigned to Balornock in the north. We were giving out posters at nine in the morning when we saw a sheriff officer's car. Our transit van chased them right into the countryside beyond Glasgow.

While we were away, sheriff officers and police descended on Germiston at 9 am. It looked like a bomb had dropped. Hundreds of local people were out in the streets. There were fifteen people at each close mouth and forty at the bottom of a Hannah's multi storey.

The four court appointed hooligans tried to storm a house in Stroma Street. My mother and the others ran from their base in

Hannah's tower block to join locals at the close mouth. 'Don't let them in. Put furniture, anything behind the door,' my mother shouted. One of the polis asked if she was refusing to let these people carry out their business.

'Damn right!' she says.

'Then you're under arrest,' says the cop. 'I hope you will not put up any resistance.'

She immediately grabbed some railings and flopped into a limp doll pose – forcing them to drag her into a police van which appeared.

We had no idea they planned to use the police on this scale. Nineteen people were arrested then, including Betty Curry, John Evans, Kay McClellan and Bob Snell also from Cambuslang. The rest were locals – like the man who jumped out of a taxi after returning from his kidney treatment at the hospital. A boy who was coming home from signing on the dole tried to intervene when he saw a middle-aged woman being dragged along the ground. His girlfriend ran down to find out why they were arresting him and she was also piled into the van. They were lifting people indiscriminately.

They even piled a sheriff officer into the back of the van. 'But you can't arrest me, I'm a sheriff officer!' he squealed.

'And I'm f****** Prince Charles' said the cop.

When Betty Curry got to the station the sergeant said: 'I'm charging you with deforcement. Do you know what that is?'

'I don't,' she said. He said to the constable: 'She knows more about it than I do, get her upstairs.' Then she heard him say, 'Go and get Sheridan!'

They found me quickly. We'd been driving the transit van back to our allocated area when we spotted the big red Peugeot we'd chased earlier. It was parked outside a house. Wasting no time, we jumped the central reservation and blocked the car into the cul de sac where it was parked. Two sheriff officers were speaking to a very nervous woman who was not even the person named in the warrant.

We told them to get lost and they got back in their car. We were walking back to the van when the police car appeared. I heard someone shout 'Get Him' and then the cop said, 'Right, Sheridan, you're under arrest.'

Meanwhile another bunch of police and sheriffs tried to storm into a third area, Barmulloch. Tam Hickey, who lives at number 76, was one of six arrested. Local pickets found themselves locked into a close with the sheriff officers. They thought they were going to be eaten but there was no violence. The polis rammed the close door and arrested them all.

They were dragged to the van in front of 300 of their neighbours who had turned out to form the human barricades of solidarity we so often talked about. Tam later wrote of his experience.

On the way to Baird Street Police Station, we asked the police why they had turned out in such large numbers. 'We're only doing our job,' was the reply. Randal Ross, a comrade in the van with me, replied, 'The last time so many people said they were only doing their job was during the Nuremberg trials!' The police had no answer to this. Some shuffled their shoes and looked at the floor.

The police returned to Germiston after arresting my mother and the others. This time they brought five squad cars to protect the fleet of sheriffs. More people were arrested. But despite the massive operation on their part, despite the thirty-nine arrests in the course of the day, they only got into one of the 400 targeted houses. Even then they couldn't go ahead because there was nothing in the house which could be poinded.

I missed all the best bits, being arrested so early. But people on the scene said every door was open that day. You could walk into a stranger's house to use the phone or just get a cup of tea. Kids on bikes took messages from one area to another. People hopped into bread vans. A couple of works vehicles turned up offering to transport pickets. As word of the arrests spread, more people flooded onto the streets.

School pupils joined us at 1pm and refused to go back to class. That was when Keith Baldassarra remembers a cry going out that the sheriff officers had been spotted round the corner: 'It's one memory that will never leave me. The whole scheme more or less emptied. Men and women, old and young people, a mixure of cars and bikes and babies buggies being pushed up this hill and round a corner. The street just filled up with hundreds of people. Just in time to see this car turn and speed away. It was like a housing scheme in revolt.'

By mid afternoon 1000 people were on the streets of Springburn. Those organisers not arrested – Kenny Weir, Wullie Campbell, Craig Beaton and Keith Baldassarra, spent the afternoon telling people to stand firm. The deadline for the poindings given on the letters was four o'clock. After the count down, they asked the 300 people out in Barmulloch to try to make their way a few miles down the road to Baird Street Police station for a rally.

This was going to be difficult. Few people in the area own cars. But they just put out their braziers, gathered up their homemade banners and headed south. Driving down, Kenny passed another spontaneous march of seventy young people from Sighthill and Royston. They marched even though the sheriffs had been too scared to come near their rock-solid barricades.

The crowd across the road from the station numbered several hundred. Gangs of young people from the different schemes had buried the tribalism of poverty. They had one purpose. Songs which were never heard before at an anti poll tax demo filtered through the cell walls. 'Always look on the bright side of life', a heavily ironic chorus sung on the Parkhead terraces at the time thundered out. There were also a couple of rounds of 'You Can Shove your British Justice Up Your Arse'.

Our campaign certainly united people across the sectarian divides of industrial Scotland. That's not surprising as much sectarianism is people trying to cling to their working-class identity – however misguidedly. Orange Bands from Bridgeton used to march alongside hunger protests as did Hibernian bands from Catholic communities. Orange Larkhall, like Republican Royston, had very strong anti-poll tax unions. Flute bands from both sides of the divide actually offered to play at our demos. We turned them all down. It would have been too antagonisic. But the unity of working people,

Protestant and Catholic that day in Springburn, showed what is possible if everyone unites in action.

We were held in the cells for thirty hours. The cells were really bad. Excrement was smeared on the walls. Tam Hickey was bitten by something in his one scrawny blanket. I remember doing press-ups and sit-ups to keep warm. The court solicitor spent seven hours trying to see us-he believed the polis wanted to teach us a lesson. They singled us up to make things worse. Time always drags when you're snibbed up on your own. At 1.30 in the morning we were all hauled out for fingerprinting.

The deforcement charge against us was archaic. It had been used the month before against anti-poll tax protesters in Greenock. Before that it was used against crofters in the nineteenth-century Highland clearances. It carried the death penalty, which caused much hilarity that night. Don't worry, we'd shout between the cells 'They can't hang you any more. It will be commuted to life imprisonment!'

When we appeared in court the following afternoon, the deforcement charges were all reduced to breach of the peace. We made a double-page spread in the *Daily Record* next day. They meant it to be negative. But we could not have asked for a clearer message to Scotland's working class.

'There were frightening scenes as police dragged screaming women away from targeted addresses to let the poindings go ahead,' wrote Tom Hamilton and Gordon Anderson. 'Sheriff officers were jostled pushed and drenched in spittle as men, women and children hurled verbal abuse at them. Their cars were surrounded. Aerials were snapped; doors were dented by kicks and punches; and windows were splattered in spittle and eggs.

One sheriff officer was taken to hospital after protesters jammed his foot in the main door of a high rise block. The officers had descended on the Barmulloch and Germiston areas of the East End of Glasgow at dawn. But the Anti-Poll Tax Federation were well prepared.'

It was a step-by-step guide on how to resist the sheriffs. People power was shown to work, and in full colour.

The comments made by Labour politicians afterwards showed their glaring lack of understanding of feelings in the poor areas. Michael Martin was quoted as saying: 'Everyone dislikes warrant sales, but I fully back Strathclyde Region in the difficult position they are in. These irresponsible protestors move into an area and encourage otherwise law-abiding people to break the law.

By following the troublemakers they could lose all their belongings which could have taken a lifetime to lovingly put together in their home.'

He was as frightening as a circus clown. By this time a minority of people in Scotland were actually complying with the tax. There were 2.5 million refuseniks across the country. Martin's hollow scaremongering was dwarfed by the *Record*'s own headline: WE'LL STILL NOT PAY!

Springburn wasn't Soweto during the rent boycott, or Santiago during the Popular Unity years or the Sandinstas in Nicaragua. It was dreich, downtrodden Glasgow. Yet here were people employing exactly the same methods of organisation as workers in those far off places: the neighbourhood committees, the human barricades, the collective principle. It was socialism in action and the people did it themselves. We just provided a little leadership.

It vindicated our decision, just a few weeks before, to set up Scottish Militant Labour. Thirty people joined the Springburn branch in the aftermath of the attempted poindings. In the course of the campaign, I found it increasingly difficult to stick to the original message of my speeches: urging people to join the Labour Party and change it from within. How could we ask them to vote for the party assisting their impoverishment? I couldn't even do it myself. I remember being extremely relieved to be away from home during the Regional Council Elections in 1990. I didn't have to vote. Talk of standing anti-poll tax candidates was discussed back then, but ruled out.

For a long time Militants restrained themselves because they didn't want to damage the movement. When an anarchist like John Cooper spoke at an anti-poll tax meeting in the schemes, his level of vitriol far surpassed anything we dared express. The audience would stamp their feet and roar approval.

Labour's internal police state blocked Federation supporters from joining – including the majority with no Militant affiliations. It really began to worry us. Here we were, involving hundreds of thousands of people in a mass movement for civil disobedience. Was it going to dissipate? Were we going to lose all that energy and anger?

You see it so often. After the miners' strike, or the big anti-nuclear movements of the early 80s, people had nowhere to go politically. Nobody showed them the way. Unless there's an organisation to give people a clear direction and keep them involved, you will lose them.

And it didn't look as if the lurch to the right would be reversed after Neil Kinnock stepped down. The same thing was happening to Social Democratic parties like Labour all over Europe. Once they were mass movements, but membership was becoming old and stagnant even in countries like Sweden where they did well at the polls.

These parties' attempts at reforming capitalism while in government had failed. Now they didn't even try. They used the collapse of Stalinist Communism in the Soviet Union and Eastern Europe as an excuse to do capitalism's bidding. It's the end of history, all the intellectuals trilled. Liberal Democracy and free market capitalism have triumphed over all the alternatives on offer.

The decline of the Eastern Bloc was not the decline of socialism. These countries had degenerated into corruption because they were economically backward from the beginning. It was very difficult for them to have a successful revolution because they were so poor. So power fell into the hands of a ruthless bureaucratic élite instead of becoming fair and open. This is what Trotsky saw happening in the 1920s and why he was hounded out of the Soviet Union and eventually murdered by Stalin's agent.

Rich developed countries like our own could transfer more easily to socialism. We have more to share. All the things we demand – a shorter working week, an end to poverty, a decent home for everyone – all these things are technically possible. The Eastern European workers who brought down the Berlin Wall thought capitalism meant a lifestyle based on the Dallas soap opera. But the harsh reality is now mass unemployment and starvation. The health service in Russia has broken down. There are epidemics of old diseases such as diptheria. Organised crime and prostitution are spiralling. Dreams of democracy and equality have been exploited by Western capitalists hoping to make a quick buck from cheap labour. The old regimes of Eastern Europe needed to be reformed but the free market will only put them in different chains.

Our experience showed people still believed in the ideals of socialism. We had built up a movement based on the discredited and dead values of collective action. We saw the most combative elements of society, like the young, looking for a radical alternative. Labour to them was the establishment.

In Pollok we extended the radicalism of our poll tax campaign into other areas of people's lives. Nazis from the BNP were run out of the area. One day George and the young team cleaned out the water tower where everyone used to go to sniff glue. Then they called a big meeting to explain the dangers of fascism – over 100 turned up.

There followed another big meeting to tackle young people's concerns. George had a speaker who had been involved with gang violence to tell them it was a waste of energy. He had former heroin addicts telling them drug addiction was just a way of keeping them down. That sparked off their campaign for better young people's facilities. Tam Diamond, one of the youths, tells the story of coming out of jail and looking for the young team in the closes. He couldn't find them because they were all at a Militant meeting. He thought he better go along too.

The Pollok posse attended the AGM of a community hall which was threatened with closure and got themselves elected onto the committee. They saved the project and now they run it themselves – George is the chairman.

We revitalised the tenants' associations and community councils – giving them a new political coherence. Unless oppositon is focused and organised, with clear political goals, it will remain opposition. Nothing will change except the tired voices of the people protesting. In Pollok we were rebuilding the types of popular movement which inspired the poll tax campaign. Why not all over Scotland?

After a long, internal debate, throughout Militant in Britain and internationally we set up Scottish Militant Labour. The name was important. We were keen to have Scottish in there because you have to recognise national identity without undermining socialism. Labour is there because it's the movement with which working-class people have traditionally identified. Militant describes the kind of Labour we want. Only Militancy can tackle the deprivation and squalor in which we live.

The French writer, Paul Valéry, said: 'Politics is the art of preventing people from taking part in affairs which properly concern them.' We wanted to turn that on its head.

9 Saughton Jail – university of revolution

Scotland's leading civil rights lawyer stared at the jars of midget gems and Russian caramels. Alan Miller is a serious guy at the best of times. But this time he was especially grave. He looked hard at me across the shiny formica table, before giving his coffee another thoughtful stir. 'It's not looking good, Tommy,' he said above the hiss of the cappucino machine.

Alan had just come from Edinburgh, where Scotland's legal élite meet in cosy clubs to trade gossip in anglicised tones. We were chatting in a less salubrious, but well-scrubbed establishment – the *Criterion* Cafe, at Glasgow Cross. We discussed my case. Abernethy McIntyre wanted me done for defying the interdict served on the day of the warrant sale in Turnbull Street. Alan had been more optimistic in October. 'People breach interdicts all the time . . .' he told me. By November the legal eagles were twittering. Alan had it on good authority they wanted to make an example of me. A custodial sentence was more than likely. The question I had to consider in the *Criterion* was whether I wanted to spend Christmas in jail. Alan could have the case called in December.

I went back to the Fed shop and discussed it with the comrades. I remember everyone being really cavalier with my life.

'Definitely go for the Christmas stint, Tam, it will make them look so mean! Show everyone how low they can sink! Loads of good publicity.'

That's universal brotherhood for you. All the same, I knew they were right. I wanted to embarrass the authorities as much as possible. And at least I wouldn't have to sing at Hogmanay. Could this be the reason for the unanimity of my comrades on the timing?

As it turned out, I was able to enjoy my mother's turkey. When the case came up in December 1991 I was not in a position to defend myself. The Scottish Legal Aid Board in their wisdom refused me funding. Lord Caplan delayed the case till January. They eventually conceded. My liberty was at stake after all. But I was denied Legal Aid to actually challenge the interdict on three occasions. It still stands today.

Basically it stops me interfering with anything Abernethy McIntyre do. If I make a speech criticising their methods and urging people to oppose warrant sales I could be in breach of the interdict again. In the old days, freedom of speech was curtailed quite blatantly. Maclean was repeatedly charged with sedition after addressing workers. At least that was honest. Now we have an illusion of democracy. No one is charged with sedition. The rich take out expensive interdicts against their critics. Unless you have thousands of pounds to challenge them, you are effectively bound and gagged.

We needed the Legal Aid money to employ an advocate to represent me in the high court. When we got that sorted out I had to travel through and meet him. Going up the steps of the high court is quite intimidating. You feel like a commoner, which is probably how you're supposed to feel. I remember looking down at my trainers and thinking I should be wearing polished shoes. There were all these guys nicking about in capes and wigs – the uniform which says: This is our exclusive club. Not for the likes of you!

The court is in Parliament Square, where the Scots parliament sat until the Union of England and Scotland in 1707. All the buildings are dark and ornate. St Giles cathedral towers up on one side. The Royal Mile runs past, linking Edinburgh Castle at the top with Holyrood Palace at the bottom. Glaswegian radicals were traditionally sent to Edinburgh for punishment. Eight shop stewards from the Clyde Workers' Committee were exiled here in 1916 after a series of strikes the *Glasgow Herald* described as: 'A vile conspiracy against the state.' Less fortunate labour leaders – like the Calton weavers – were whipped through these streets.

I was reminded how little had changed since Maclean and others walked up these steps. In her biography of her father, Nan Milton describes the opening of the court case in 1916, when Maclean received three years imprisonment for campaigning against forced conscription during World War One: outwardly he was alone facing overwhelming odds, but in his mind's eye he could see ranged on his side the powerful historical forces which would one day sweep aside all this awe-inspiring pomp as so much worthless junk.

We met Derek, the advocate, in a vast room with a timber roof and dark oil paintings of old men in wigs. This is where advocates meet their clients. They pace from one end to the other in a military way. This was parliament hall, where the Scottish parliament occasionally met until the Union.

Derek Batchelor led us down a spiral staircase into the cubby hole which was his room. He seemed an okay guy. I doubt we had much in common politically. But I got the sense he had a bit of respect for our moral stance. The first thing he did was advise me to plead guilty. That could have got us off on the wrong foot but Alan had warned me on the train he was duty bound to do this. Derek explained the judge might take a more lenient view if I admitted my guilt. I might get off with a fine.

No way was I going to plead guilty. I was not going to accept that what I had done was unlawful. I remember reading about the pressure Maclean was under in his cases. Strike a deal. Plea bargain. Get off lightly. But he was absolutely firm – to admit guilt to these people would be to submit to their laws. In 1916, Jimmy Maxton and Jimmy MacDougall pleaded guilty to sedition after telling workers to strike during a big demonstration at Glasgow Green. They gave an unjust law legitimacy and still ended up being sentenced to a year each.

Obviously you have to keep things in perspective. I did not face the same hardship as those fearless men. Maclean's health and eventually his life was taken by hard labour and semi-starvation in Peterhead Prison. But the principle remains the same.

Derek accepted my decision. Now we had to prepare a defence. Given the overwhelming evidence against me, it would be a challenge. Half the country's television viewers saw me tear up the interdict on the Scottish news. Sometimes people say I shouldn't have ripped up the paper – but my attendance alone was a breach of the interdict – tearing it up just told them what I thought.

My preferred defence was moral: we were in Turnbull Street to protect someone who could not defend herself. We were also making a point about the far-reaching effect this could have on other people threatened with warrant sales. But morals have no place in a court of law. Or, at least, our morals have no place in their courts. Our defence had to be in law. Derek consulted his case histories and came up with a sound legal argument. The interdict banned us from interfering with the warrant sale. But the sale never took place – it was cancelled just before 11 am. So how could we interfere with something that never happened? Well, it was credible enough on paper.

Having sorted that out, I hardly gave much thought to the trial. We were so busy at that time. On 20 January we stopped fifteen poindings. On 22 January we were all up at 5.30am to leaflet South Nitshill for a meeting that night. The General Election could be called at any time and I was the SML candidate for Pollok.

The hearing began on Thursday 23 January. Most of the day was spent viewing the police video of Turnbull Street, along with the already familiar Scottish Television footage. The court saw a bois-terous but determined crowd. There was only one worrying clip. A guy in a brown leather jacket was aggressively pushing people from behind. But it turned out he was an undercover cop. There were ten of them mingling with the crowd that day – in addition to the dozens in uniform. You could spot him disappear behind police lines. Agent Provocateurs have been used to discredit working-class protest for hundreds of years. John Maclean asked the audience at his meetings to check the shoes of the person next to them – if they were shiny and well-heeled they were likely to be a police agent. Agents were also used in Trafalgar Square and on most picket lines.

On Friday a police inspector gave evidence to say there were three ringleaders of the demo: Sheridan, McNeilage and another. He insisted I'd said: 'Fuck the interdict' as I ripped it up. They played him the video tape over and over, but not once could the expletive be heard. 'I could read his lips' he insisted, to much laughter.

I can swear as good as anyone but not usually in public and not with scores of journalists and a couple of TV cameras in tow. Swear words have little place in speeches, though sometimes I can't help referring to bosses and certain members of the ruling class as bastards, because that's what they are.

Freda Reilly and big crowbar McIntyre were not convincing witnesses. Freda's gaffe was the most entertaining. 'Do you see anyone in court who was in Turnbull Street that day, apart from Sheridan?' She pointed to Alan Miller, who was sitting behind me taking notes. He had visions of *Daily Record* headlines saying: 'Civil liberties lawyer implicated in poll tax riot!' Where the hell was he on 1 October? Fortunately he remembered and told Derek.

'Are you quite sure about that, Mrs Reilly?' asked Derek. She said she was sure. Would it surprise you to hear that Mr Miller is a lawyer who was in Dumfries Sheriff Court on the day in question? She still insisted he was there. Derek later said her evidence was hardly reliable because she even implicated Alan. Counsel for Abernethy McIntyre stood up and said: 'We all know Mr Miller. We know he is a lawyer. That's all we're prepared to accept.' It was a cheap jibe against a principled man. The establishment hate anyone who breaks ranks.

Derek was beginning to think we had more of a case. He advised us not to blow it by calling defence witnesses. More than fifteen witnesses were waiting to say their piece in my defence. I reluctantly agreed not to call them. But I was determined to take the witness stand.

Convinced I would be found guilty anyway, it was the only way to get our message across. It was quite nerve wracking. I'd been in sheriff court witness stands loads of times, but this was different. Crown counsel kept pushing me on the issue of violence. 'You were prepared to use violence to stop this warrant sale, weren't you?' I was a bit cheeky and said: 'Did you see any violence on the video?' I was asked: 'Who's cross-examining who?'

I was getting asked things like: Were you aware that this was an interdict to ban you from the warrant sale? Of course I could have played daft and said: Naw, I wisnae aware of that. I could have said If I'd been aware I wouldnae have went. But I had to think of the wider implications. People in England and Wales were going to prison for following our campaign. I couldn't rat out of it. My evidence was enough to convict me. Alan Miller said I was the best prosecution witness of the lot. But I think he would agree with me that the decision to send me down was taken long before the court case.

The court room was mobbed for the summing up on Tuesday. There must have been around 100 people on the public benches. By this time the charges against my co-accused, David Landels, had been dismissed. This was further evidence of the political nature of the hearing. Davie had been served an identical interdict. Like me it barred him from attending the sale, and like me he turned up in Turnbull Street that morning. But the court was only interested in making an example of one person – it was nothing to do with the evidence or the rights and wrongs of the thing.

I looked around and saw the familiar faces – my mum, George, Coco, John Cooper from Castlemilk, Dave and Betty Curry who had become like aunt and uncle to me. I couldn't feel alone with such solid support.

I was carrying a little Clydeside Press book for inspiration: *All for the Cause*. It was the story of Willie Nairn, who pioneered Marxism in Scotland until his death in 1902. Revolutionary activity meant he could not keep a job. So he worked as a stone breaker. After this exhausting and repetitive work, he spoke at six or seven meetings a week. And he still found time to write extensively on Marxism, the vibrant new philosphy sweeping across Europe. Reading about his life stopped me feeling sorry for myself.

All the same, I felt quite shaken when Lord Caplan delivered the sentence at 2.30pm. Six months! Predicting the length of my incarceration had become a source of endless lunchtime entertainment in the course of the hearing. I think someone might have had a book on it. The prosecution evidence was so bad that they had settled for three months maximum. Talk about a false sense of security! I was pretty gutted. But I couldn't show I was upset. I knew from others that my mum was very worried about the whole business. I didn't want to make it worse for her.

Lord Caplan gave a little lecture. 'In a democratic society it is the rule of law that shields it from anarchy and mob rule . . . many forms of political protest are available but ignoring court orders and obstructing sheriff officers are not among their number.' What a pompous man. He said I was lucky it was not a more severe sentence. If it had been proven I was involved in damaging the van, then I would have got longer.

I wanted to jump to my feet and shout: 'Who elected you? Who are you accountable to? It's people like you who undermine democracy. Sitting there in your horsehair wig and your £93,000 a year salary.'

All the things you wish you'd said at the time . . . I wanted to say 'Hasta la Vista, Baby' like Arnold Schwarznegger in *Terminator*. But I couldn't be sure of getting the correct pronunciation. So I said something like: We'll be Back. I wished later I'd said more.

I was taken to a tiny room underneath the court. Alan and Derek appeared. They told me the sentence was too severe. This was grounds for appeal. Alan agreed to come and see me the next day, then they were gone. I was left with two policemen and a well-thumbed Wullie Nairn. Out of nowhere they produced a pair of handcuffs. It took me by surprise. It seemed like unneccesary humiliation. 'Do you think I'm going to run away?' I asked. But they said nothing.

I was led through a low door into a narrow corridor which seemed to open onto the road. I could hear the crowd singing as I got nearer, and cheering as I came into view. I so wanted to stop and say a few words of encouragement. I think I managed to give an awkward thumbs-up despite the handcuffs. But all the time I was being pushed from behind into the back of the waiting van.

When the doors were shut I realised I was in a cage. The side of the van vibrated with a few dull thuds as we drove off. Saughton here we come. What would it be like? I didn't know what to expect. But at least I was mentally prepared. I knew what I was doing was right. Imagine how it must feel for a young guy getting put away for the first time?

After a few minutes the van stopped. Were we here already? No, the cop – a different cop from the ones in court – was asking me if I wanted to come up to the front of the van. So I sat behind him and his mate. They took the handcuffs off. 'A bit severe, six months, isn't it? All you did was tear up a piece of paper,' said one. The other offered me a fag. This was to be the first of many hundreds of small acts of humanity I would come across in prison.

Entering Saughton Prison is like going into a huge factory; except this plant processes people. The reception area resembles a production line, with endless rows of clothes. These belong to the cons, who must leave the last traces of individuality hanging on the rail.

I was back in handcuffs when they passed me over to prison reception. 'We've been expecting you,' said the screw. We all smiled. They asked my waist and shoe size then told me to strip and take a shower. It's a bit daunting, because the shower is in the middle of the reception area and not really screened. The screws and the cons who work there take it for granted. But you feel vulnerable by yourself, when everything is strange to you. I changed into the regulation stripey blue shirt and these terrible trousers that look like denim but are just floppy cotton. Belts are forbidden – in case you try to commit suicide or attack someone. I remember being instructed to remove my watch and jewellery – I wear my mum's wedding ring on my pinkie and another which belonged to my granda Peter on my right index finger. One of them was stuck and the guy says, 'You'd better be careful, I've heard of people getting their fingers cut off for less around here.' I gave him a disbelieving look. Was he trying to wind me up? 'I'll take my chances,' I replied.

They put me in what they called the dog box. It's like a tiny cupboard with a wee wooden seat in it. When they shut the door you're sitting in pitch darkness. Nothing happens. You wait and you wait for what seems like ages. The systematic nature of prisons is designed to subdue and control inmates. The dog box was a way of cooling off a prisoner through sensory deprivation. After being left in the dark so long you become compliant – you're so glad of human contact.

It was a relief when they finally opened the door and handed me my Community Charge Exemption form – prisoners don't need to pay. What a load off my mind that was! We all had a good laugh about it and one of the officers said: 'Listen, we'll try and get you a job here.' I found out later it was a really generous gesture, because reception jobs are popular. You get better cells, and can take your meals when you like. Most important of all, you get to meet people. Human contact is highly valued in prison, as I was to discover.

Cell 28 in B Hall was to be home. Everyone called the cell their peter. (I think it means safe place.) Ricky, my cell mate, was also new and even more nervous than me. He'd got a year for assault – his first offence – at the age of forty-seven. Apparently, some guy started noising up his wife in the pub. Ricky told him to stop but was challenged to a fight. In the course of things he picked up a tumbler and smashed it in the guy's face. Yet he seemed a really mellow character.

We were locked up until 5 pm when you could go for tea. Around that time I heard a voice outside: 'Sheridan! Sheridan! Come out.' The screw opened the door and the con standing there said: 'My name's Cat and I'm fae Govan – come along tae the peter and have a wee cup of tea.' It turned out he was Ian MacLean and got his nickname because he'd been a goal keeper on Govan shipyard's football team. He even knew Mr Davies, father of my best pal, Billy, who had worked beside him.

Next thing Cat's calling in others and the cell is getting crowded: 'Meet Tam, you know, he's the anti-poll tax guy!' I was a bit like the circus act. All the cons are giving it: That's terrible, you shouldnae be in here. They were offering me baccy and powdered milk and tea bags. That night, when I crawled between the scratchy prison blankets on the squeaky iron bed, I felt strangely relaxed. Maybe it wouldn't be so bad.

You are wakened at 6.30 am when the keys turn in the door. First thing you do is empty your piss pot and wash your hands and face. Prisons are designed to dehumanise people in small ways – like forcing you to do the toilet in front of someone else – and then sleep with the stench. This practice is now banned in European law – another piece of progressive legislation ignored by this government.

The cell doors are closed again until 8 am when you go down to breakfast. Everyone has their own chair, and I didn't want to aggravate some big guy by stealing his place. Luckily, Cat's mate Dave kept me a seat. Monday to Friday you get lumpy porridge, which is inedible after the first three spoonfuls. You don't get sugar unless you bring your own. You must take your own cup as well, or you get no tea. At weekends you are allowed cornflakes – with enough milk to drown a fly. Food is always boiled: anaemic carrots, flaccid cabbage, powdery potatoes. It's very bland. Having said that, I ate three meals a day in Saughton, which was more regular than outside on the broo.

Prison makes you appreciate all the wee things you take for granted. I wasn't able to shower for days and kept having to borrow soap. You just feel really manky all the time. The cheap razor blades hack at your face. Worst of all was not being allowed a watch – having no idea of time. Everyone loved to have a radio, to give them a sense of time passing. You are not allowed pictures of yourself in case you use them to make a Colditz-style passport to escape. Some of my political opponents or even my friends for that matter might suggest this was the greatest deprivation of all, but I survived. By day two I was scribbling all the things I'd need on the back of an envelope: radio and deodorant being top of the list.

'You made the front page' shouted Cat who was out sweeping the corridor. He pushed the *Daily Record* under my peter door: 'Downfall of the Dodger' said the splash which then talked about a 'Smirking Tommy Sheridan, getting his comeuppance.' I later heard the paper got a lot of calls of complaint. The editor completely misjudged the working-class readership. It pretends to be a people's paper, but really it's just an establishment rag. To think its former owner, the arch crook Robert Maxwell, died with a Labour Party membership card in his bulging wallet. That really hurt.

The *Record* never carried anything on the federation's press conferences about warrant sales. Suddenly I was newsworthy. But they did me a favour because they let everyone know I was inside.

A screw came late that afternoon and told me I was being moved to D Hall. I asked him what it was like and he said: 'Do you know the difference between heaven and hell?' I said: 'Naw, is the jacuzzi a different temperature?' I shouldn't have laughed. B Hall's cells were clean and comfortable. I was going into a dungeon.

First, the noise hits you. It's a much younger population and there were loads of guys shouting. The stench as they open the cell door was overpowering. Everything was dark, cold and boggin'. The floor felt sticky beneath your feet. Jam was plastered over the walls. Prisoners are not allowed blu tack or glue – in case of abuse – so they steal jam from the canteen to put up posters.

The first thing I did was take down the pornographic pictures. They made me feel uncomfortable. Every cell I visited was decorated with pornographic photographs. Some guys offered me books, with the same kind of material in them, almost as a sign of friendship.

Engaging anyone in an argument about the exploitation of women would not have been wise under the circumstances. You have to be very careful in prison. It's considered natural to swap porn mags and you might be considered unnatural. Still, I refused.

D hall was dirty because it only held a transient population of remand prisoners. The guys in B Hall were serving sentences between one and five years – it was in their interests to keep the place clean. I was in D Hall because civil prisoners were not supposed to mix with convicted criminals. Until then I did not understand the distinction. Civil prisoners are rare in Scotland and I was the first in Edinburgh for five years.

Cat and the boys told me about my rights. They said civil prisoners were entitled to their own television, clothes, chairs and tables. They liked to see one of their own getting his due. They were really annoyed at a radio report saying I was living in the lap of luxury. Strangely enough, for someone locked up for defying authority, I was initially nervous about making demands. Maybe the system was getting to me.

Although the perks due to a civil prisoner were not forthcoming at that stage, I was suffering the drawbacks. Apart from D Hall, which was so cold I spent the night rearranging the blankets, the visiting arrangements were like something from the Gulag. Normally prisoners meet their families in a big room with lots of long tables. But because I was segregated, I met my first visitors – Mum, Hannah McArthur and Davie Archibald – in a room reserved for anyone suspected of smuggling drugs. There was a big glass screen between us, and an officer on either side. There's just enough space for your fingers to touch underneath the partition.

Terry Fields, then MP for Liverpool Broadgreen, said I'd find more humanity in prison than the House of Commons. Terry had done time in England for poll tax non-payment. Now I knew what he meant.

I made loads of friends among the remand prisoners. There was Mick and Curly and Jimmy from Fife, who spoke to me as soon as I arrived. Then there was Fitzy, who did a lot of reading and lent

me his *Economist* and *Newsweek*. Or Harry, from Greenock, who
sweated it out with me during circuit training. He talked about the
yards where he had worked, and how his life changed when the
redundancy money ran out. All the stories had the same threads
twisting through them: unemployment, deprivation and alcohol.
But most guys didn't make the connection until I brought it up.

Often we'd get together at tea break, about six or seven to a cell,
and the lads would pass round their charge sheets. One guy was
charged with sticking a screw driver through someone's head. When
I asked what happened he said: 'Tam, I was blotto, out my heid . . .'
Another prisoner was a turbo mechanic – a highly skilled job – yet
he was accused of deliberately driving over someone – reversing back
just to make sure. The victim walks with a limp now. This mechanic
was a thoughtful type who did a lot of reading. Yet he couldn't
remember the night in question. He was in a drunken stupor.

Jail made me want to change the way alcohol is so accepted in
society. I'm a non-drinker. I think it stems from my childhood,
through seeing other people's fathers paralytic. Mums and dads
would fight and it was horrible.

I got drunk once at the age of ten. It was during a New Year
party at my house. I was in a bad mood about something and spent
all night sitting under the table, sipping from everyone's drinks.
Then I visited Mrs Jack next door who gave me a Breaker malt lager.
It finished me off. When I came back home I fell over in the hall.
The whole family laughed and thought I was joking. But their
laughter turned to outrage when they saw me crawling to the toilet
where I spewed my ring. My mother wanted to kill me but Gran
Rose leapt to my defence. She produced some liver salts and told
them all to leave me be. I decided early on I never wanted to feel
like that again. I always want to be in control of my faculties.

In jail I met warm, friendly people. Drink turned them into the
nutcases who destroyed other people's lives with blades and broken
bottles. It's no coincidence that the big breweries are among the
largest contributors to the Conservative Party. That's why advertising
for drink is so prevalent. The early socialists were mainly teetotal.

They saw alcohol as a way of enslaving the working classes. In many ways that's what it does. Why else did employers once pay their workers in the pub?

In South Africa the Apartheid state subsidises cheap beer halls in the black townships. These were wrecked by youths during the uprisings – they recognised them as a tool of oppression. The temperance movement in Britain wanted to built an alternative social life – their halls were used for everything from ILP meetings to weddings. Nobody wants to be a killjoy. But alcohol is a dangerous, legalised drug which needs to be handled very carefully. The news of my release came over someone's radio and was round the canteen before I heard myself. One guy came to congratulate me then asked if he could have my sugar. Alan Miller had been trying for interim liberation pending appeal, but I had not been optimistic. My QC's agent said there were political shenanigans at the High Court. Certain people were determined to keep me inside. Derek overcame these establishment obstacles and next thing I knew I was being interviewed at the prison gates.

I told the press we would fight this unsafe conviction. I also said I was looking forward to playing football next day with Dalzell, the amateur team I played with. This upset the manager, Geordie, who phoned up later and said: 'What do you mean? Who says you're picked?' But the entire Scottish press corps were coming to cover our clash with Coatbridge next day. Geordie's arm was twisted and I was in the team. Fortunately we won, so the big man was happy enough.

Scottish Militant Labour had a more important contest to train for in those few weeks – even more important than football. We decided soon after our launch that I would stand against Jimmy Dunnachie in Pollok. The immediate reaction of the Labour right-wing was ridicule.

Stewart Maclennan, Dunnachie's election agent, compared us to the prostitute Miss Whiplash. 'We already have a fringe candidate – the Corrective Party'.

Pat Lally, the leader of Glasgow District council, said if we came out in the open we might muster enough supporters to fill a telephone box.

We'd have to see what happened. At first we thought I might still have freedom during the general election campaign. Appeals on civil cases usually take a long time to come to court. A gap of six months between the conviction and the appeal hearing is quite normal. In my case the creaking wheels of justice began to whir. My appeal was in a month's time. They were determined to bang me up again before polling day.

Those weeks leading up to the appeal hearing were a blur of street meetings and early morning leafleting. I spoke a great deal about how the law works differently for rich and poor. For example, Ernest Saunders, the Guinness chairman, embezzled £6 million. He was given five years – but the appeal court halfed his sentence on the grounds that he was suffering from Alzheimers' Disease at the age of fifty-five. He eventually only served ten months. After his release, Saunders astounded the medical world with his recovery from what is supposed to be a progressive disease. He was playing tennis and launching a legal battle to clear his name. Maybe his £75,000 annual pension from Guinness cheered him up. It only made three leading psychiatrists more concerned – they criticised the diagnosis saying his spontaneous recovery from dementia was unprecedented.

Compare Ernie's treatment to that of Marie McGregor, a thirty year-old mother from Govan. I don't know her. I read about her in the *Evening Times*. She admitted stealing three packets of meat from Littlewoods in Argyle Street. Her agent said she had three children and only £39 a week plus family allowance to live on. She had no money left to buy food that week. The sheriff jailed her for sixty days.

There were lots of other examples. While I was jailed for defying the law, lots of supermarkets in England and Wales were trading illegally on a Sunday. No judge or magistrate lectured them before handing out a six month sentence. Most ironic of all was our own attempt to turn the tables on Strathclyde Regional Council. They had banned the Federation, and then SML from hiring any of its premises – a ban which is still in force three years later. This is a travesty of democracy because schools and community centres run by the region are often the only public buildings in the big housing schemes. Militant took out an interdicts at our lawyers' suggestion. Charlie Gray was completely contemptuous of the court. He told the papers we could do what we liked we still weren't getting in. Someone suggested we could end up sharing a cell. But the law works in mysterious ways. Charlie heard no more about it.

The weeks flew by until suddenly it was the night before the appeal hearing. I addressed a crowd of 200 people in a pensioners' hall in Arden. Three generations, all with hope in their eyes, sat in the tiny room. Some of the women were crying. Our community had placed their faith in us. What a huge compliment. After so many years of being ignored and disappointed, they had every right to be cynical. Instead, they had embraced our values of sharing and struggling together for a better way to live. I say embraced, but in fact these values are woven into the daily fabric of working class life. Militant did not invent them. I was determined not to let them down.

Naturally, I lost the appeal the next day. This time three judges upheld the original hearing. Four noble lords had now decided I was a threat to the democratic process. So it was back into the handcuffs, the van, the dog box, the open plan shower and the stripey shirt before being snibbed up in peter 23 of D Hall. That was 6 March. The election was on 9 April. What timing. It was also my 28th birthday on the 7th of March, the next day.

How could I campaign from a smelly mattress in a prison cell forty miles away? The cell was even worse than the one in January. At least the jam on the walls was fresh then. This stuff was caked black, having given years of adhesive to pornographic pictures. Peter 23 wasn't much of a campaign head-quarters. There were no screaming telephones, no harrassed canvassers popping in and out, no detailed wall charts of our progress. Keith Baldassarra was my election agent. To reach him I had to use a bit of political manoeuvring.

We were not allowed to phone from prison after a certain time at night. Keith was at meetings until late, so to catch him I'd have to bluff the screw: 'I've got permission from the governor. He said it's okay to call after nine!' I'd grin while clutching my prison issue phone cards. Clearly, this flannel wouldn't work more than twice. Alan Miller gave me a little book on the rights of civil prisoners. These rights, along with the Representation of the People's Act, allowed me to fight the election from prison.

The last person to do this was Bobby Sands, the Irish Republican hunger striker who won Fermanagh and South Tyrone from his cell on 9 April 1981. But my political inspiration came from the Clydeside socialist, John Maclean. In 1918 he stood in the Gorbals while still locked up in Peterhead where he was being forcibly fed through a rubber tube. Maclean was on hunger strike in protest against the five-year sentence he received that year for making seditious speeches encouraging workers to take control like their brothers and sisters in Russia. Maclean had made a famous speech from the dock. He said the war was really about the two capitalist powers, Britain and Germany, who were fighting to gain markets for their products. Millions of young men were slaughtered in the trenches for this greed. 'I am not here as the accused,' he told the court. 'I am here as the accuser of capitalism, dripping with blood from head to foot.' The Gorbals Labour party wanted Maclean as their candidate, despite opposition from London. He was released shortly before polling day, a very sick man. He got 7,436 votes.

Maclean was unable to contribute to his campaign while locked up. It was run entirely by Willie Gallagher. I was more fortunate in many ways. I was living in an age of mass communications which could, in theory, pierce the prison walls. The Representation of the Peoples Act gave me certain rights. As a civil prisoner, I could request utensils. But was a vodaphone a utensil? The assistant governor did not blink as I listed my requirements: a phone, a fax, a writing desk, a radio cassette, a television, access to my agent and the press. Keith was later told by the governor he could have everything he wanted for the duration of the campaign – except his candidate. I got the impression they were bending over backwards to appear liberal. I wouldn't be able to kiss any babies. But our campaign wasn't about kissing babies anyway.

Our opponents sneered: Look at Sheridan, with his vodaphone, his video messages and his press conferences. Who does he think he is! In fact, it was a great victory for us. You have to remember I was put away because the authorities didn't like what I said. Yet here we were, breaking new political ground. We put it down to our support: all the letters piling in, the visits from MPs like Terry Fields, Jim Sillars and Dick Douglas. All this pressure meant they might lock the problem away, but could not make it disappear.

I was twenty-eight the day after I was jailed. Kenny Weir and some guys at the Celtic vs Morton cup tie at Parkhead chipped in £10 to have a message put over the electronic notice board above the ground. 'Happy Birthday, Tommy Sheridan, from three million friends and supporters – you'll never walk alone.' My only gripe was that a similar message was not relayed at Ibrox. But Charlie Gray was fizzing in the *Daily Record* the following Monday. Under the headline 'Paradise Puzzle' he said: 'Celtic should think again about accepting that kind of political advertisement since it is extremely one-sided in the run-up to a general election.' My being slammed up was not sufficient – he wanted me shut up as well. Our supporters collected a fortune at that game. While we expected the sentence, the general public was outraged. Like the polis who drove me into prison, they couldn't understand all this iron heel treatment for simply tearing up a bit of paper. They dropped fifty pences and pound notes in the collecting cans while making points about child abusers and muggers who had got off more lightly.

After about a week the prison governor brought good news. I would be moved to a place more suitable for the purposes of a political campaign. My new residence would be in the Training for Freedom Unit, a section of the prison where lifers prepared for release. Inside the self-contained building, prisoners made their own decisions about how to run things. They stayed in their own rooms, which locked from the inside. They had freedom of movement within that two storey building.

Jimmy Marr, the officer in charge of the TFF unit, led me across the yard and showed me to my room. The door opened to reveal this incredibly muscular and unhappy looking guy removing the last of his possessions. These were two enormous dumb bells – they looked like bar bells to me, but he was carrying them easily in fists the size of footballs. His name was Ronnie and this was his room. He was cleaning it out to make way for me, while he was being bumped upstairs. He gave us a cold stare as he passed.

I was already feeling nostalgic for the smell of urine and dried-up strawberry jam in D Hall. Officers in the TFF unit left the building at 8 pm, allowing the lifers to organise themselves behind the locked main door. I felt a bit out of place. My presence was causing discussion to say the least.

Peter, a really friendly guy in his late forties, whom everyone called Plum, explained some of the frostiness when we met at dinner that night. 'There's a bit of a problem with you coming here, but it's nothing to do with you,' he said. TFF was supposed to be all about consultation, and they weren't consulted about me coming. They were simply told.

Most of the TFF prisoners went out on day release to work for charities and community projects around Edinburgh. That left me alone in the unit with Ronnie, the big guy whose home I had taken. Unlike the others, he had no release date. He was the pass man for the building. It was like a caretaker's job, making him responsible for keeping the place clean, fetching food and so on. I soon bumped into him in the corridor while he was mopping up. He was really warm and friendly and explained the earlier cold stare. He was refused an outside pass that weekend to attend a family christening. After knocking him back they said: this prisoner, Sheridan's, coming over – you don't mind doubling up to make way for him, do you? You don't talk back in prison, not if you value your parole chances.

Ronnie and I spent a lot of time together and became close friends. Every morning after mopping up he'd come into my room with a poached egg on toast. We'd talk for hours and he'd tell me stories about life inside. He'd already served eleven years of a life sentence in twelve different prisons. These stories opened my eyes to a different world. He came from a rough part of Edinburgh and always felt he had a reputation to live up to. When he was a teenager he actually broke into Saughton to see his father, who was himself serving a life sentence. Needless to say, it caused the authorities great embarrassment. Ronnie talked about the Ghost Train: being moved from prison to prison without seeing family or friends. About losing touch, becoming rootless within the system. And the repetitious violence of it all. He had a lazy eye, it looked like glass sometimes. That was from an attack early on, in Wormwood Scrubs. Three gangsters jumped him in the shower. They stuck a biro pen in his eye and hit him over the head with a battery inside a sock – the standard offensive weapon in prison. He would have been killed but for the soap in his hair which caused the battery to slip. Surviving such attacks meant Ronnie knew how to handle himself. Just being his mate protected me from the attentions of the small group of bullies you get inside every prison.

I really suffered with him whenever a meeting of the parole board came up. Ronnie saw all these guys pass through TFF to the outside world – where his own wife and four kids were waiting. He never knew when he would cross the line. Being in TFF is really tantalising, even for someone like me serving a short sentence. I took days to adjust. It seemed like freedom. But it stretched a finger out to you, when really you wanted to grab the hand – a real mental battle.

Like a lot of guys he would take out his frustrations in the gym. The previous year he organised a million kilo lift for charity involving several cons in the prison gym. Now he worked with the bench press and weights he'd set up in the toilet upstairs. Physical exercise becomes really important to you in prison. I was obsessive about it. I started to work out with Ronnie and I suppose that sealed a kind of a bond.

Ronnie told me how he used to have a temper which led him into trouble in his younger days. He wanted to escape from his aggressive Edinburgh reputation, so he moved to London where he set up a business restoring furniture. He had been happy and stayed out of trouble for three years. Then he was charged with murder. He showed me a lot of the paperwork relating to his trial and, in my opinion, the evidence made for an unsafe conviction.

Ronnie had been inside for so long, I think he was glad to find someone a bit different he could talk to. Years in prison can make people emotionally crippled and unresponsive. One guy of thirty came across like a seventeen year-old – he just hadn't developed since starting his sentence.

Ronnie, by contrast, was a complex individual. A hard man with a soft heart. He once wrote some poetry just to prove to me he could do it. He helped me fit into the system and was full of prison folk wisdom: 'Always be the hunter, never the hunted.' Once, after a press conference, he advised me to make more of my imprisonment. I didn't want to to play the martyr, but Ronnie said: 'Look at the bars on those windows. Try to open the door. You can't just walk out of here and see your friends.'

I became more painfully aware of my captivity when the election really got underway. Keith Baldassarra became my eyes and ears in Pollok, as well as my voice. He would debate in my place on the hustings. One night he'd be arguing freedom of choice in an abortion debate before a middle-class audience in Shawlands. Then next he'd be in the Sikh Temple, discussing the poll tax campaign.

I longed to be on the streets to catch the buzz. We got the result of a canvass showing nearly thirty-five definites in the first week of the campaign. We recruited 140 new members in Pollok in the short time since I went back inside. Our people were young and fresh, many with no experience of a political campaign. Within days they had mastered the Reading system of canvassing.

As in the anti-poll tax campaign, we stirred a lot of people who were reminded of the socialism of their youth. One old man travelled from Possil in the north of Glasgow because our methods reminded him of his days in the ILP. Alan McCombes canvassed the street in Priesthill where he lived as a kid. Everyone there was voting for us. Old neighbours of his parents, people he'd always considered set in their ways, all right behind us. Even anarchists, like John Cooper and Andy Dick, leafletted for us because of the circumstances of my imprisonment. Later, when my mother held a vigil outside the prison, John offered to sell his car to get something for her to shelter under. Some Labour party members put our yellow and red posters in their windows. Stewart Maclennan was apparently sending window checkers round to catch the disloyal.

The gang running the show from my house in Linthaugh Road were always answering the door to find someone new offering their services. A couple of ten year-olds sat for hours licking envelopes. Another two eight year-olds wrote a song about me! Apparently the place was ablaze with red and yellow – some gardens even had billboards. Keith said we stopped the traffic with massive car cavalcades which made Pollok look like Notting Hill on carnival day.

We launched the Scottish Militant Labour manifesto in the prison conference room on 23 March. Eight of us commandeered the place, decorating the drab prison walls with posters. When the doors opened at 11.30 the entire media circus charged in – around thirty in all including two film crews. We were a bigger attraction than the Scottish Secretary, Ian Lang, who conducted a misjudged photo session with some penguins at Edinburgh zoo the same morning. I spoke for about ten minutes on what we stood for. But most of the questions were trivial. What did I miss most? Could I play football? What was the porridge like? The sub-editors loved it – lots of pithy headlines about captive audiences appeared next day.

Sometimes journalists said our campaign benefited from the novelty of a stay in hotel Saughton. 'You want to be in prison', they taunted. Sure, we made the best of things. We held another five press conferences, and numerous individual interviews inside the jail. We made the front page of the *Scotsman* and the *Independent*. We got a good show in the *Guardian*. Unfortunately few among my electorate in Pollok read these papers. When they picked up the *Record* or the *Sun*, there was hardly a column inch. Despite the novelty, despite the wall-to-wall monotony of the other election stories, the editors of these two papers ignored us.

We are used to that treatment. But at least when I was free I could go and speak to people directly. If I have any talent I think it's for public speaking. We tried to overcome this enormous disadvantage. I recorded a video message to be shown at an eve of election meeting. When we held a big rally in Pollok I spoke directly on the vodaphone, which was broadcast through a loudhailer. I remember being really nervous, which never happens when I'm actually on a platform. The transmission was so bad Davie Archibald insists it was a wee man shuffling in the gravel behind the stage, Wizard of Oz style. But everyone cheered. We made history, despite the feedback.

I was allowed use of a vodaphone for the 3-week duration of the election campaign. One to one calls were more successful. We put my Saughton vodaphone number on the back of a leaflet and told voters to call anytime. Lots did. I even had a few poll tax queries. I think I was more accessible to Pollok voters from the jail than the other candidates, who retired to their bungalows in residential areas at night.

The calls and letters from Pollok were full of enthusiasm. They really thought we were going to win. I hoped they would not be too disappointed on the night . . . I knew from Keith we were failing to pick up the votes in Shawlands and Pollokshields. That's when I missed being in the thick of things. I desperately wanted to speak to those voters, to convince them of our sincerity.

Election day came. Keith realised he had been so caught up in the politics he'd forgotten to get rosettes to wear on the platform. So he spent part of polling day trying to find somebody who'd make them in our red and yellow colours. He was successful – so we stuck political niceties on our lapels at least.

The vote, when it came, was incredible. We were second with 6287 compared to 14,170 for Labour. Their vote was slashed from 23,239 in 1987. Dunnachie looked really shaken according to my mother and Keith Baldassarra. His agent had compared us to the Corrective Party, now *they* were suffering the whiplash.

Nobody was paying much attention to Dunnachie's speech – you'd think we'd won. We could have come very close. Alan McCombes calculated we lost 5000 votes through people who kept their names off the register to avoid the poll tax. Richey Venton, a Militant organiser from Liverpool who helped in the campaign, met folk who were turned away from the polling station because they weren't down to vote. Still, we were the only people in Scotland celebrating that night – apart from a few Tory MPs whom everyone predicted would be wiped out . . . Our celebrations were, of course, couched in real and deep disappointment that Labour nationally had again failed to beat the Tories. Us and our class would suffer the consequences, the really harsh consequences Kinnock and the other right-wing leaders would face little fundamental change to their comfortable lives.

David Dimbleby conducted a live interview on the election show the next day. I spent half of it correcting him when he said I'd been jailed for not paying the poll tax. The press conference we held inside on the Friday was packed. We said we now had a mandate to speak for the schemes. Our people would never be neglected again.

It didn't take long for the despondency cloaking the rest of the country to reach Saughton. I didn't write in my diary for a week, struck dumb by the thought of five more years of Tory government. Scotland United was set up during this period, by a group of artists and politicians from different parties. They called for a multi-option referendum to allow Scotland to decide its future, pointing out that seventy-five per cent of Scots voted against the Tories. A huge rally was held in George Square shortly afterwards and our supporters were there – making sure red flags fluttered among the saltires.

I immediately liked the slogan. Working-class people are drawn towards unity – a fact cynically exploited by their leaders. But I was overcome by *déjà vu*. Scotland United was under the political wing of the STUC – none other than Campbell Christie and Bill Speirs. The very people who'd attempted to sabotage the Federation in the early days. Charlie Gray, who a year earlier was castigating sheriff officers for not hammering the poor hard enough, was talking about mass civil disobedience.

My suspicions were well founded. After the initial furore, all these people resumed their comfortable places in the Tory-sanctioned Scottish establishment. They had successfully contained the panic. Within a year, all the energy had been sapped out of Scotland United. No mass, democratic movement materialised. When the European leaders came to Edinburgh for the EC summit in December 1992, the STUC staged a big demonstration.

Why did they not bring the capital to a standstill, like the people of Leipzig? Why did the STUC leaders at the forefront of the campaign not organise a one-day general strike? Because Ian Lang told them not to embarrass Scotland on her big day? Might it put off potential investors? Civil disobedience was off the agenda. It was a job well done as far as the STUC was concerned.

But there was no time for despondency in April 1992. Scottish Militant Labour planned to fight the district elections in May on the basis of our Pollok vote. We contested every seat in the working-class part of the constituency. I stood in North Pollok, Nicky Bennett in South Nitshill, Angie Black in Arden and Bill Bill in Cowglen. Chic Stevenson and Jim McVicar, our two councillors who were expelled from the Labour Party, contested their own seats against imposed official candidates. Ann Lynch, secretary of the Drumchapel Anti Poll Tax Union, stood in the Summerhill part of that scheme.

I was desperate to win, mainly for the comrades and the people in Pollok. There was the added factor of my opponent, Stewart Maclennan, whose main reason for standing seemed to be stopping Militant. He published material attacking me personally.

Not that many Labour party canvassers actually set foot on Pollok doorsteps. We saw a few tired, old men on polling day. Rumour had it they were paid a tenner to stand there. We had to make sure we got our vote out on 7 May. Scotland was so depressed by the general election result. There was lots of talk of working-class voters staying at home for the district elections. Richey phoned on the morning of election day to say things were going to be close. What did he mean, close? I scrawled in my diary: 'Surely the turnout will affect everyone?'

In fact, we were getting people out who hadn't bothered to vote in years. Jack Jardine took several families to the polling station who had missed the last two elections. Now they believed their vote might make a difference.

I spent the day playing five aside, working out, answering letters. At 10.40pm I turned on the television. They said we were the only story in Glasgow. At 11pm I got a call from Alan McCombes who had borrowed the *Scotsman*'s phone at the count in the Scottish Exhibition Centre. Donald Dewar had just walked by him, looking even more grey about the gills than usual. Summerhill, the Drumchapel ward where Ann Lynch stood, had just gone to a recount. We had lost it by forty-six votes, but what an achievement! We did not expect that kind of support in virgin territory. I watched and waited. My mother was carrying a huge colour photograph of me and annoying every Labour Party member in the hall. I think it reminded them of scenes from distant countries – where political prisoners are represented by images.

The phone bleeped again shortly after 11pm. 'Can you get me a hoose?' It was Alan. I'd won. Ronnie came down from his room and congratulated me. 'It's a victory for the underdog,' he said. We sat watching the rest of the coverage. Scottish Television had sent a phone into the prison as the one I used in the general election was returned due to the expense. Bernard Ponsonby was to interview me live, but the batteries were failing fast. It won't be long now, said the producer at the other end when I explained the power problem. I was watching Bernard beam from the screeen – almost blinded by his polka dot tie.

'Now we're going over to Saughton Prison for the first interview with the new councillor for Pollok,' said Bernard. 'Councillor Sheridan – how do you feel tonight?'. At that very moment, "phut" The phone packed up. Bernard was looking out of the screen anxiously. 'Councillor Sheridan?' 'Can you hear me, councillor . . .?'

By this time Ronnie and I were bent double. Ponsonby turned to Pat Lally. He reminded the Glasgow council leader of his earlier comment that Militant supporters would be lucky to fill a telephone box if they stood under their own banner. 'There are an awful lot of telephone boxes in Glasgow tonight, Councillor Lally . . .'

Our success proved challenging the system earns votes as well as respect. We were no longer a single issue organisation. This provided us with the opportunity to raise the banner of genuine socialism and embarrass Labour in its own marble citadel. At every turn, we would expose the way the party was implementing Tory policies, the very policies Labour insisted they had no mandate to impose. A very proximate finger would now be pointed at the self-servers who claimed to be socialists. There were four of us on Glasgow District Council – Nicky, a community activist, won in South Nitshill. Our two sitting councillors regained their seats. We missed becoming the official opposition by those forty-six votes in the Drum.

They had been threatening to move me back to D hall after the election. The Scottish Office itself was discussing my future accommodation. It was ridiculous, here I was responsible for all these people, answering housing queries and dictating mail, and they were going to lock me up again for eighteen hours a day.

Someone saw sense in the end and I was allowed to stay in TFF. My mail was arrived unopened for the first time. All prisoners' mail is opened in case it contains something forbidden, like money or stamps. The authorities are not supposed to read it, but I'd been told of cases in various prisons where prisoners' marital problems would be cast up by some screws. I was receiving so much mail I think they were getting a bit fed up sifting through it all. After my election, they agreed to open it in front of me in case there was anything confidential from a constituent.

During my time inside I received 1,606 cards and letters. I replied to every one, spending a fortune on stamps and ending up with a permanently swollen forefinger. The lifers who worked outside used to post it because the prison mailing system took days to process things. From church ministers, to pensioners, and young kids – I was surrounded by messages of love and support.

Many told me about their lives. A seventy-two year-old from Edinburgh, Jimmy Cranston, wrote of his attempt to join the International Brigade in Spain at the age of sixteen. His brother and many friends went to fight Fascism in Spain. Jimmy was desperate to go but was told he was too young. He tried everything – he left home and went to sign up in Glasgow – but his family brought him back. He eventually got to Spain many years later on a holiday with his wife. It still grated on him and he seemed to admire any demonstration of youthful rebellion. 'I am now a grandfather,' he wrote: 'Ready to take advice from my grandchildren and I will never stand in the way of their approach to socialism.'

He wrote again reminding me that the Labour Party leadership had expelled the entire Labour League of Youth in the 1930s for working with the Communists to fight fascism. An offshore worker who had been suspended for his part in the earlier platform sit-ins wrote amazing letters about conditions offshore. Despite his earlier treatment he took copies of the OILC newspaper, *Blowout*, to distribute on the rigs.

A Glasgow man called James Lafferty sent £20, but left no address. He had just read an attack on me in the *Herald* by the Euro MP, Janey Buchan, who said I was not a real political prisoner.

He summarised the sentiments in so much of my mail: 'Her spiteful letter makes you wonder, but not much, how political most politicians are. It's obviously never occurred to them that masses of people, who are not physically chained, not physically tortured, who will never see physically the inside of a prison, nevertheless *are* political prisoners.' But the most moving of all these letters came from Elaine Boden, a woman in her early forties who ran a Blackpool boarding house. I met Elaine in the early days of the campaign in England. You tend to think of seaside landladies as being quite well off. But they are really hard-working people who were hit hard by the poll tax. Elaine was outraged at the tax and organised opposition all over the north west of England.

But while I was inside she wrote to say she had cancer. She never said it was terminal. But you could tell from her letters it wasn't looking good. She wrote in capitals because of a trapped nerve in her arm. She had just had a course of radiotherapy and was told it would be four months before she felt any benefit. She was tired all the time and the morphine for the pain made her even more drowsy. Yet her letters were so cheerful- she was only concerned about keeping up my spirits. Her commitment to the ideals we were fighting for was stronger than ever. 'The doctor got me a wheel-chair,' she wrote on 12 June. 'Ha! Well, I had a spin out in it. It was good on the prom and at least it got me out for some sea air. This lovely sunny weather and I can't sit in it! Because of the treatment all my right lung and back is burned and covered in prickly heat. I have cream for this, so it cures the itching. The side effects are not too bad. It's all worth it, if it gives me more strength in November. I shall have to learn some patience! I am thinking of you, Tommy. Keep that brave chin up! We shall break this sick system – it will not break us – Never.'

Elaine died the week before my release.

When my release date finally arrived on 1 July, I had mixed feelings. I was very sad to be saying goodbye to Ronnie. Though I knew I would see him again and we've remained close friends. Shortly before I left, he gave me some more advice: 'I was worried when you came in here, Tommy, wondering how you'd cope,' he said. 'It's been water off a duck's back to you. But please, please, don't give the impression that prison was easy. You know it's not. There are lots of young people who look up to you. Don't give them the idea that prison isn't hard.'

I thought about the young team in Pollok – I wouldn't want to see them in D Hall. So I went out of my way to say jail was an unpleasant experience – my toned-down version of *Angels With Dirty Faces*. The full James Cagney 'I don't wanna die' routine would have been a bit inappropriate to say the least! At the same time, I couldn't give the authorities – or our supporters – the impression I'd knuckled under. I said I was prepared to go to prison again over the issue – warrant sales are barbaric and should be banned.

The whole day of my release was very emotional. Mum, Keith and Ronnie Stevenson, the secretary of Scottish Militant Labour, were waiting outside with a crowd of supporters. After loads of hugs and press photographs, it was off to the house of a Militant member who lived nearby. Ecky and his wife Pat, a COHSE shop steward, had kindly laid on sandwiches and tea. I remember they had a wee dog – I hadn't seen an animal for months. It felt really good just to touch and stroke it.

Perfume was all I could smell in the house and on the train back to Glasgow. The only smells in prison are sweat and disinfectant. Now I was really sensitive to every single cologne, no matter how subtle.

When we arrived in Glasgow, they told me to wait on the train for five minutes – so I could come down the platform myself. All I could hear were chants of No! No! Warrant Sales! echoing under the station roof. As I got nearer there was this enormous roar. It was just a mass of people, cheering and waving banners. My Gran, Rose, was there. So was my sister, Carol, with my niece and nephew who gave me a wee bunch of flowers.

George and Matt Smith hoisted me onto their shoulders and carried me across George Square to the City Chambers. It was in the middle of the summer break so no Labour councillors were around. The policeman who had been duped when we put up tents for the hunger strike two years before said: 'Good to see you,' – he'd mellowed! We went upstairs to the council chambers and sat in the leader's seat – 'This is where Scottish Militant will be soon' I said.

After going round to see everyone in the Fed shop, we all took a No 9 bus home to Pollok. I sat upstairs with George, Coco, James and Tam Diamond. They had been doing my house up and were kidding me on about the mess they'd made. Saying it was all these terrible colours. When I walked round the corner to Linthaugh Road I saw a big crowd of my neighbours. Their kindness was overwhelming. Women gave me packets of biscuits, cakes and loads of cards.

I walked in the door and the house was transformed. It had been a right mess before I left. It must have got worse after being headquarters for two election campaigns. But they'd all clubbed together for the decoration. It was a marvellous gesture. One supporter from Govan, Pat Spence, made all the curtains. Coco fitted the carpets. Eddie Gribben did the painting and George put up the wallpaper. Cause the rooms are so damp, it started to peel off within a few months – and it's now held up in the bedroom with brass tacks. I used to kid them on: 'Whit did ye hang it wi – spit?' And they'd be all annoyed: 'We used loads of paste, honest – it's thae false walls!'

It was a lovely sunny evening and Keith had arranged street meetings in schemes all over the constituency. Every meeting was the same – folk were so warm. Remembering the scenes in the city chambers that afternoon, it all added up to something. It was almost as if the people were taking over.

10 The legacy – continuing to point the finger

'You're still as poor. There's no more in the pot.
You're not being cared for. You can't accept your lot.
Are things looking up, then? No, they're not:
It's a drop in the ocean, that's what.'

From 'Ballad of a drop in the ocean' by Bertolt Brecht

'Are you the anti-poll tax woman? Can you look at ma wean's nappy?'

Ann Lynch arrived home from work one night to this greeting. It came from a young mother who'd just moved to Drumchapel. Her newborn baby had dysentry. The girl was frightened to go to the doctor in case it was taken into care. But Ann's successes in keeping out the sheriff officers gave her a reputation as someone who could handle a crisis. She'd know what to do.

That's just one example of how the anti-poll tax campaigners began to take up the political agenda of the housing schemes. And the reason why Ann came so close to winning the Drumchapel Summerhill ward in the district elections. This particular case demanded practical help – Ann made sure the child got medical attention. Otherwise the disease would have left the baby dehydrated and dead within a day.

Even Scottish Militant could be accused of underestimating the level of political discontent in 1992. We should have put up candidates in areas like Springburn, Royston, Rutherglen and Cambuslang while I was inside. Jim Cameron should have stood. So should Willie Campbell in Springburn. We could have ended up with ten seats on Glasgow District Council. But resources defeated us. Some people thought we were already stretched to the limit. It was difficult for me to argue with the voices on the ground. I was banged up inside. I wasn't faced with the immediate problem of financing the printing costs for each district contest.

Chic Stevenson thought we should have stood everywhere. He was already a councillor, a man with forty years involvement with the Labour movement. It was a constant topic of discussion when I got out. Chic was saying: 'We'd have won! We'd have won! Don't you understand the shit being piled on the communities? People really feel they've been taken for granted.'

I thought: Chic's sixty-five. He's been through a lot . . . he must know. He had been the first comrade to really highlight the importance of the poll tax as an issue, so when it came to the regional council by-election in Gartloch/Easterhouse, we were determined to stand. It was one of the poorest areas of the city: people who live there are twice as likely to die before they are sixty-five than the residents of wealthy suburbs like Eastwood a few miles away. Success was not guaranteed. The electorate of a regional seat is much larger than the district wards we already held. And we had to find a candidate. We had local activists like Liz Murray. Liz and her husband, Ronnie, were moved to run down maisonettes in Cranhill after their Garthamlock council house was handed to private developers to be done up and sold. She is an ordinary battler, a thirty-one year-old mother coping with cramped conditions, dampness, burnt-out waste-chutes, while finding a safe place for the kids to play. She'd have been a brilliant candidate. But she was reluctant to stand. Lots of good working-class people feel they are not expert enough to go into politics. But it's only when they've replaced the public-school experts that politics will mean anything.

Christine McVicar, who became our candidate, also had all the right credentials. Before having kids she was shop steward in the

McKellar Watt sausage factory which once employed hundreds of women from the East End of Glasgow. Christine was thirty-five, a powerful speaker and married to one of our councillors, Jim McVicar. She led the anti-poll tax union in Baillieston, her local area. The entire Baillieston Labour Party branch was suspended on orders from London when they refused to withdraw their support for Jim. Christine was feeling a sense of duty and loyalty to SML but didn't feel up to being councillor. Most of her time was cut out looking after three young children. She'd been ill and Jim was quite worried about the stress of an election. She said yes twenty-four hours before the nominations closed. 'There's nae chance of you winning,' was the clinching assurance from Alan McCombes.

It was September 1992. My first opportunity to campaign for Scottish Militant Labour on the street. No prison walls to dull the message. We'd canvass the long queues outside the Post Office – people waiting to cash their benefit books on Monday mornings. We had three street meetings a night for five nights in a row. All done from the back of Kenny Weir's battered Yugo or Richey Venton's Lada. It was like the poll tax revisited.

But this was a much broader political campaign. Christine spoke at meetings about her mother and father-in-law. How they were all members of the Labour Party and how she was worried they'd be angry that she was standing against Labour. But when she went to talk to them, her mother-in-law said: 'Look hen, you're not turning your back on Labour. Labour's turned its back on us.'

All the Easterhouse anti-poll tax activists came to the meetings: Flo Reilly, Alex Poland, Gerry McMahon's parents. One of the common points older people made was: 'You lot stood up for us. It's time for us to stand up for you.' It was really touching. But also a big responsibility.

There was also a feeling of 'at last, someone's listening to us.' Youths on the streets helped in the campaign just like the Pollok posse who had delivered Poll Tax leaflets after football on the light nights in Pollok. This wasn't just an election for us. It was a chance to build our mass movement where it mattered. At meetings we said: 'Whether you vote for us or not isn't the most important thing. We want you to join with us.'

They had never heard of this before. Politicians usually wanted your vote and nothing else.

Young people like Kenneth Malcolmson and April McCafferty got involved. They had just moved to Easterhouse from Castlemilk. Kenneth was twenty-one, and April, nineteen, with a young child. They didn't have a stick of furniture when they arrived and got nothing from the social fund. They managed to buy some basics with back-dated money April's mother had been due from the social.

Kenneth's father had a spare suite. They got one carpet – all the other rooms had bare floorboards. You are talking two generations of a family with no income besides benefit. Kenneth's father was a binman until he damaged his back lifting. His older brother had been disabled since birth.

Kenneth had only ever known Youth Training Schemes. Never a real job. Ironically, his YTS was sweeping floors in a carpet factory. He was booted out after a couple of weeks for reporting a fire hazard.

The couple said Militant had opened their eyes. It was like that for a lot of people.

Easterhouse was a model campaign for us. I was really impressed with how organised the comrades were. We'd meet every Sunday before canvassing to talk about the issues. Then afterwards we'd meet again to discuss what was actually coming from the doorsteps. Housing conditions were raised often: 'Naebody's dae'n anything', was repeated at every door. One of our canvassers remembers groping her way up one close. There was no lighting. The stairs were slippery. Up at the top, in the only occupied flat, she found a young single mother and her three kids. The woman locked herself in at three o'clock until the next morning. She was terrified. What kind of life is that for a supposedly developed democracy in the 1990s.

There were loads of upsetting cases. Christine remembers one home where the young woman's bathroom, hall and kitchen were all bare brick. She had extractor fans on for three months trying to dry out the walls. Every now and again council workmen would appear and remove more crumbling plaster. Each time they said it would be sorted. But it never was. She had three kids, all with asthma, all sleeping in the one room. Black mould crept up behind their beds. Their mother pulled out bin liners to show Christine who was nearly knocked out by the stench. They were full of children's clothes. 'I just felt so sad,' said Christine, who was brought up in a single end in Shettleston. 'I was thinking of my own three wee kids.' We shouted at the housing department and actually got her moved. But so many others' houses are the same.

Hands Off Our Water

The poll tax was still a big issue then. But by this time the government was threatening to privatise Scottish water. We in turn promised to lead a mass campaign of civil disobedience. We wouldn't pay private water bills. They were soaring in England and Wales. People with skin conditions, arthritis and kidney disease were getting bills for hundreds of pounds. The privatised companies in England had disconnected the water in 21,000 homes in 1991. People just couldn't afford to pay. So excrement was thrown out of the windows of Birmingham tower blocks. A threefold increase in reported cases of dysentry was recorded. By this time we had made our position abundantly clear and had begun the process of launching the Scottish wide campaign which was later baptised as the HOW (Hands Off Our Water) Campaign. Attempted water disconnections would be stopped by forming the same human barricades which prevented poindings. That went down a treat.

All the other parties were hesitating and prevaricating. Labour had an information pack on how much it costs to water the lawn, use your dishwasher and wash the car. This must be what they meant by making 'An historic compromise with south of England voters'. Well, it doesn't go down well in their traditional heartlands. You could count the number of dishwashers in Easterhouse kitchens on one hand. There are no private lawns. And very few Easterhouse residents own cars.

Labour were so out of touch. This is hardly surprising. They only had seventy-five members in the whole of Provan, the constituency which encompasses Greater Easterhouse. Jimmy Wray, the local MP, lives in Newton Mearns, a wealthy suburb to the south of Glasgow. He turned up in Easterhouse shopping centre during the campaign with Donald Dewar and the new Shadow Scottish Secretary, Tom Clarke. Christine heard about the VIP visit from the waitress who usually served her in the wee cafe. 'Here's your beefburger, Christine,' said the woman. 'See what you were saying the other day about this election putting Easterhouse on the map? You were right. Andy Cameron was in here the other day!' After a minute's confusion, Christine realised she meant Tom Clarke. The leader of the Scottish Labour party had been mistaken for a Glasgow comedian. It's a pity Clarke wasn't as good a political leader as Cameron is a comic.

The shopping centre was a safe, controllable space. You'd never catch them venturing into the scheme itself. Can you imagine Donald Dewar holding a street meeting in Drumchapel? Or Tom Clarke addressing the masses from on top of a post box in Easterhouse? They'd be crucified on their own broken promises. Labour never seem to call public meetings in Scotland anymore. They prefer to rely on buttered-up journalists with the same middle-class outlook as themselves. Politics is a series of press releases, internal party debates and fundraisers for the dwindling number of faithful. For this chattering class of socialists it's a lucrative career or a kind of recreational activity – like golf or wine tasting. Scottish Militant don't treat it as a game. We took our message to the streets, doorsteps, and the shopping centres.

Christine McVicar polled 1791 votes. Labour got just 941. We slashed their share by forty-two per cent and won fifty-three per cent of the votes cast. The SNP were marked absent. It caused uproar. Militant could sweep through every Glasgow scheme. We weren't just winning in our Pollok stronghold, or where we already held seats, like Queenslie and Baillieston. Within a month Willie Griffin won the other Easterhouse regional council seat,

Queenslie/Barlanark. He took over forty per cent of the vote. In Govan on the same day, we took thirty per cent of the vote. The SNP, who had built up a strong local organisation under Sillars, took the seat from Labour by less than 100. If we had not stood, they would have won more convincingly. We took votes from the Nationalists as well as Labour. We also fought two good campaigns in Dundee, coming from nowhere to second place in the district council Blackshade ward.

Our sprint into the political premier league led Dr Michael Dyer, from the Unit for the Study of Scottish Elections in Aberdeen University, to write in the *Glasgow Herald* in February 1993: 'Militant is the only political party in Scotland with reason to be greatly impressed by its own efforts.'

Labour has changed its rhetoric since getting those bloody noses. Jack McConnell, the new Scottish general secretary, is a clever wee character. He's begun to talk a bit more on issues like poverty and water. But given Labour's record on the poll tax and their continued attempts to collect it, these utterances are hollow. When Jean McFadden replaced Pat Lally as leader of Glasgow City council, she launched an anti-poverty strategy saying there would be more emphasis on housing and less on opera. Yet her administration meanwhile spends thousands on treating councillors and their wives to the high life. They spent £12,000 in January 1993 sending councillors, officials and their wives to a Burns Supper in Rostov-on-Don. 'A junket's a junket for a' that!' as the immortal Rabbie would probably have said.

Siren voices can be heard from the other parties at election time. But Scottish Militant Labour are about raising consciousness all year round. One thing mass movements have in common, if they are successful, is building bricks. They start from the bottom. You help people get a bit of control over their lives in the areas where they live. Then they are radicalised. They question authority more quickly. You really can go from wanting to change the street lighting to wanting to change the world.

During the poll-tax campaign, we compared our street committees to the defence groups set up in Chile between 1970 and 1973. Chile was run by a democratically elected Marxist government in those years. It was a speech about this inspiring period that recruited George McNeilage into Militant and changed his life. While the Popular Unity president, Salvador Allende, took the banks and mines into public ownership, workers themselves set about changing their day-to-day existence. Those with nowhere to live began squatting on undeveloped land in the cities just like the Glasgow squatters' movement after World War Two. The Chilean government supported them, provided building materials and refused to protect the property rights of rich landowners. Neighbourhood committees and women's groups were set up to distribute food and build health centres.

Glasgow's Marxist councillors – SML – are closely involved in community campaigns. Because we live in the schemes we understand the relevant issues. That's why we knew we could build a successful non-payment campaign when others in the Labour movement said it couldn't be done. By 1992 we were applying our local knowledge to issues other than the poll tax.

It is particularly difficult to organise people in big schemes like Easterhouse and Drumchapel. That's partly because of poverty. But it's also because any money coming into these areas is controlled by development companies called initiatives. These are made up of representatives from the regional and district councils and non-elected bodies like the health board, the Scottish Office, Scottish Homes and what is sycophantically referred to as the business community.

After our election successes, we had three councillors on the Easterhouse Initiative. The Labour establishment panicked. Their members could be outnumbered if we voted with the five independent community reps who were also on this body. One of the first things we tried to do was change the way grants were handed out by a committee meeting in secret in the city centre. We suggested it meet in public, in Easterhouse itself. Locals could then see who was getting what.

The regional council responded to this outbreak of democracy by changing the structure of the initiative. 'You people are getting nothing as long as we're in control,' said Bob Gould, the new leader of Strathclyde Region. So they brought on Labour councillors from outside the area. They gave extra weight to the non-elected bodies including the Scottish Office. They would rather work with the Tories than working-class people who talk back to them. Labour councillors bleat about the erosion of local democracy. The Tories currently plan to set up new single tier local authorities which favour the electoral areas where they are strong. They have blatantly gerrymandered the boundries, carving out little Tory islands where none previously existed. Water will be taken out of democratic control and placed in the hands of non-elected boards. How hypocritical for Labour to oppose this while they practise it at local level.

But folk aren't daft. They see through the hypocrisy. They know who will stand up for them. If there was an election in Easterhouse tomorrow, we'd get an even bigger vote than in 1992.

Labour used to talk about Militant parachuting into communities. But the fact is, we're part of the community. That's what they can't stomach. Our councillors are not seen as politicians, but ordinary working-class people who are taking on the establishment. Mary McQuaid and Ann Curran, from the Bellshill Anti-Poll Tax Union, have now set up a local branch of Scottish Militant Labour. They were finding people called them if they had trouble paying the gas bill. Women with violent partners would also call asking for help. Shortly after she was elected, Christine McVicar was invited to open a women's refuge in her ward. She knocked the door and and a voice said: 'Just push and come in.' A group of women were sitting around the table chatting and Christine joined them. After a while one of them said: 'Where's this dignitary who's supposed to be opening this place?' They were really surprised and a bit embarrassed when she said: 'I'm sorry, I left my twinset and pearls behind.' Everybody laughed. But it demonstrates how working-class people have been conditioned to expect the middle classes to speak on their behalf. That is changing now.

Road Safety

By mobilising the housing schemes, we are stirring up a confident, radical and very powerful brew. Our method is a transitional one. The right campaigns raise the demands and expectations of the participants.

Road safety may not be a political issue in villas where there's a garden for the children and a car in the driveway. But if you live in a scheme, you are unlikely to have a garden for the children. Most mothers are terrified to let kids out of their sight. Parks can be dangerous places especially at night. The street is their playground. But it is not quiet and suburban with lots of ramps and sleeping policemen. It could be on a busy bus route. Or a wide thoroughfare, like Linthaugh Road where I stay. Cars race past at fifty and sixty miles per hour. Chances are these vehicles are from outside Pollok, just like those which race through Easterhouse or Drumchapel.

Christine worked closely during her election campaign with a group of mothers who wanted a pedestrian crossing on a busy road. They were ridiculed by the local Labour functionaries – they were told they didn't understand the issues because they hadn't seen the paperwork. But Christine took their case seriously and has managed to get the traffic slowed down with the types of islands and ramps you see in middle-class areas.

Militant activists have helped lead similar campaigns in South Nitshill and Dormanside in Pollok. In South Nitshill, a little boy was killed. We helped his uncle organise a campaign which eventually led to safety features being installed. George McNeilage, now head of the North Pollok community council, helped organise a sitdown protest involving more than 100 people on the busy Linthaugh Road. Another child had been knocked down and angry parents called the protest. Despite police threats, the traffic was blocked for several hours. The regional council eventually gave commitments on safety features. Within twenty-four hours, workmen were out painting slow signs on the road. Yet Linthaugh had been a speedway for years. People have been quietly lobbying the authorities for years. They were ignored until they took matters into their own hands and, in a small way, defied the law. Just like we did over the poll tax. What else can you do when democracy fails you?

The Campaign Against Dysentry

Labour never take up any issue which really matters to people in the schemes. Donald Dewar became known as 'Sewer Dewar' in Drumchapel because he refused to see the dysentry outbreak as a political issue. It was left to Ann Lynch and two community activists called Tommy Reilly and Jackie Church to get the scandal on the national media.

Ann is in her thirties and for a long time worked in unskilled jobs – as cleaner in a hospital, a barmaid and in a pickle factory. One day she got TB and nearly died. While she was lying in hospital she said: 'There's no way I'm going back to scrubbing floors after this. I'm going to college.' As well as doing that, she joined the Labour Party and then Militant. Sixty-six Drumchapel people were hospitalised with this Third World disease in 1992. One victim, a woman in her late sixties, was suffering a second time. She first caught dysentry when pregnant thirty-eight years ago. It then caused premature labour and her child was still-born. 'I never thought I'd see it return in this day and age', she said. The disease left the lively pensioner so weak her family say she has never properly recovered.

Local councillors tried to play down the epidemic and accused Ann of political scaremongering. They did not want to admit the outbreak was caused by broken pipes spilling raw sewage into the back courts. The council refused to fix the pipes properly. In a house where a nine-month old baby was hospitalised, the cracked pipes had been repaired with clingfilm. Other patch-up attempts involved empty baked bean tins and old copies of the *Daily Record*.

'Nothing to worry about: it comes in cycles. Just remember to wash your hands, said the authorities. Why then was it concentrated in the worst housing? Pollok was one of the other areas affected. The young kid across the road from me was off school for months.

Children in India die from dysentry because they play beside open sewers. The bacteria is also passed by flies feeding on effluent. These were the conditions in some Scottish housing schemes in 1992. Only Militant stood up and shouted about it.

Enterprise v Education

Drumchapel was also fighting the closure of its schools at this time. Strathclyde earlier announced its intention to rationalise education provision across the region because of falling roles. Schools in housing schemes are a community resource. They provide facilities for sport and adult education. Ann and the others kept asking why they needed to close two of the scheme's three schools when the education budget was underspent and children could benefit from smaller classes. After the bulldozers moved in all became clear. The land on which Waverly High once stood was sold to Bellway Homes for more than £300,000 for private housebuilding. This is partnership with the private sector in action.

Labour try to convince us that such collaboration is the sensible way forward. The Labour councillor in Drumchapel, Charlie Gordon, told public meetings that the local community would get a spin-off from the private developers. Business would replace what they lost. But Bellway Homes have ignored Waverly Community Council's letters asking for a youth facility. Of couse, the property deal was struck after the district council elections. Ann missed taking the seat by forty-six votes and gave them a real fright. She would have won if people had known about Labour's behind-the-scenes deals.

Private enterprise has offered Drumchapel few spin-offs. The scheme's only bank shut recently – no profit in it. It was replaced by a Job Centre. When you walk into the shopping centre you are confronted by second-hand clothing shops, off-sales, pubs and bookies. Ann recently campaigned with the community to stop the council allowing a second betting shop to take premises in the centre. They just wouldn't listen.

The Child Support Act

Militant was the only political party to lobby and occupy Department of Social Security offices when the Child Support Act was introduced in 1993. We distributed advice notes to people at Post Offices and supported the picket at the launch of the CSA at the luxury Moat House Hotel in Glasgow. This was organised by single-parents groups like One Plus in Strathclyde and Gingerbread. No Labour or SNP representatives bothered to show. To make an issue of it you need to be in touch with the communities. There are 20,290 lone parents in Glasgow: one in four of all households with children, according to the district council's 1993 Poverty Audit. Seventy per cent of them claim income support. I don't think there's a big scheme now where less than a third of the population are one parent families. In my area of Pollok it must be forty to forty-five per cent. This is an issue at the heart of the schemes. But it was peripheral to the big parties.

Disgracefully, opposition politicians neither spoke nor voted against the Act when it passed through parliament. They'd swallowed the moral argument that you need to get hold of these irresponsible young men with two to three kids with different women. But the Child Support Act isn't about absent fathers. It's about reducing the level of income for families.

If a woman is on income support, the act tries to get the father to pay instead. The children don't get any more money. If the father has a second family, those children could also be impoverished by this act. Single mothers who refuse to co-operate stand to have their benefit cut by nearly £9 a week. We advise women, many of whom have suffered domestic violence, to take a friend along if the CSA demands an interview. The act says you don't have to co-operate if you fear harm or distress. But it's up to the interviewing officer to decide who he or she believes.

If the single parents in Pollok could get the same deal as Princess Di or Fergie there would be no problem: you get a big house and a private income as long as you don't talk about your old man or his mother. The Social Security minister, Peter Lilley, is now telling us to attack the 'something for nothing brigade'. Does that mean slashing the biggest family allowance bill in the country – for the Royal Family and all their hangers on?

Morality is being applied selectively when it comes to this issue. Relationships have changed. Men and women are less likely to stay together if they are very unhappy. Often that's the best decision for the children. When a middle-class wife chooses that route she's a fine upstanding women of substance; she's brought up that family on her own. Done a great job. She's a professional. But if she's living in Pollok on benefit, she's a scrounger. 'You've only had the wean to get a house.' My neighbours should be applauded for bringing up their kids so well in such difficult circumstances. The facts don't show that benefit-dependent single women are bad parents. Recent research by Richard Kinsey, a criminologist at Edinburgh University, showed their kids were less likely to commit an offence than those whose parents went out to work. It all boils down to low pay, lack of cheap childcare and all the other things that go with poverty. Tory policies have led to family breakdown. The idea of getting married, settling down and bringing up kids was always linked to a bit of security. With a steady job and a steady income, you could have children. It's not like that any longer. Most people aren't getting steady jobs. There's nothing to plan ahead for. So single parent units are almost the norm.

Housing

Another Militant campaign which was once central to the movement, is now ignored by Labour. Half of all the homes in Scotland suffer some form of damp or condensation, according to the government's own 1993 House Condition Survey. Mild condensation sounds like something you get when the kettle boils. According to this report, it is 'traces of mildew on clothes and furniture'. The civil servant who drew this up had obviously never had 'traces of mildew on his clothes or soft furnishings. It is stinking black mould. It means you have to throw out your children's clothes. It's the reason why the woman downstairs from me had to discard a new wardrobe within nine months. This is not a mild inconvenience for people with no spare income at all. Imagine how bad the 95,000 houses officially Below Tolerable Standard must be?

In Glasgow thirty-seven per cent of the housing is damp and another 12,900 council houses are Below Tolerable Standard. It is estimated that to maintain adequate comfort levels a young single person would have to spend seventy per cent of their weekly benefit on fuel. Most tenants can only afford to heat one room, according to the Povery Audit. That's because the average income of a Glasgow District Council tenant is less than £3,900 a year. Eight out of ten claimed some kind help with their rent and rates in September 1993.

This is not a minority problem. More than half the population of Glasgow – fifty-eight per cent – still lives in public housing. Glasgow District Council has estimated it would cost £1.62 billion to put its housing right. It will be lucky to get a fraction of that from the government.

Does that mean we have to stand by and watch as our asthmatic kids in the schemes struggle for breath? Should we just shrug when we see their education suffer through constant illness caused by the ingestion of spores from the mould that lines the walls? One consultant at Yorkhill Children's hospital in Glasgow now advises families just to sue the local authority. He is fed up with his letters to the council on behalf of young patients being ignored.

Despite their poverty and the poor state of their homes, Glasgow's tenants have seen their rents rise by forty per cent in the last ten years. Seventy pence of every pound they pay goes to service the city's housing debt. The debt rises every year and currently stands at £1.1 billion. This year the council will hand the banks £135 million, mainly in interest with a tiny repayment.

This municipal millstone is going to get heavier every year. Each time a council house is sold, the debt passes on to the remaining tenants in the city. The debt burden per family was £4,800 in 1986. It is now £8400 – Pollok's share is some £53 million.

Mere words of opposition won't cure our kids' asthma. So we're saying to the district council: 'Cancel the Debt – Don't Pay the Interest.' The first is directed at the government – the second at the council to at least force the government to come to the negotiating table. 'Homes Fit for Humans, not Profits for Parasites' should surely be the guiding principle for a socialist council.

For just one year's interest payments, every house in Glasgow could have central heating, double-glazing and a new bathroom suite. Of course the Labour council will say it's illegal. But we ask: 'What law are you keeping?' Our tenancy agreement states that we will live in wind and watertight homes. The council is breaking that law every day. Why does it meet its obligation to the bankers but not to its own tenants?

Writing off debt is not such a big deal. The government happily cleared the £4000 million debts owed by British Gas when it was privatised. It also used public money to wash away £5000 million owed by English water companies at the time of their privatisation.

It is particularly ironic that the government recently wiped out £250 million owed by Scottish Homes, the housing agency charged with privatising public housing. Scottish Homes encourages tenants to transfer to housing associations. These housing associations will be forced to raise rents to carry out repairs as their government grant is cut each year. In England and Wales, this process is quite far advanced. The average rent for a housing association flat has jumped from £48 to £64 a week in two years. Who can afford that?

The housing associations will also borrow heavily from banks to finance their spending. So this idea of community ownership is a sham – the banks own the houses. In a few years' time they could be selling off homes to Japanese developers.

Our campaign will encourage people to question community ownership of housing. It's a cynical phrase because it uses working-class people's collectivist sympathies to effectively privatise their homes. Our 'Cancel the Debt – Don't Pay the Interest' campaign will radicalise those who get involved. They will ask, How do we cancel the debt? We break the law. Then they will ask: Who is the debt paid to? The banks. Fine, let's nationalise the banks. So you move from a local, concrete demand for dry, warm housing to challenge capitalism's economic foundations.

It was like that during the rent strikes. They moved from demanding fair rents to wanting municipal housing. The second demand challenges the nature of property ownership. It says private landlords will never be able to meet our housing needs.

Towards A Socialist Scottish Parliament

There are several other big campaigns which could transform people's lives. I've already mentioned Hands Off Our Water. I believe it was our threat to build a mass campaign of non-payment of private water bills which led the government to back away from all-out flotation. That doesn't mean we accept these new boards which control water. They will 'assume ownership' of the reservoirs and infrastructure. If someone walked into your house and 'assumed ownership' of the TV, you wouldn't be very happy. We will not accept the backdoor privatisation of a resource which is so plentiful in Scotland. We don't want to see people getting their water cut off in a country which is literally sodden with the stuff. If necessary we will refuse to pay bills issued by unelected, unaccountable, un-democratic and overpaid water boards, filled with Tory placemen.

All these campaigns are necessary because parliamentary democ-racy is so ineffective. The Tories were elected in 1992 on a minority of the vote – forty per cent in Britain as a whole. Even in England it was only forty-five per cent. Parliament does not represent the will of the people. It had no moral authority to impose the poll tax. It still has no moral authority to impoverish us by parliamentary decree.

In Scotland the failure of democracy is even more glaring. The Tories only captured twenty-five per cent of the vote in 1992. By September the following year their support had slumped to thirteen per cent in the *Scotsman*'s opinion poll. Yet opposition politicians still talk about working within the framework of democracy.

248

248

If they took the will of the people seriously, they would convene a Scottish parliament tomorrow. It would not be the old 1707 version, full of corrupt aristocrats who sold out the people. Nor would it be like the dusty old Constitutional Convention, full of self-apppointed politicians and church ministers who are accountable to no one.

This should be an assembly of real Scots: trade unionists, community groups, the unemployed. In one fell swoop we'd settle all the arguments about local government reorganisation. People in Scotland are just waiting for someone to take a lead. Remember, seventy-five per cent of them consistently say they want either a devolved Scottish parliament or complete independence from England and Wales.

I myself do not support a complete break from England and Wales. Capitalism crosses boundries to exploit people. Workers need to link arms across the world to fight back. A socialist Scottish Parliament would also inspire our brothers and sisters in England and Wales who are suffering under this democratic dictatorship. But it mustn't be the Edinburgh talking-shop proposed by the Labour Party. Not another Strathclyde Regional Council, administering Tory policy in the northern territories. I want a Socialist administration in Scotland that means something: – one which would take the North Sea oil wells into public ownership – along with all the banks and insurance companies which make Edinburgh a financial centre. With all these resources – £125 billion in the top 15 institutions alone – distributed equally among the people, we could offer a real future to the 42% of Scottish children under five who, according to research at Edinburgh University, are currently living in poverty.

The Timex Experience

A Scottish parliament has not been achieved because the leadership are not prepared to defy the government, hold a referendum, and bring it into being. The Timex dispute in Dundee showed what can be done when people assume leadership themselves – as well as what happens when national leaders let you down. The dispute encapsulated all the problems Scottish and British workers face in relation to employment rights, wage levels and trade-union recognition.

There, you had a multi-national company which once had two factories in Dundee employing 5000 people. That was gradually run down in the course of the 1980s to one factory employing 240. Watch making was transferred to low-wage economies like the Philippines. The workers remained well-organised in the engineering union. Despite this, they went along with the company's demand for further redundancies at the end of 1992. The workers wanted the lay-offs rotated. The company wanted to select who was sacked. They walked out. But after a ballot for industrial action decided to return. In a sense they were too timid. If you keep running, they'll keep chasing you. The management made new demands. Workers would have their bonus payments cut along with their pensions and facilities like a subsidised canteen. Still, they decided to return under protest. They found the gates locked. They were sacked.

People who had worked for Timex for thirty years were replaced by scabs on a fraction of the pay. With hindsight, Timex provoked a dispute in order to either break the union or close the plant. Peter Hall, the managing director, was hired as executioner. He had already sunk two firms so he wasn't employed for his managerial expertise.

The strike committee called daily pickets against advice from the national union. The AEEU head office said Timex workers were breaking the law. So the strike committee just changed the name. They were having demonstrations, not mass pickets. Nothing illegal in demonstrations.

Guerrilla warfare methods similar to the anti poll tax federation were employed. They tried to blockade the gate with a van. At one stage they were inside the factory. They tried to occupy the scab buses.

All this really radicalised the women on the picket line. Some walked for miles from their homes to get there for 7.00am. They moved from a personal hatred of Peter Hall, who patronisingly handed out sweets on St Valentine's Day, to questioning the entire strategy of the American based company. 'This has changed us from poodles to rottweilers', they would joke.

Scottish Militant Labour came to be closely associated with the dispute. I was twice called to speak on the picket line. We printed and distributed strike bulletins. We offered our opinion on how the dispute should progress and were listened to with respect. We took Timex workers to speak at meetings around the country. We helped mobilise people to attend the mass pickets. On March 23 we helped delay two double decker buses full of scabs from getting into the factory. We held them up for an hour and a half.

I was arrested along with others from around the country. The television news that night talked about picket-line violence. If sitting down in front of a bus is violent then Gandhi was a dangerous man. If we had stayed behind police lines the dispute would have remained unreported. That day turned it from a localised dispute involving a couple of hundred workers into an international story.

We should really question the amount of money spent on policing that dispute. Tayside Region was paying for police to clear the way for Timex, a multi-national company, to sack local people and drive down pay and conditions.

Why are we subsidising an all powerful multinational? These companies have an annual turnover similar to the industrial output of a small country. They do what they like. They can switch investment across continents with the flick of a switch. They now go where labour is cheap and unorganised – that's why Timex prefer The Philippines to Dundee. In the Philippines trade unionists and socialists are regularly gunned down by death squads in the pay of the government.

What happened in Timex was part of a wider trend. If it's time for Timex today, it will be Hoover's time tomorrow, Yarrows the next day, Albion the day after that. Every major work-place in

Scotland is threatened. And because all workers are affected, all workers should respond. That is why it was right to hold mass pickets involving people from all over the country. Militant argue that a general attack merits a general response. We wanted other trade unionists to stop work in support of the Timex workers.

Local workers at factories like National Cash Registers recognised the correctness of this. They walked out unofficially. But the STUC failed to produce a general response, such as a one-day strike. They called a Scotland-wide meeting of shop stewards, but postponed it so many times the eventual meeting was ineffective.

The AEEU were unhappy about the local strike committee's radicalism. So Jimmy Airlie, the Scottish executive officer, stepped in to 'negotiate' a deal with the company. It entailed a 27% pay cut. But the workers had months of real leadership from local organisers like father and son, John Kidd senior and junior, among others. They rejected this insult. Airlie, a long way from his Upper Clyde Shipbuilding days, said: 'Maybe being down in London you get a wee bit out of touch.' It's nothing to do with being in London! It's to do with earning XXk a year. Gavin Laird, the leader of the AEEU, is very similar to Howard Davis, head of the CBI. They dress the same, live in the same type of surroundings. We shouldn't be surprised if their outlook is the same.

Laird and Airlie take the 'poor jobs are better than no jobs line.' That's the way trade-union leaders have helped create the conditions for continuing job shedding and the replacement of manufacturing with unskilled, poorly-paid work. Perhaps the trade-union leaders would act differently if they had to take the type of twenty-seven per cent wage cut they 'negotiated' for their members at Timex. All trade union leaders should live on the average wage of the people they represent. Then they would fight a bit harder.

They tell us industrial militancy is a thing of the past. That it doesn't work. It doesn't work because well-paid trade-union leaders play within the rules set by the other side. Just like local authorities played by the Tory's rules in collecting a poll tax designed to cripple local democracy. The tax could only be defeated by breaking the law. Likewise, you cannot win an industrial dispute unless you break the law. The law prevents secondary action. It stops workers acting together even though the bosses act together.

The one thing that working-class people have over their bosses is labour power. It is the source of all wealth in the world. That's why this government has passed so many laws to prevent workers withdrawing their labour.

But there are positive developments. Some ordinary workers are acting independently of their leaders. The Joint Sites Committee in London co-ordinated unofficial action on building sites while Ucatt, the official construction union, did nothing. The OILC was formed by offshore oilworkers frustrated at the squabbles of big unions. They preferred fighting each other to tackling the oil multinationals responsible for the deaths of hundreds of men on Piper Alpha and other rigs.

Trade unions are merging into big units. Unison, which covers the public sector has 1.4 million members. It would be the equivalent of a general strike if they all walked out in response to the government's decision to freeze their wages. Anyone who thinks industrial action cannot bring down governments should remember the miners strike of 1984–85. The miners failed. But the government had to spend millions to defeat them. It had stock piles of coal. It had to deploy thousands of police to defeat pickets. It had to use all the resources of the courts, the Department of Social Security and the media to win the confrontation. Yet it still took them twelve months. The NUM at that time formed one per cent of the organised British workforce. Think what twenty per cent or even fifty per cent could do?

But how do we get them to do it? A lot of people say the dominance of the mass media means there can never be any social change. The same people, like Rupert Murdoch, own all the television stations and the newspapers. Every news bulletin you listen to gives the same line. Journalists censor themselves. They filter out socialist opinions.

Scottish Militant regularly hold press conferences advocating a socialist society – we argue for things like nationalising the banks. Nobody reports them. Every day you'll find out what Labour's saying about the railways, the banks or about Europe. Because we are attacking the system itself we are ignored by the media.

But I'm an optimist. Sometimes the mass media works against itself. It's a blizzard of information. It's wallpaper politics. Even if you are allowed a little space, your message is lost if not compromised. It is possible to stand outside that blizzard and speak in an alternative voice. Speak directly to people. They respect you for it. And they listen.

We print our own bulletins in the communities. Lots of people comment on the clarity of our material, as in the poll-tax campaign. Many movements have been built in countries where the media has been directly censored. Look at Chile. General Pinochet was forced to step aside by an opposition which depended on secretly-printed leaflets. Solidarity, the Polish trade union, had its own underground radio station. People Power brought down the Berlin Wall with no help from the television news. We just have to trust our own ability to educate and organise outside parliament. It cannot be the same as the past. We don't have the thousands at Albion Motors or at Govan in the engineering works. They existed in a period of history when people worked in big units and organisation was therefore a bit easier. Now organisation isn't as easy.

During Harvey Duke's election campaign in Dundee, I got speaking to a group of young people standing round one of the chip shops while we were doing street meetings. They were talking about the Timex dispute. 'If I got offered a job there I would take it,' said one. I was saying: 'But it's somebody else's job.'

'But they don't want the job.'

I don't think they would have said that twenty or thirty years ago. Then their parents would have had jobs. They would have instilled them with values about the labour movement protecting everyone. But these young people were from a second generation of unemployed. They were so different from the young people from

Pollok we took to Timex with us. Colin and James McGregor, Tam Diamond and Eddie Gribben didn't have jobs either. But if they ever do have jobs, they want them to be decent and well-paid.

But they have been educated in the value of solidarity. The first time they went up to Dundee, the bus was held up in Pollok at 5 am. A local pensioner had her house broken into and the video was stolen. The guys gave chase across the back courts and retrieved it for her. A form of direct action. A few years ago they might have had a different attitude to housebreaking. Now they hate it because it's stealing from our own. That's solidarity. If you can extend it to the workplace then we'll be well on our way to creating that different kind of society.

Conclusion: A Vision For The Future

We've been successful in keeping young people behind our banner because we involved them in so many different initiatives. Take the water campaign. Who else has raided the offices of Quayle Munro, the chartered accountants, who drew up the privatisation options for the Scottish Office? Who else has cut off the Scottish Secretary Ian Lang's water? Who else has taken over the stock exchange in Glasgow, stopping trading for several hours? It was the same as the sheriff officers' occupations during the poll-tax campaign.

Young people like being defiant. Breaking the law for its own sake is not very positive. It might mean throwing stones at boarded-up houses and smashing into someone's living room. Better to channel their energies into positive and constructive defiance like breaking bad laws.

Otherwise they could vent their frustrations in very dangerous ways. The rise of the far right in Europe is due to the hopelessness felt by many young people. There is forty per cent unemployment in areas of Marseille where Jean-Marie le Pen's National Front is strong. Racists lay the blame for social ills on black people. That distracts attention from the fact that big business is deliberately keeping people poor and unemployed.

We have campaigned hard against the rise of fascism in Britain. I'm very proud of the part Scottish Militant has played in physically stopping the Nazi British National Party organising public meetings or rallies in any of Scotland's cities. Now the BNP have won a district council seat in Tower Hamlets in London. Anyone who claimed the wave of Nazi hatred stopped at the English Channel should feel ashamed of themselves. Young members of Militant Labour initiated the setting up of Youth Against Racism in Europe to mobilise all young people, not just Militant members, against the fascists. Their main slogan is 'Jobs Not Racism'. Its aim is to educate them about the real causes of unemployment and involve them in physically stopping organisations like the BNP.

Winning battles, whether in the communities, in the workplace or in politics generally, requires good leadership. Members of Parliament are shop stewards for the people they represent. They should be paid the average industrial wage in their constituency. MPs might stand up to things like the poll tax and wage freezes if they lived on £250 a week instead of the current £90,000 worth of salary and expenses. Militant MPs Terry Fields and Dave Nellist were paid this way. Every other MP is quite happy to take the full salary and allowances. Maybe this explains why Labour have become, in the words of the Tory Home Secretary Michael Howard, 'Just a paler version of the Conservative Party.'

Labour don't want to change society. They don't want to change the world. But that's what politicians are supposed to be about: changing and shaping the world. Instead Labour have accepted hook line and sinker the existing socio-economic system. The system which tells you to trust in parliament. The system which claims capitalism can be gently reformed. That's the system which has resulted in one Glaswegian in three being dependent on income support in 1993.

This is the harsh reality of the system which Labour supports. Their health spokesman, David Blunkett, thinks they should be the party of 'self-reliance'. Blunkett is proposing to make the long-term unemployed work for their benefit. This will make it easier for the Tories to impose American-style workfare.

The Tories want to cut benefits because they know unemployment will remain high – above two million, even when the current recession ends. High, long-term unemployment, along with cutting welfare, is part of a trend which also affects Europe and America. Half of Europe's seventeen million unemployed in 1993 had been out of work for more than a year (OECD). This isn't just because of the recession. It's because of the way capitalism is moving across the world.

For the past ten years the output of European economies has grown. But no new jobs have been created. Economists sometimes call this post-industrialism. Basically, it means that manufacturing jobs are in decline. We make less things. Low-paid service jobs are on the increase. We buy more beefburgers. There is a change in the global division of labour. Multinational companies will move work to where they can buy labour cheapest. Or they will bring in machines to do the work. Machines don't ask for rises.

In Europe and America this process has resulted in big social divisions. The number of Americans living in poverty has grown from 24.5 million to 32 million between 1978 and 1988. That's a jump of twenty-eight per cent. The Child Poverty Action Group estimate that the number of families living on half the average income in the UK more than doubled in the 1980s – from five million in 1979 to twelve million in 1988.

Conservative policies have all been designed to speed up this process. The government's New Earnings Survey shows that the gap between the top and bottom tenth of salaries is wider than when records began in 1886. This has been achieved by attacking the organised working class by closing pits and shipyards and steelworks. They cut benefits to force people into these new junk jobs. They've already done it to sixteen and seventeen year olds. Some young people are working for as little as £1 an hour. They call this a flexible labour market. It's really a low-wage economy. Britain is much further down this road than other European countries. A recent advert in German newspapers exposed the sad truth. The advert was placed by the UK government. It was meant to attract inward German investment. The biggest selling point was the fact that Britain had 'cheap wage costs'.

So when Labour support welfare cuts, they are supporting this push towards poverty wages. Other European social democratic parties are following the same road. Sweden cut its benefits for the first time in 1993. In Spain the supposedly socialist prime minister, Felipe González, is reducing employment protection so business can hire and fire at will. Not all out of work people are punished in this way. Robert Horton, the one time chairman of BP, didn't suffer too badly when he was kicked off the board. He got a £1.5 million pay off. He had, of course, overseen the sacking of thousands before departing.

Is this what John Smith means by rewarding individual ambition? He seems comfortable with the divided society the Tories have deliberately created. Maybe he thinks he can write off the poor. Maybe that's why some of his shadow cabinet advocate workfare. It's certainly why the Tories push these policies. By castigating the long-term unemployed and talking about an underclass they try to divide the working class. This is a time-honoured tactic. Victorians talked about the deserving and undeserving poor.

The Tories use this divide tactic to convince a section of workers that their economic interests are more in tune with the very rich. An example would be Margaret Thatcher's tax cuts. The propaganda was directed at the middle-income worker. Labour's own research shows that the bottom fifty per cent of income earners got fifteen per cent of the tax cuts. The very rich top one per cent of earners got twenty-seven per cent of the cash!

But the disadvantaged are not a minority underclass. Two thirds of Britain's population are on less than average income. Even if you're among the minority of skilled workers who earn more, your future is threatened.

Job shedding is happening all the time to maximise profit. In the first two weeks of September 1993, Daimler Benz, the biggest industrial company in Germany, announced 40,000 job losses. British Gas announced 20,000, Rolls Royce 3,100 and Air France 4000. No wonder skilled workers are wondering whether they'll be next.

Capital will go on replacing European workers with cheaper Third World versions or else with machines. There's nothing wrong with new technology. It's who controls it that's the key. Rather than sacking 500 car worker to make way for robots, we should lower the working week. Why should you have to put in forty-four hours to earn a half decent wage? Why has this become the norm? That's the way capitalism works. But it is not natural or acceptable.

We can stop this process by taking control of the technology and the factories ourselves. Conventional political parties like Labour kid people that moderate investment in industry will make everything OK. They talk about achieving full employment, but how? Capitalism has decided it no longer has a use for a third of Glasgow's population, the people who, less than a generation ago, sweated gold to line someone else's pockets. Labour say if we become more competitive, invest moderately in education and training, we will win the jobs back from the Far East. But that's just accepting the rules laid down by the market. You can't win when you are competing against slave wages unless you undercut them.

The only solution is for working-class people to run the economy to meet everyone's needs instead of the profits of a few multinational companies. You can only control something if you own it. John Smith has said the ownership of industry is 'an irrelevance.' I don't think the head of ICI or the Hanson Trust or Rio Tinto Zinc thinks ownership is irrelevant. They know how important it is to have their greedy paws on the levers of economic power. Competition doesn't just waste vast sums of money and throw people out of work. It kills. One child dies of starvation every four seconds in the world today according to the charity, Christian Aid. Yet there is more than enough food in the world. Much of it lies rotting in warehouses. People in the Third World cannot afford it. They starve because they cannot compete.

War is caused by greed and rivalry. The First World War was about economic rivalry between Britain and Germany. The Gulf War was about who controlled the oil wells in the Middle East. Without the competition which leads to war, scientists could use their talents productively. They could spend their time finding cures for diseases instead of making weapons. Under our new society I look forward to the day when they rattle collecting tins to try and pay for nuclear bombs, not kidney machines.

It's not much of a leap of the imagination. Some people say it's not workable. That doesn't mean they're right. Copernicus got roasted on the spit for saying the earth circulated round the sun. Saying that was tantamount to witchcraft around that time but it didn't stop the earth circulating round the sun.

But do we need to change the whole car? Can't we just tinker with the engine? The Labour Party prefer the latter option. In fact, they would go for a service rather than replacing any parts to make it run more smoothly. They claim capitalism is basically a good system if it is managed properly. But they have already had their chance to deliver a caring capitalism and it failed.

The welfare state as we know it was introduced by the Beveridge Report at the end of the Second World War. Then there was the NHS, introduced in 1947, which made healthcare free and available to all. The package included Keynsian economics, based on the writings of John Maynard Keynes. This encouraged governments to generate demand in the economy. If the state made sure people had enough money to spend, there would be more demand for industrial products. Industry would benefit and more people would be employed.

But it was simply a stopgap measure to keep capitalism on its feet. John Maynard Keynes and William Beveridge were not socialists. Keynes frankly admitted his theories were designed to save the world from Communism. In the 1930s, when he was writing, capitalism appeared near to total collapse just like it does today. Now Keynsianism itself has failed. It caused inflation. The shift towards cheap overseas manufacturing meant even when British workers had money, they spent it on Japanese and Korean products. Now even the Labour Party have abandoned Keynsianism. So where do they turn? The only alternative offered within the system is the rule of the free market.

The Tories are so confident that capitalism will survive, they don't feel they have to buy people off with gestures towards collectivism. That's why they are running down the welfare state. Even the NHS is being attacked. Competition has been introduced with disastrous results. People are dying because the money principle is applied to human life. Just one example from 1992 was contained in a letter to the *Guardian* from Mary Lambert of Essex. Her husband Bert died after being told that St Barts could not afford to treat his urgent heart condition until the new financial year in April. He originally sought treatment in January. He didn't make it to April. His condition worsened and he was rushed to hospital in February. He died. The cornoner's report read 'cardiac arrest'. It should have read – 'Cause of death: budget constraints'. The free market is murdering people.

The NHS, the welfare state, a commitment to full employment through government intervention in the economy – all these things lasted just a few decades. They were little compromises the ruling class made to the working class in order to hold on to all the power and wealth. They could be taken back at any time. Democracy is just something the ruling class grants the rest of us as long as it does not challenge their power. Since 1979 any gains of the working class have been attacked. That's why we wanted labour leaders to head a mass movement for profound change – one that transfers power away from the ruling class for ever.

The Labour Party and most trade union leaders have shown they are not willing to do this. We wanted them to abandon reformism. They did this but not to embrace revolution. They stopped trying to reform capitalism and embraced big business itself!

So our mass movement will have to be unofficial – just like the anti-poll tax campaign. Only the scale of our ambitions is bigger. We have to convince people that if we all pull together we can make a difference. It's not going to happen overnight. But working-class people know the rich screw the poor. If you can articulate that and explain how the rich do it, why they do it and how to change it – if you can do all that, people will support you.

When the *Scotsman* newspaper asked an unemployed twenty year-old in Easterhouse why he voted for Christine McVicar, a Marxist, he replied: 'Marxist? Does that mean we all get the same wage? I'll go for that.'

Enough people would *like* to see our kind of society: one built on love and cooperation, on satisfying people's needs instead of private profit. But many others who want it have been convinced this is an unrealisable utopia. Just like the wee woman at the back of the poll-tax meeting all those years ago who said: 'I agree wi' ye son. But ye'll never dae it.'

It's easy to become disillusioned when there's so much stacked against you. But if we had taken that attitude at the beginning of the poll tax campaign – we can't break the law, no one will support us, we've no resources – then we'd have done nothing. The tax would still be with us today.

If you know your history, you keep going. One of my most inspiring moments came when I was on my way to the first meeting of the Hands Off Our Water Campaign in 1992. I was a bit nervous about what the turnout was going to be like. I'd posted invitations to every tenants group and anti-poll tax union I could think of. It was a bit hit or miss. My mind was wrapped up in these thoughts when I was about to enter Glasgow City Halls. Then I heard a woman's voice call my name. 'I'm sorry to interrupt but there's someone here who wants to meet you, Mr Sheridan', she said. Her name was Ann Gellatly and she wanted to introduce her husband, John. He was ninety years old and began to explain how he had been involved in the Unemployed Workers' Movement in the Gorbals in the 1930s. He had taken part in the hunger marches and was arrested at one of the demonstrations in London. Willie Gallacher mentioned him in his book. He also knew Maclean, McShane and Wal Hannington. He knew them all.

'I really wanted to meet you,' he said. 'Because I never thought I'd see the same fighting spirit again. I never thought I'd see it in my lifetime.'

I was completely floored. Here was this ninety year-old who had lived through the time which inspired us so much. He was not saying – 'Who do these people think they are!' He was confirming that our struggle was the continuation of the one he waged all those years before. He wanted to join Scottish Militant Labour.

After speaking to Mr Gellatly I stopped worrying about the turn out at the meeting. There would be other meetings. Sure, we'll have zigzags in our development. But I'm absolutely confident that we can build a mass movement for change. We might be ridiculed and laughed at but all of the ridicule and all the criticism don't change the fact that the system is rotten and corrupt and can't deliver the goods any longer. Eventually people will realise that the most capitalism can offer them is a tiny drop in a vast ocean of riches. They will look for change.

Bertolt Brecht wrote this in the 1930s. It's even more relevant today.

'Are you being fobbed off?
Are you being consoled?
The world is waiting for you to put your demands
It needs your discontent, your suggestions
The world is looking to you with its last shred of hope
It's time you firmly said you will not
Accept the drop, but must have the whole lot.'

Appendix 1

How We Stopped the Warrant Sale

DONATIONS WELCOME.
All proceeds to the Strathclyde Anti Poll Tax Federation

A Day in the Life of a Pensioner, 1st October 1991

Alice Sheridan had phoned me on Sunday morning. "Betty, there is going to be a warrant sale in the Old Jail Square on Tuesday. Can you be there? Can you pick up Jo, she's just round the corner from you?" "Sure", I said, "See you at the Federation Shop".

We set out at 7.45 am, Tuesday, a cold, wet, windy morning. Wouldn't you know. Arrived at the Federation Shop. Standing room only. We squeezed our way through to have a cup of tea. It's great being old, they just say, "O.K. doll, in you go".

A few minutes later we all moved along to a 'Pen'. A pen is a space left in old buildings, where you could drive a horse and cart through to the back of the building. The wind was howling through this opening, but at least we were out of the rain.

Tommy Sheridan addressed us. What did we think? It was just 8.15 and the sale wasn't to take place till 11am. We were just about a 100 strong, we are expecting folk in from out-lying districts of Glasgow, would we wait till about 9 to give them a chance to arrive and assemble later. The majority agreed that we disperse till 9.15 then gather outside the Federation shop.

Standing in that pen I had a look round me. What drew my attention was one young lad standing near me was literally shaking with the cold. I thought of all the woollen scarves I had in the house, and wished I had brought a bag full. One of the women took off her gloves and gave them to another young lad. I heard they had been there since 6am. My heart bleeds for the youth of today. They are in a no–hope situation, something like the times when I left school in 1935.

Jo and I got a cup of tea and a roll, we expected it to be a long day and we wouldn't get any more to eat.

At 9.15 we gathered outside the Federation shop. Our numbers had increased quite a bit. There wasn't the same joviality as on other occasions. An Interdict had been issued against Tommy Sheridan forbidding him to go anywhere near the scene of this warrant sale, or he faced arrest. Faces were tense, after all, these young and middle aged people didn't know what lay ahead of them. One pretty young girl standing beside me said, "Are you sure you will be alright?", meaning "Shouldn't you be at home with your knitting". I said, "I'm OK. We must see this through to the end". "I wish I could take you home to my grandfather", she said, "you could have a talk to him about this". I wondered about her grandfather, if he was my age, was he one of the troops pulled out of Dunkirk, or was he a Desert Rat, or was he on the submarine-infested Atlantic Run. Maybe he had enough fighting to last him a lifetime. Thank God for the young lad with the effigy of Margaret Thatcher. He had put a placard in her hand. It said, "NO POLL TAX HERE". That eased the tension a bit.

We marched off singing, "We're no paying the Poll Tax, da da da da". Down at Jail Square the gates were closed. The sale of goods was to take place in this square. Someone climbed up the gates and stuck a few placards on, saying "NO WARRANT SALES HERE". I noticed a woman about my own age standing alone and I joined her. Then suddenly we were all surging through the gates. "How did they get the gates opened?" I asked. "The police opened them", someone said. I think it was a joke, but being of a very suspicious nature, I decided to get outside the gates again.

Just then a slight scuffle took place and this was the only incident of the morning. The police surrounded Tommy Sheridan and the people around him closed in, among them, his mother and sister. There was a wee bit of pushing and shoving. At this time the police could have bundled everyone out, there was enough of them, or they could have caused mayhem by resorting to violence. To their eternal credit, they did not.

By this time I was standing at the gates again, and someone had closed them. I didn't think this was a good idea, so I opened them. "You've opened them the wrong way", said a disabled lady standing just outside. It doesn't matter I said, this is the only way out of that square, there is nowhere else to run. Just then Tommy Sheridan got up on a crash barrier to speak. "Look folks, it's all cool in here, move back in. Our fight is not with the police, we're here to protest about the scum who are attempting to carry out this barbaric practice of selling off this woman's household goods. Then he tore up interdict order.

Babs and I, the lady I had just met that morning, I think we were the oldest people there (she is 68 and I am 70) moved into the square again. It was bitterly cold, the rain was slashing down and the gales still blowing. My teeth were chattering, I don't know if it was the atrocious weather, or the fear of the unknown.

Did I mention the number of police there. I wish I had taken a rough count of them. They were all linked arm in arm down the side of the square and I'm sure there was as many again inside, because there was a single decker bus and 4 or 5 mini buses outside. It was so scary all these tall, well-built men towering over me. When I contrasted the way they were clad, and remembered the boy standing beside me shivering with cold, I thought what would our men and women of the past who fought so long and so hard for a fair deal for the working class, think of the situation now, heading towards the year 2000.

My friend of the morning and I stood against a pillar under the shelter of the carport and passed the next hour talking about our early years. Her father had been working in the coal mines at the age of eleven.

Just before eleven o'clock a cheer went up. The Warrant Sale had been called off. Tommy got up on a crash barrier again and announced the victory, thanked everyone for their support and said again we would fight every Warrant Sale attempted in Scotland.

We all left the Square after a few more cheers, but going out I noticed that there had been three rows of crash barriers put across the exit so there would have been some stampede getting out of there. Tommy got up on some scaffolding, and spoke again for the benefit of the people outside the Square, thanking them and saying our fight was not with the police, that probably some of the relatives were not paying the Poll Tax. Here I must say that the Glasgow Police did not at any time take up a threatening attitude. When I think of what could have happened in that small Square, had there been a few hot heads there, I tremble at the knees, it could have been a blood–bath. We walked back to the Federation shop to return the pink umbrella I had borrowed, and forgot to put up in the excitement. When I was alone, I got into my car to wipe the rain and tears from my face. Then I noticed my friend Jo standing with Alice Sheridan. I joined them to say I was leaving. Alice just put her arms around my neck and said "Thanks". I said that I had feared for her son this morning. She answered, "How do you think I felt?", and for the second time that morning, tears ran down a woman's face. Jo and I got into the car and headed for home.

Betty McEachin

Betty Mc Eachen

Govan Pensioner, Member of Govan A.P.T.G.

**STRATHCLYDE ANTI POLL TAX FEDERATION
69 LONDON ROAD
GLASGOW**

HOTLINE: 041 552 1179

PAY NO POLL TAX

TORIES IN CRISIS – WE ARE WINNING

SHERIFF OFFICER'S LETTERS – IGNORE THEM! – JOIN THE CAMPAIGN

Over 400,000 people in Strathclyde have recently received letters from different firms of Sheriff Officers. These letters contain idle threats and are deliberately meant to frighten you. Some give 3 days to pay, while others give 7 or 14. The fact is they are desperate people determined to make a living from the financial misfortune and despair of others. The advice of the Strathclyde Federation is simple – DON'T LET THEM FRIGHTEN YOU – IGNORE THESE LETTERS AND GET INVOLVED IN THE CAMPAIGN.

After all, why should you struggle to pay a poll tax that make Thatcher and the rich even richer and you and the rest of us even poorer? NO WAY – DON'T PAY.

WHAT ABOUT MY WAGES?

Your wages can only be arrested if the Sheriff knows where you work. Don't tell them. They have no access to personal employee details and have to rely on underhand snooping. If they do find out where you work they can only legally arrest a certain amount. They can take only £13 p/w from £100 net weekly wage, £14 p/w from £105, £15 for £110 and so on. Get your trade union to fight any wage arrestment.

WHAT ABOUT MY BANK ACCOUNT?

Again they do not have a clue where your account is. Don't tell them. Change the name of your account from that on the poll tax register. Have your wages paid into the new account. They have only a 6% chance of finding a non-payer's account through a 'speculative' arrestment.

WHAT ABOUT MY BENEFIT?

The only benefit that can be arrested is Income Support. State Pensions, Unemployment Benefit, Disability Allowance, Sickness Benefit and Child Benefit cannot be arrested at source.

Over 54,000 people in Scotland currently face benefit deductions, only 9,100 have been carried out so far. They can only deduct a maximum of 5% off your Income Support. Today that means £1.85 p/w from a single person and £2.90 from a couple. Benefit deductions are a dammed disgrace and should be appealed against. Appeal letters are available from the Federation. The councils should be ashamed of themselves for this action.

CAN THE SHERIFF OFFICER COME TO MY HOUSE?

Sheriff Officers may try and visit your home to try and frighten you into paying Thatcher's tax or to conduct what is known as a poinding.

What is a Poinding?

A poinding is the pricing of someone's 'non-essential' goods in preparation for a warrant sale to meet a civil debt like the poll tax. Only certain items can be poinded. Anything 'reasonably necessary' in your home is exempt. They cannot poind cookers, washing machines, fridges, clothes, suites, beds, bed linen, anything used to store or prepare food, anything used to store or prepare clothes, or carpets. They can only poind luxury goods that belong to you. A T.V. or video on hire purchase is exempt. Other similar type goods you can prove don't belong to you are exempt.

CAN THEY COME WITHOUT SPECIFIC NOTICE?

Yes, these thugs in suits can come to your home without specific notice.

What should I do if they come to my door?

DON'T LET THEM IN. If you see them through a spy-hole or window then don't even open your door. If you do open the door tell them it is an 'inconvenient time' and slam the door in their faces.

WHAT IF THEY THREATEN TO GET THE POLICE

This happens very rarely, but can happen. YOU HAVE TWO CHOICES:

(i) Contact the local anti-poll tax union and the Federation. Get people to your house to blockade it with a physical wall of human solidarity.

If this cannot be arranged then you must take the second choice;
(ii) Lock your door and leave your house empty. Make sure you are
well out of sight in case they return.

**Can they force entry if I am still in the house when they
return?**

Yes they can. That is why the above advice must be followed.

Can they force entry into an empty house?

The Debtors (Scotland) Act 1987 Schedule 5, Section 3 (1) states
clearly that despite having a summary warrant "a sheriff officer shall
not enter a dwellinghouse to execute a poinding if, AT THE TIME
OF HIS INTENDED ENTRY, there appears to him to be nobody,
or only children under 16 years, present there, unless, AT LEAST
4 DAYS BEFORE THE DATE OF HIS INTENDED ENTRY,
he has served notice on the debtor SPECIFYING THAT DATE."

WHAT DO I DO IF I GET SUCH A NOTICE?

Contact your local campaign and the Federation. IMMEDIATELY.

Can we stop poindings?

YES, EVERY SINGLE TIME THE FED HAS BEEN NOTIFIED
PRIOR TO A POINDING ATTEMPT WE HAVE STOPPED
THEM. WE HAVE NOW STOPPED OVER 30 ATTEMPTED
POINDINGS.

IS A POINDING THE SAME AS A WARRANT SALE?

No. A poinding is only the first part of a warrant sale. In order to
conduct a warrant sale the Sheriff has to issue you with a clear 14-day
notice of the date of the intended sale. That gives us the chance to
mobilise a huge turnout to stop any warrant sale from taking place.
DON'T FORGET, AFTER 20 MONTHS OF NON PAY-
MENT NOT ONE SINGLE WARRANT SALE HAS TAKEN
PLACE IN SCOTLAND. WE INTEND TO KEEP IT THAT WAY.

How big is the Mass Non Payment Campaign?

Huge and growing every week. Over one million people have not paid or are in serious arrears for 1989/90's poll tax in Scotland. After the first 8 months of 1990/91 Strathclyde Region has had to issue 500,000 Final Notices. 65% remains unpaid. The non payment level in Glasgow is officially over 45%. We believe it is actually over 50%.

IS NON PAYMENT THE REASON FOR POLL TAX RISES?

Definitely not. The Poll Tax will rise every year regardless of the level of non payment. Thatcher continually underfunds local government to force the level of Poll Tax to increase OR the amount of local government jobs and services to be slashed. WHAT IS NOW HAPPENING IS A COMBINATION OF BOTH. The Regional Council is faced with at least a £112 increase in Poll Tax to £337 next year because of government underfunding. Even allowing for the effect of 3 years non payment it still only accounts for £42 per head.

In other words, EVEN IF EVERYONE PAID THE POLL TAX THE REGIONAL POLL TAX WOULD STILL HAVE TO RISE BY £70 TO SAVE CUTS IN JOBS AND SERVICES BECAUSE OF TORY CUT-BACKS.

WILL THE REGIONAL POLL TAX RISE BY £112?

No. The Region will introduce a disgusting package of cuts amounting to over £75 million. By slashing jobs and services they will keep the increase down to nearer £60.

They will then mislead people by blaming non payers for most of the increase.

WHAT IS THE FEDERATION'S POSITION?

We demand NO CUTS IN JOBS OR SERVICES. The reason we are in this problem is because the Labour Regional Council implemented Thatcher's Poll Tax in the first place. They should have had the political guts and honesty to refuse to implement it on the basis that what is happening now is exactly what we warned would happen. The Tories are forcing a Labour council to not only increase the Poll Tax but also to slash jobs and services. They know a £112 increase would finish the Poll Tax off and thus incur the wrath of Malcolm Rifkind and therefore are making cuts of £75 million, increasing the Poll Tax to around £295 and then intend to blame the non payment campaign. WE SAY – NO CUTS – STOP IMPLEMENTING THIS POLL TAX SLAUGHTER.

What is the likely level of Poll Tax next year?

When you add the likely Regional increase of around £63 to the likely Glasgow District increase of around £40 and the water charge increase of around £6 you have a probable Poll Tax bill in Glasgow next year of around £430. THAT MEANS A POLL TAX OF £35 A MONTH, OF ALMOST £10 PER WEEK.

We appeal to all non payers to stand firm and get involved in the campaign and we appeal to those who are paying to stop paying and join the campaign. Remember this Poll Tax is evil, unjust and immoral. DON'T CONDONE IT BY PAYING IT. DEFEAT IT BY MAKING IT UNWORKABLE AND UNCOLLECTABLE. THE MORE NON PAYERS THE QUICKER THE WHOLE THING WILL COLLAPSE AROUND THATCHER'S EARS.

SCOTTISH DEMO
TWO YEARS OF RESISTANCE
SATURDAY MARCH 9TH
GLASGOW, GEORGE SQUARE
11.00 AM

ALL BRITAIN DEMO
14 MILLION NON PAYERS
SATURDAY, 23RD MARCH
LONDON
FLEET OF COACHES LEAVING
GLASGOW

MONEY!

We have no rich backers. We rely on you to fund us and help pay
for material like this. Don't let us down. PLEASE SEND US A
DONATION. S.A.P.T.F. 69 LONDON RD. GLASGOW

Bibliography

Adams, Ian. *The Making of Urban Scotland*. Croom Helm, 1978.

Beynon, ed, Huw. Digging deeper: *Issues in the Miners' Strike*. Verso, 1985.

Brown, Gordon. *Maxton*. Mainstream Publishing, 1986.

Butler, David & Kavanagh, Denis. *The British General Election of 1992*. St Martin's Press, 1992.

Crick, Michael. *Militant*. Faber & Faber, 1984.

Croucher, Richard. *We Refuse to Starve in Silence: A History of the National Unemployed Workers Movement*, 1920–46. Lawrence & Wishart, 1987.

Donnachie, Ian, Harvie, Christopher and Wood, Ian S. *Forward: Labour Politics in Scotland*, 1888–1988. Polygon, 1989.

Duncan, Robert & McIvor, Arthur. *Militant Workers: Labour and Class Conflict on the Clyde, 1900–1950. Essays in Honour of Harry McShane*. John Donald, 1992.

Dickson, ed, Tony. *Scottish Capitalism*, Lawrence & Wishart, 1980.

Forster, Les and Savage, Hugh. *All for the Cause – Willie Nairn, 1856–1902.*

Howell, David. *A Lost Left: Three Studies in Socialism and Nationalism*. The University of Chicago Press, 1986.

Hutchinson, Gerard and O'Neill, Mark. *The Springburn Experience*. Polygon, 1989.

Kay, Billy. *Odyssey: Voices from Scotland's Recent Past* Polygon.

Keating, Michael. *The City that Refused to Die*. Aberdeen University Press, 1988.

King, Elspeth. *The New Factor: The Hidden History of Glasgow's Women*. Mainstream Publishing, 1993.

Lenman, Bruce. *An Economic History of Modern Scotland*. B T Batsford, 1977.

MacDougall, Ian. *Voices from the Hunger Marches, Vol II*. Polygon, 1991.

McLay, ed, Farquhar. *The Reckoning: Beyond the Culture City Rip Off*. Workers City/Clydeside Press, 1990.

McLay, ed, Farquhar. *Workers City: The Real Glasgow Stands Up*. Clydeside Press, 1988.

Miliband, Ralph: *Parliamentary Socialism – A Study in the Politics of Labour*. Merlin Press 1972.

Milton, Nan. *John Maclean*. Pluto Press, 1973.

Morton, A L & Tate, George. *The British Labour Movement*. Unwin Brothers 1956.

Orwell, George. *The Road to Wigan Pier*. Penguin.

Pilger, John. *Distant Voices*. Vintage, 1992.

Reynolds, Maureen. *Uncollectable: The Story of the Poll Tax Revolt*. Greater Manchester Anti Poll Tax Federation, 1992.

Rosen, Michael and Widgery, ed, David. *The Chatto Book of Dissent*. Chatto & Windus 1991.

Scotia, Bar. *First May Poetry Prize*. Taranis Books 1992.

Slaven, Anthony. *The Development of the West of Scotland, 1750–1960*. Routledge and Kegan Paul 1975.

Smout, T C. *A Century of the Scottish People, 1930–1950*. Collins 1986.

Taaffe, Peter and Mulhearn, Tony. *Liverpool: A City that Dared to Fight*. Fortress 1988.

Trotsky, Leon. *My Life: An Attempt at an Autobiography*. Penguin.

ALSO: *The Scotsman, The Herald, The Glasgow Evening Times, Scotland on Sunday, The Guardian* and *The Financial Times* from 1987–1993. Special thanks to the *Evening Times* picture desk.

Material on the Pollok witches in Chapter 4 comes from the Stirling Maxwell family papers which are held in the Mitchell Library, Glasgow.

Index